THE CHURCH AND ITS MISSION

THE CHURCH
AND ITS
MISSION: A

SHATTERING
CRITIQUE
FROM THE
THIRD WORLD

Orlando E. Costas

TYNDALE HOUSE PUBLISHERS, Inc.
Wheaton, Illinois

COVERDALE HOUSE PUBLISHERS, Ltd.
London, England

Library of Congress Catalog Card Number 74-80150
ISBN 8423-0275-1 cloth; 8423-0276-X paper
Copyright © 1974 by Tyndale House Publishers, Inc.,
Wheaton, Illinois 60187. All rights reserved.
First printing, June 1974
Printed in the United States of America

To the faculty and student body of
Gordon-Conwell Theological Seminary;

and especially to

the members of the 1973
"World Mission of the Church" class,
whose stimulating encouragement
and constructive criticisms
contributed greatly to the
writing of this book;

and to

Dr. and Mrs. Nigel Kerr,
whose friendship, openness,
and warm hospitality
toward my wife and me
helped to make January 1973
one of the highlights of our ministry.

CONTENTS

FOREWORD

by Paul S. Rees
Vice-president at Large
World Vision International

Is mission at the edge of the Christian Church's life or is it inherent in the very nature of the Church?

Is it possible to account for the Church's worldwide penetration and growth without focusing on her sense of mission?

How can today's Church both survive and utilize the theological and tactical tensions that have developed within her ranks in relation to her own work and witness in the world?

These are in fact the major questions with which the author grapples in the following chapters. Admittedly, other authors have wrestled with these issues—ably and vigorously.

What makes this book arresting and timely is that it springs from the informed mind and the aroused conscience not of a European or a North American but of a Latin.

Orlando Costas is a significant representative of a small but growing breed. Standing firmly yet graciously within the Protestant evangelical community of Latin America, identified staunchly with the fundamental and enduring insights of the Reformation, he brings together in a living whole that kind of thinking that is at once theological and evangelistic. If anyone reading these lines has ever prayed, "Lord, give us some theologically minded evangelists and some evangelistically minded theologians," Costas is an answer to your prayer.

He *thinks* theologically; he *acts* evangelistically. No ivory-tower theorist, he is an activist in evangelism. He teaches it, practices it, stimulates it.

All this he does, however, in a context of Latin American culture, evangelical creativeness, and, using the term in its older classical meaning, ecumenical concern.

My willing response to the author's request for a Foreword to this book can be explained *chiefly* by the fact that he speaks as a Latin evangelical on sensitive issues with respect to which North American writers have been, and are, highly (sometimes shrilly and shallowly) articulate.

We have needed this book. We do well to listen to it with humble honesty.

To give total assent to it is asked neither by the author himself nor the writer of this preface. As my esteemed friend, the Rev. Jack Shepherd, education secretary for The Christian and Missionary Alliance, remarked to me, with a knowing twinkle in his eye, "There is something here to offend everyone!" He is trenchantly right.

He would have been equally right if he had said, "There is something here to instruct and to stimulate everyone!"

Tolle lege! Take up and read, in the words of Augustine.

FOREWORD

by C. Peter Wagner
Fuller Theological Seminary
School of World Mission and
Institute of Church Growth

Scarcely could Orlando Costas have written this substantial work on missiology at a more opportune time. I have little doubt that one of the major developments (if not *the* major one) in world missions during the decade of the Seventies is the awareness of the rise of what some call Third World missions. The Western monopoly on foreign mission work is now being broken by scores of new missionary societies and hundreds of new missionaries from the peoples of the world in Africa, Asia, and Latin America who not too long ago were referred to as the "heathen" nations.

Milestones in this process are appearing. In early 1973 James Wong published the first preliminary world survey in Singapore under the title *Missions from the Third World.* The survey located 210 agencies sending out over 3,000 missionaries. Later on in the year, twenty-five Asian leaders from thirteen countries held a summit meeting in Seoul, Korea, called the All-Asia Missionary Consultation. These are two of the historic milestones.

Perhaps the third milestone will be *The Church and Its Mission.* Few of even the most enthusiastic backers of Third World missions would have dared predict that so early in the process a textbook on missiology would be produced by an authentic Third World mission theorist, but Professor Costas has risen to the occasion and given us such a book. The missionary world (and finally it *is* the world!) will long be his debtor.

Not that Costas' book will be acclaimed by all Third World leaders as representing their point of view on all issues. Not that missiologists from the North Atlantic nations will unreservedly endorse everything he says. Parts of it will rub some evangelicals against their grain. Parts of it will irritate ecumenists to the core. I myself would have written many parts differently. Costas' material is not missiological Pablum, it is strong meat and it must be read and studied as such. He writes with an enviable combination of courage and conviction, and he addresses himself to the major missiological issues of the day. But whether they cheer or groan, readers will certainly recognize that we now have a welcome contribution to the theory of missions that has aided the cause of the fulfillment of the Great Commission.

ACKNOWLEDGMENTS

Few are the authors that write books without any help from others. This one is no exception. I want to acknowledge, therefore, my indebtedess to all those who contributed in one or another way to the publication of this work.

To my lovely and faithful wife for her decisive role in the preparation of the manuscript. Not only was she admirably patient with me for the long hours I spent in preparation at the expense of family activities, but was willing to spend many long hours herself in the typing and correction of the manuscript.

To my friend, colleague, and student, A. William Cook, Coordinating Secretary of the Institute of In-depth Evangelism, for graciously agreeing to take over my classes for a semester at the Latin America Biblical Seminary in order that I might be free to work on the preparation of the manuscript.

To the many friends and colleagues who read the manuscript entirely or in part and offered valuable suggestions and constructive criticism. I am particularly indebted to colleagues Richard Foulkes, Kenneth Mulholland, Mervin Breneman, and W. Dayton Roberts for their penetrating insights and encouragement; to my former teacher and friend, Dr. Carl F. H. Henry, who graciously read the manuscript overnight during his visit to Costa Rica as part of a Latin America tour and offered very constructive criticisms; to the Rev. Alfred Krass, of the United Church Board for World Ministries, Jack Shepherd, of the Christian and Missionary Alliance, and Günter Dulon, of the German Missionary Council, for their feedback and suggestions; and to Prof. C. Peter Wagner, of the School of World Mission of Fuller Theological Seminary, for his enthusiastic encouragement, promotion, and publishing contacts, and for his Foreword to the book.

To Tyndale House Publishers, and its Managing Editor, Dr. Victor L. Oliver, for their willingness to break out into a new type of publication.

To Dr. Paul Rees for his willingness to write a Foreword.

Grateful acknowledgement is also given to the following publishers for permission to quote copyrighted material from the titles listed below:

Abingdon Press, Nashville, Tennessee, for permission to quote from *The Dynamics of Church Growth* by J. Waskom Pickett,

xvi ACKNOWLEDGMENTS

International Review of Mission, Geneva, Switzerland for permission to quote from articles in Vols. LX, LXI, LXII, Nos. 237, 241, 243, 246 (June, 1971; January, July, 1972; April, 1973).

Lincoln Christian College Press, Lincoln, Illinois, for permission to quote from *Verdict Theology in Missionary Theory* by A. R. Tippett, copyright 1969.

Lutterworth Press, Guildford, Surrey, England, for permission to quote from *Solomon Islands Christianity* by Alan R. Tippett, copyright 1967; and *Witness in Six Continents* by R. K. Orchard, copyright 1964.

MacMillan Publishing Co., Inc., New York, New York, for permission to quote from *The Secular City* by Harvey Cox, copyright 1965.

Moody Press Publications, Chicago, Illinois, for permission to quote from *Crucial Issues in Missions Tomorrow* by Donald A. McGavran, copyright 1972; and *Church/Mission Tensions Today* by C. Peter Wagner, copyright 1972.

National Council of the Churches of Christ, New York, New York, for permission to quote from *Where in the World?* by Collin Williams, copyright 1963.

Orbis Books, Maryknoll, New York, for permission to quote from *Theology of Liberation* by Gustavo Gutiérrez, copyright 1972.

Prentice-Hall, Inc., Englewood Cliffs, New Jersey, for permission to quote from *Missionary, Go Home!* by James A. Scherer, copyright 1964.

Revista Bíblica, Buenos Aires, Argentina, for permission to quote from "¿Contaminación? En torno a una definición de la religión (Santiago 1:27)," by Rodolfo Obermüller, copyright 1972.

Ediciones Sígueme, Salamanca, Spain, for permission to quote from *Teología del mundo* by Johann Baptist Metz, copyright 1970; and *El culto cristiano* by Jean-Jacques von Allmen, copyright 1968.

Tierra Nueva Editorial, Montevideo, Uruguay, for permission to quote from *Opresión-liberación: Desafío a los cristianos* by Hugo Assmann, copyright 1971.

Tidings Publishing Co., Nashville, Tennessee, for permission to quote from *Beyond the Either-Or Church* by Alfred Krass, copyright 1973.

C. Peter Wagner, for permission to quote from *Frontiers in Missionary Strategy,* copyright 1972.

The Westminster Press, Philadelphia, Pennsylvania, for permission to quote from *The Misunderstanding of the Church* by Emil Brunner, copyright by W. L. Jenkins, 1951, translated by Harold Knight; and *Missions in a Time of Testing* by R. K. Orchard, copyright 1964.

William Carey Library, Pasadena, California, for permission to quote from *Church Growth Through Evangelism in Depth* by Malcolm Bradshaw, copyright 1968; *The Warp and the Woof* by Ralph D. Winter and R. Pierce Beaver, copyright 1970; "The Theology of Salvation at Bangkok" by Peter Beyerhaus and "Thinking Aloud About Bangkok" by Paul Rees in *The Evangelical Response to Bangkok* by Ralph D. Winter, copyright 1973.

Word Books, Publisher, Waco, Texas, for permission to quote from *Eye of the Storm* by Donald A. McGavran, copyright 1972.

World Council of Churches, Geneva, Switzerland, for permission to quote from *Main Lines of a Biblical Theology of Mission* by Johannes Blauw, copyright 1960; and *The Uppsala Report 1968* by Norman Goodall, (ed.), copyright 1968.

World Vision International, Monrovia, California, for permission to quote from articles in the March, 1973 issue.

Zondervan Publishing House, Grand Rapids, Michigan, for permission to quote from *Shaken Foundations: Theological Foundations for Mission,* copyright 1972; and *Which Way? Humanization or Redemption* by Peter Beyerhaus, copyright 1971.

To all of them, my deepest and sincerest appreciation. And to all those who read these pages, the acknowledgment of my personal and sole responsibility for all the "errors" and "heresies" that they may find.

Orlando E. Costas

INTRO-
DUCTION

1/GOD'S REDEMPTIVE MISSION TO THE WORLD

THE WORLD OF MAN AS THE OBJECT OF GOD'S MISSION. This is a book about mission: God's redemptive mission to the world. By *world* I do not mean the world of the cosmos, although God's redemptive missionary presence in the world does have a cosmic dimension. The cosmos is part of God's creation and is therefore the object of his love. Yet the world which is the *direct* object of God's mission is not the world of things but of man. Mission is concerned with the world in its anthropological purport —man's world.

But man is a historical being, not an abstraction. To say that mission is oriented toward man is therefore to refer to a task that must concentrate on concrete situations. It must not look for man in the world of ideas but of action. Further, it cannot consider him a single homogeneous unity. Man is a complex phenomenon.

Our first task is therefore to try to characterize this creature who is the object of God's mission. To do justice to the many situations in which man finds himself, we must approach him from at least three angles.

First, it is imperative to see him from the perspective of change, for it is indisputable that man is characterized by his capacity for change. As Rubem Alves says,

> Man is a historical being. He is not born in the world of things, persons and time as a finished product. His being is not prior to history. He becomes what he is through the history of his relations with his environment. He is not, therefore, simply a being *in* the world; he comes into being *with* the world. Man changes because he is not a monad. He is receptive. Due to this condition he is able to respond and not merely to react.[1]

Several aspects are at present changing in the life of modern man. Man is changing in regard to his *self-image.* Dietrich Bonhoeffer was among the first contemporary thinkers who began to point out this reality. Shortly before his death, Bonhoeffer wrote a letter in which he described man as coming of age. He saw modern man entering a period of maturity, reflected by a growing tendency to affirm his moral, philosophical, political, cultural, religious, and scientific autonomy. Hence, concluded Bonhoeffer, modern man no longer needs God as a working hypothesis.[2]

Bonhoeffer's analysis was prophetic, although somewhat overstated. Nevertheless he was pointing to a new stage in the history of mankind. Man is undergoing a process of change, basically because his *categories* are

---

1. Rubem Alves, *A Theology of Human Hope* (Washington: Corpus Books, 1966), p. 3.

2. Cf. Dietrich Bonhoeffer, "Letter of July 16th, 1944," in *Letters and Papers from Prison* (New York: Macmillan, 1953), p. 214.

changing. His scientific and technological efforts have led him to discover a new language, which differs radically from the religious language of the past. He no longer contemplates reality through mythic or metaphysical lenses (although this statement is somewhat relative in light of the revival of the occult in Western society). The questions man is raising are more "flesh-and-bone" than metaphysical inquiries. Modern man, Harvey Cox says,

> . . . sees the world not so much as an awesome enigma, evoking a sense of hushed reverence, as a series of complex and interrelated projects requiring the application of competence. He does not ask religious questions because he fully believes he can handle this world without them.[3]

We must be careful not to generalize. Although it is true that change is basic to man, not all men change in the same way. In other words, man must be viewed as a heterogeneous being. His heterogeneity becomes evident in at least three areas.

Contemporary man's heterogeneity is reflected in the fact that he lives in different historical stages. Thousands of men and women today are living in pre-modern, not to say primitive conditions. Others live far ahead of their time; they belong to what has been called the post-modern world. This reality works against any triumphalistic conception of the progress of mankind. The truth is that for the greater part of the world's inhabitants modernity is no more than a dream.

This is apparent in the uneven socioeconomic situations in our world. The daily-growing gulf between the economic affluence, political power, and superdevelopment of some nations as contrasted with the poverty, impotence, and underdevelopment in the rest of the world, undercuts the validity of equating the technological-scientific progress of the modern world with its socioeconomic

---

3. Harvey Cox, *The Secular City* (New York: The Macmillan Co., 1965), p. 63.

reality. The social, economic, intellectual, religious, or racial segregation (either covert or overt) in so many societies, makes conspicuous the heterogeneous situation of man in our era.

Heterogeneity may also be seen in culture. Modern man's world-view, language, customs, and creations are continuously changing because of an unlimited number of variables, both external and internal. These variables are determinant factors that dynamize modern culture and force contemporary man to reevaluate, modify, and change his values. Despite the continuous changes it is forced to go through, however, culture is a powerful creative motor. It unifies peoples at the same time it accentuates their differences. As the world's cultures expand and develop, they become an outstanding symbol of man's social heterogeneity.

Contemporary man is not only a changing, heterogeneous being. He is also homogeneous. His homogeneity appears in almost all areas of existence: the physical, psychological, social, cultural, political, and economic. As a receiving agent, man is capable of responding to all sorts of stimuli. He is influenced by nature: rain, drought, fire, cold or heat, calm or storm, hurricane or earthquake. Man is homogeneous in that he has to face the world of things, has similar biological needs, and above all, is incapable of surviving without his neighbor. The latter is true not only with regard to his psychosocial life, but also, and especially so, with respect to his political and economic relationships. Modern man is politically and economically interdependent. He needs and is needed by his neighbor. His political and economic sovereignty is relative. Even when he attains a strong political and economic position in the world community, as the USSR and the USA have done, he is dependent on peaceful coexistence and on what men of other nations produce.

JESUS CHRIST AS THE CENTER OF GOD'S REDEMPTIVE ACTION. It is the world of this complex phenomenon, man, which God so loved that he gave his only begotten

Son "that whosoever believeth in him should not perish, but have everlasting life" (Jn. 3:16). The incarnation of Jesus Christ can be understood only in the light of God's redemptive concern for man. This is what is meant by the Gospel narrative when it records Jesus as saying that he came not to do his own will, but the will of him who sent him (Jn. 6:38; cf. 4:34, 5:30). God's will is that all men have everlasting life through faith in his Son Jesus Christ. To make this possible, Jesus went to the cross, descended into hell, rose the third day from the grave, and ascended into heaven to sit at the right hand of the Father.

THE HOLY SPIRIT AS THE EXECUTOR OF GOD'S MIS-SION. Following the resurrection and ascension of Jesus, God's redemptive mission to the world continued in the coming of the Holy Spirit. Hendrikus Berkhoff has described the Spirit as the powerful and dynamic movement from the one to the many.[4] Paul says that he is the very Spirit of Christ (2 Cor. 3:17). That is, the Holy Spirit makes the loving Lord present in the many situations in which men and women find themselves. Having been active in the life and ministry of Jesus, he is also the one whose specific function is to point all human beings to him as Lord and Savior. Thus, just as Jesus Christ is the center of God's redemptive mission to the world—since it is through him that God made possible the reconciliation of mankind—so the Spirit is the executor of God's mission. In other words, he is the force that extends redemption, which has its center in God, out into the world. He is the centrifugal-centripetal force that takes Christ to the world and calls the world to become part of Christ. The ultimate goal of the Spirit's ministry is to fulfill God's redemptive purpose in Christ, namely, the creation of a new humanity.

THE CHURCH AS THE AGENT OF GOD'S MISSION. Out of this dynamic movement from the one to the many, and

---

4. Hendrikus Berkhoff, La doctrina del Espíritu Santo (Buenos Aires: La Aurora, 1969), p. 37.

the ingrafting of the many into the one, the church is born. She is the "firstfruits" of the new creation. The church is also, and particularly so, used by the Spirit as an instrument of God's mission. The church is thus that portion of humanity who experience God's grace in Christ made present by the Spirit. And because of this, the church is called to witness to the world about her marvelous experience in Jesus Christ.

THE ROLE OF THE CHURCH

This book is particularly concerned with the role of the church in God's redemptive mission to the world. It focuses on the church as an agent of the Holy Spirit, the great executor of God's mission. With an eye on the historical, heterogeneous, yet homogeneous character of contemporary man, it asks about the church's specific role as a missionary agent in the light of her historical dynamics.

This inquiry is further reduced to three specific concerns. The first has to do with the relation of mission to the church's essential nature. The second, with the phenomenon of the church's expansion as a direct result of her involvement in mission. The third, with the most pressing tensions experienced by a considerable segment of the church today as she seeks to understand and participate in the work of mission.

In the following pages it will be shown that the church is basically a missionary community, *i.e.,* her fundamental character can only be understood from the perspective of God's mission to the world. There is an intrinsic, inseparable relation between the church as such and her calling. In other words, the church is a miraculous redemptive community. Not only is she the product of God's redemptive action in the world, but from the beginning she has been called to be the Spirit's instrument in the activity out of which she herself was born. Her participation in God's mission involves the transmission of a message imbedded in her own miraculous experience. The character, calling, and message of the church are discussed in chapters two, three, and four.

The second section of this book emphasizes the phenomenon of church growth as the evidence and result of God's redemptive missionary presence in man's multiple life situations. An examination of the witness of biblical theology to the imperative of church growth is followed by a critical analysis of a contemporary missiological school of thought which has zeroed in on this important dimension of the church's involvement in the task of world mission.

The third section deals with what I consider the two most pressing missiological tensions in the contemporary *Protestant* expression of the church.[5] Both of these tensions, it will be shown, are directly related to the complex situation of contemporary man. For although the church has come out of the world, she is nevertheless *in* the world, and as such she is not exempt from the conflicts of mankind. As a matter of fact, the character of the church, her vocation, her message, and the success of her missionary endeavor force her to be concerned not only with the tensions of her world but also to be involved in these tensions. Otherwise the church would not be, as Scripture says she is, a community on the march, a project in the making, or the "firstfruits"—the new order which has come but not yet in its fullness.

Thus the tension that develops in the relationships between the church-in-mission (the missionary society, etc.) and the church arising from mission (the offspring of the missionary enterprise) has direct bearing both on the

---

5. This is not, however, due to sectarian or unecumenical conviction. It is simply a choice I must make, given the fact that contemporary Catholicism faces other tensions which deserve separate treatment. I also recognize that the selection of these tensions is rather arbitrary. Other tensions in Protestantism may be considered just as crucial, *e.g.,* the charismatic movement, the generation gap, the tension between paid and nonprofessional clergy, etc. In my personal opinion, however, these tensions are not so strong in contemporary Protestant missiology as the ones chosen for analysis.

growing consciousness of a world in search of its own identity and on the incarnational character of the Christian mission. Such issues as indigeneity and ecumenicity are not only the by-products of a world that wants to be itself and yet is conscious of the danger of provincialism and nationalism. These issues are also an expression of the internal dynamics of a church that must be at once indigeneous and universal.

Likewise, the issue of the liberation of man deals with one of the worst tensions in a world divided between haves and have-nots. God's redemptive mission is oriented to such a situation. Jesus' message at Nazareth (cf. Lk. 4:18ff.) leaves no doubt about it: God is concerned for the plight of the downtrodden. This issue poses the question of *how* the church should participate in God's mission in the midst of situations of oppression and exploitation. Is there a direct relationship between mission and the struggles of so many millions around the world to liberate themselves from their poverty-stricken, unjust, oppressive, and humiliating conditions?

The question of the kinds of relationships that ought to exist between the missionary societies and their offspring will be analyzed in chapter eight, while the last three chapters will be devoted to the mission-liberation issue.

THE SPECIFIC CHARACTER OF THIS BOOK

A CHALLENGE . . . This book attempts to be a challenge for wholeness in missionary theory and practice. It tries to call the attention of the church in the North Atlantic[6] to the unity of the gospel and to the undichotomous character of the church's role as an instrument of God's mission.

There is an increasing tendency among contemporary Christians toward a polarized, dichotomous, either-or view

6. That is, Western Europe and North America.

of mission. Several contemporary authors have addressed themselves to this issue in recent publications, especially in relation to the question of evangelism and social action in North America.[7] This book attempts to deal with the same problem, but in relation to world evangelization and from the perspective of one who lives and ministers in an area of the world where commitment to a holistic concept of mission is not only necessary but urgent.

The writer seeks to challenge the church in the North Atlantic to be more integral in her view of mission, because the non-affluent, poverty-stricken, exploited, and oppressed world is challenging Christianity (identified with the affluent world) to be consistent with the message she proclaims. The question is no longer what is the church's "primary" task, but what is her *total* task. The issue today is not whether or not people are being converted to Christ but whether this is happening as part of a total process: is the church a community totally committed to and involved in the fulfillment of the gospel in the context of the concrete historical situations in which men and woman find themselves?

. . . FROM A LATIN AMERICAN. Then there is the particular perspective from which the book is written, *i.e.,* that of a Latin American evangelical churchman who lived and studied for many years in North America, who served for the last four years as a professor of missiology in a Latin American seminary and who is presently a member of the staff of an indigenous evangelistic organization. I write as one who appreciates the hospitality given to him from the moment of his arrival in New York City as a member of a Latin American family who migrated to the North in search of better economic conditions. Although my parents were Christians, it was not until four years later that I met Jesus

---

7. See Ernest Campbell, *Christian Manifesto* (New York: Harper & Row, 1970); David Moberg, *The Great Reversal* (New York: Lippincott, 1972); and Alfred Krass, *Beyond the Either/Or Church,* Nashville: Tidings Publishing Co., 1973.

Christ as Lord and Savior. I am deeply grateful for this experience, for the pastoral care I was given, for the fact that there I was called to the gospel ministry, discovered my own people by ministering in several Latin American churches, and became burdened for Latin America as a continent. Even though I returned to my own country for college training, I went back to the North to study in seminary. I am grateful for the fine graduate theological education I received in the United States and for the fact that it was not an isolated experience, but one that was connected with a fruitful, dynamic, and exciting ministry in the heart of a large urban community. I also appreciate the interest that the friends from these years have had in my ministry in Latin America, praying for and supporting it financially.

I would be dishonest, however, if I were to leave out the other side of my experience in North America, for this too is part of the picture, and a very important part! As a member of a forgotten minority,[8] I experienced the awfulness of ethnic prejudice, the harshness of poverty (in a country where the great majority have over and beyond their needs), and the oppression of an impersonal, culturally alienating educational system.

When I decided to go back to my own country to finish my college training it was because deep inside I sensed the need to pull myself together. I majored in Latin American history and politics, and discovered that my situation as a migrant in North America was much better than the history of exploitation and oppression of continental Latin America under the imperialism first of Spain, Portugual, and other European countries,[9] and later of the United States. As a college student I had an opportunity to travel to the Dominican Republic during the 1965-66 conflict. I had a chance to see for myself how a powerful nation quenched the hopes and aspirations of a people who have been

8. The expression is borrowed from Julio Samorra, *La Raza: Forgotten Americans* (Notre Dame, Ind.: Notre Dame University Press, 1967).

9. For example, England, France, Holland.

dominated in one way or another throughout their history by oligarchies and foreign powers. Later on when I began to travel more extensively throughout the rest of Latin America I began to see how the story repeats itself over and over. I further realized that it was not a situation caused by a single nation, the United States, but by a bloc of nations who are part of the same system, who have a similar history of colonialization, and who have become extremely rich, partly as the result of their business and economic deals with the oligarchies that control these countries.[10]

The sad thing about this is that these countries have also been largely responsible for the expansion of Christianity in the Third World. We know, of course, that the church has always suffered from the tensions of society. It ought not surprise us to see coming out of the same land a movement of domination and exploitation together with the message of freedom imbedded in the gospel. What is hard to take, however, is the way that the values undergirding the imperialistic philosophy and practice of these nations make their way into the church, distorting the gospel sometimes beyond recognition, and setting up what some of my Latin American friends would call ideological and/or cultural roadblocks to the understanding of biblical faith.

This tendency may be seen not just among missionaries. In a sense, the latter are no more and no less a reflection of the attitudes and overall philosophy of the missionary societies, churches, and individual Christians who

---

10. Henceforth, the expression Third World will be used to designate Asia, Africa, and Latin America. The idea behind this expression is that of their common economic plight vis-à-vis the two powerful blocks in the world, that of the NATO nations and that of the WARSAW PACT. Generally speaking, the Third World represents the "underdeveloped" countries of the world. A better description, however, would be the nonaffluent, economically, politically, and culturally "dominated" countries of the world. (Someone has rather pejoratively likened the situation of these nations to that of a cow. The First World (NATO) is the "milk man" and the Second World (WARSAW PACT) the "butcher".)

sent them. Having lived and studied in North America I can understand why so many missionaries think and act as they do. (And from what I understand, the situation is similar in the case of missionaries from Western Europe.) They are part of a syncretistic religious culture. I say syncretistic because many of the values inherent in this culture are definitely not Christian. Yet they have been made to appear as *if they were.* Worse yet, these values have permeated the mental structure of the great majority of North Atlantic Christians and particularly their theological methodology.

This is not the place to discuss the seemingly Christian values of the North Atlantic community in general and North American society in particular.[11] It will suffice to point out that they have not only been used to serve as a theological justification of colonialism, and more recently of neocolonialism,[12] but have been the basis for a paternalistic relationship with national churches; a culturally alienating religiosity; an ethic of neutrality and noninvolvement; and an evangelism that is either totally divorced from the gut-issues of an oppressed society or that has a one-sided orientation to the "beyond," or an evangelism that is reduced to social assistance (a "band-aid operation" as

---

11. For a general treatment of the problem of values in Christian religiosity in the North Atlantic see, among others, the following sources: David Moberg, *Reversal,* pp. 54-56, 101, 132; *Inasmuch* (Grand Rapids: Eerdmans, 1965); *The Church As a Social Institution* (Englewood Cliffs, N.J.: Prentice Hall, 1962). Also, Richard Niebuhr, *Christ and Culture* (New York: Harper and Row, 1951); *The Social Sources of Denominationalism* (Cleveland: The World Publishing Co., 1967); and Paul Tillich, *The Protestant Era* (Chicago: The University of Chicago Press, 1957); Peter L. Berger, *The Noise of Solemn Assemblies* (Garden City, N.Y.: Doubleday, 1961), pp. 39, 57-157.

12. Of course, this is not new in the history of Christianity. As I point out in Chapter X, the history of modern Christian missions is filled with case after case in which the missionary enterprise has been used to justify economic and political imperialism, from the conquest of the Americas, to the missionary endeavors of the maritime commercial companies of England and Holland during the eighteenth and early nineteenth century, to the private business ventures of some missionaries in the twentieth century.

some would call it), paying little attention to the real causes of the problem (both spiritual and structural), and refusing to penetrate into the deeper dimensions of the gospel (life, death, guilt, reconciliation, etc.).

The situation in the Third World, particularly in Latin America, is no better than that which Moberg, Krass, and Campbell describe in their respective publications about the either-or-ness of the church in North America. Because we are so dependent on the influence from the "North," and more positively, because no church exists in a vacuum (the church is one and thus feels the consequences of any movement from any of its parts), the church in the Third World is affected even more by the dichotomous either-or, heavily syncretistic values of the North Atlantic Church. At no level is this felt more than at the level of missionary theory and practice. The hard fact of the matter is that even though the church is one, and therefore the task of mission ought to be a joint enterprise of the church *in the six continents,* nevertheless, contemporary missionary theory and practice, whether liberal or conservative, verticalist or horizontalist, is shaped by the church in the North Atlantic.

THE OBJECTIVE
OF THIS BOOK

Sensitive to this reality, I decided to insert a parenthesis in my writing and teaching program within the church in Latin America to address myself to the church in the North, whom God used so greatly in my life and to whom I feel I ought to try to minister at this time. This book should therefore not be taken as one more lash at the North Atlantic church but as a positive challenge from one who was once challenged by her. More specifically, it is aimed at the evangelical wing of this church (the sector I know best), particularly to those who are involved directly or indirectly in the task of world mission:

—laymen who pray fervently and support sacrificially the missionary enterprise;

—pastors who are trying to lead their congregations into greater involvement in mission;

—seminarians who are considering their own role in the church's mission to the world;

—professors of mission in Bible institutes, colleges and seminaries who are responsible for the study and interpretation of mission in the context of today's world;

—missionaries who are on the cutting edge of the church's evangelistic outreach;

—missionary agencies in general; and

—missionary executives who are responsible for the formulation and implementation of the policies that shape the work of their respective missions.

Here are then, succinctly and concretely, the two basic objectives of this work.

1. To provide a personal, evangelical, Latin American, holistic interpretation of the church as an instrument of God's mission to the world[13] in the light of the witness of Scripture, the phenomenon of church growth, and the most outstanding tensions in the fulfillment of her responsibility.

2. To challenge Christians in the North Atlantic, particularly evangelicals, to a more integral and committed

---

13. That is, an integral, undivided, and organic interpretation of the church's role as an instrument of God's mission. By this I mean that I am interested in looking at the church's mission in its totality and not in pieces. Yet one cannot take a holistic approach to the church's missionary involvement without rediscovering the wholeness of the gospel and the holistic perspective of Scripture on such concepts as man, Christ, sin, and salvation. This is to recognize the need of rediscovering the unity of the biblical theology of mission.

One word about the term "holistic." I have chosen to use it in this form (without a "w") in accordance with *Webster's Seventh New Collegiate Dictionary* (Springfield, Mass.: Grand C. Merriam Co., 1963), p. 365, which defines it: "Of or relating to wholism. Emphasizing the organic or functional relation between parts and wholes (rather than atomistic)."

approach to the church's involvement in God's mission to the world.

THE ORIGIN
OF THIS BOOK

The basic material used for this book originated in connection with an invitation I received from the Department of Mission and Evangelism of Gordon-Conwell Theological Seminary to serve as visiting professor of the "World Mission of the Church" during the January, 1973 Intersession. Besides considering this kind invitation from one of the leading evangelical schools in North America an honor and privilege, I welcomed it as an opportunity to structure the ideas that are elaborated in the following pages. The fact that the class was so representative of North American church life[14] made it an excellent laboratory for the testing of the book's basic ideas in a North American setting. The feedback received from the students was stimulating and challenging. In addition, I had the privilege of having with me my faithful wife, who served not only as a very special private secretary but also as a co-worker in the development of the course. And as if this was not sufficient, I was given the privilege of sharing some of these thoughts with faculty members, other students not enrolled in the course, and with my friend and former student, Edesio Sánchez of Yucatán, México, who was at Gordon-Conwell as an exchange student from the Latin American Biblical Seminary. They all were an effective and challenging "sounding board."

---

14. There were 118 seminarians enrolled in the course, many of them involved in pastorates, youth ministries, Christian Education, evangelism and other ministries of the church. This was by no means a homogeneous group. Indeed, it represented a broad spectrum of Protestantism in North America, although the majority would identify themselves as evangelicals.

THE TENTATIVENESS
OF THIS BOOK

Finally, it must be said that under no circumstances should the reflections that follow be taken as a final word. Rather they should be understood as the words of a fellow traveler sharing with friends what he has seen in their common journey. No doubt they too have their own thoughts about him and will most likely find loopholes in his analysis. Hopefully our mutual insights will strengthen our performance as instruments of God's mission to the world.

GOD'S MISSION AND THE CHURCH'S NATURE

2/THE CHURCH'S CHARACTER*

Summary p.35

What is the church? For those who confess Jesus Christ as Lord and Savior this question is of utmost importance. For to "be in Christ" (2 Cor. 5:17; Rom. 8:1; Phil. 3:9; 1 Cor. 15:22; Eph. 1:4) is to be incorporated into his body, which is the church. To ask "What is the church?" is for the Christian as basic as a person's understanding of himself, the nature and origin of his family, his cultural background, and his national distinctives.

This question deals, therefore, with the problem of identity. Every person and group needs to know itself. For the Christian this is imperative, since his own being

---

*This chapter summarizes parts of ch. XII of my edited work, *Hacia una teología de la evangelización* (Buenos Aires: La Aurora, 1973).

and vocation are inseparably linked to the church's nature and mission.

We are concerned in this chapter to explore the meaning of the church. This meaning, however, cannot be discovered in her contemporary expressions or in the history of Christianity, but in the Scriptures, especially the New Testament. The New Testament must be our norm, our "rule," because it is the fundamental testimony of the origin, nature, and mission of the Christian community. As Emil Brunner said several years ago:

> So far as the contingent historical fact implied in revelation is concerned, the crystalization of the tradition in writing, the primary witness of the New Testament Canon is the standard means by which tradition operates. All later accretions must be judged by the measure of their conformity with this fundamental testimony: the canon is the "rule," the norm of tradition. Certainly it is true that oral tradition preceded Scripture and also that in this sense the Church preceded Scripture. The New Testament was the product of the primitive community. But such considerations do not affect the fact that this tradition fixed in writing must be and must remain the sole criterion of all later oral developments. Otherwise there is no guarantee that the same fate might not be in store for the Christian Gospel as overtook, for example, the teaching of Zarathustra or that of the Buddha—namely, that in the course of oral development something utterly different was evolved out of it.[1]

Our task is therefore reduced to the question: what is the essential character of the Church in the New Testament? There we find at least four general concepts that characterize the church. Let us consider them.

---

1. Emil Brunner, *The Misunderstanding of the Church* (Philadelphia: Westminster, 1951), p. 36.

First, the foremost image of the church in the Scriptures is that of God's people. This is primarily derived from the Old Testament. Nevertheless, the clearest reference to the church as the people of God is found in the New Testament:

> But you are a chosen race, a royal priesthood, a holy nation, God's own people, that you may declare the wonderful deeds of him who called you out of darkness into his marvelous light. Once you were no people but now you are God's people; once you had not received mercy but now you have received mercy (1 Peter 2:9, 10).

Note how the image of "people" permeated these verses. In verse 9, three nouns with similar meaning are used: *genos* (race, but more specifically a particular people); *ethnos* (nation, but understood not so much politically and geographically as culturally and sociologically; hence, a group of people); and *laos* (people, but in the biblical context it is used with reference to a *specific people* in contrast to the other peoples of the earth). *Laos,* repeated twice in verse 10, is used in biblical thought to distinguish God's own people from the other peoples of the earth. This particular use of *laos* is carried over from the Hebrew concept of *'am,* the noun used in the Old Testament to distinguish Israel from the *goyim* (the gentile nations).

These verses point out clearly that the church is a people with deep historical roots. Her origin goes back to the Old Testament concept of the people of God. The apostle uses three Old Testament passages (Ex. 19:5; Is. 43:20; 61:6) to show (1) how God's plan for the salvation of the world was *not* frustrated by the failure of Israel and (2) that a new community founded around Jesus Christ, whom God has made the principal cornerstone in the construction of his new temple (cf. vs. 5ff.), has taken the place and inherited the honors and names of Israel. It is in the community of Christ that God's intentions for Israel become clear.[2] The church has become the "new Israel" and God's plan of salvation is being fulfilled in her missionary endeavor.

The fact that she has taken the place of Israel is indicative of her election in Christ ("a chosen race"). The church's election can be understood only in the context of God's mercy: "Once you were no people but now you are God's people; once you had not received mercy but now you have received mercy" (1 Pe. 2:10). The church is a people whom God has chosen through his sovereign will. These Old Testament words are thus applicable to the church:

> It was not because you were more in number than any other people that the LORD set his love upon you and chose you, for you were the fewest of all peoples; but it is because the LORD loves you and is keeping the oath which he swore to your fathers, that the LORD has brought you out with a mighty hand, and redeemed you from the house of bondage (Deut. 7:7, 8a).

This people, chosen in God's grace and sovereignty, is a pilgrim community (cf. Heb. 13:13). The church is a community "on the go." She has been called to live "outside the camp" (that is, in the wilderness), to travel lightly. Rather than settling in the earthly city, she is to look for the city which is to come (Heb. 13:13), a "city which has foundations, whose builder and maker is God" (Heb. 11:10). This means that the church is oriented toward the future salvation of the Lord. She is thus an eschatological community. For this reason, she cannot be satisfied with the present. She must be critical when the transient and

---

2. Cf. Johannes Blauw, *The Missionary Nature of the Church* in *Cross Roads in Missions. Key Reprints of a Decade* (South Pasadena: William Carey Library, 1971), p. 128.

temporal are given an absolute character. She cannot give absolute commitment to the state, to political ideologies, economic theories, or cultural distinctives. As a community of the future, she is called to witness to the coming glory and to criticize the present in the light of the coming future.

> Hence the Christian community does not live from itself and for itself, but from the sovereignty of the risen Lord and for the coming sovereignty of him who has conquered death and is bringing life, righteousness and the kingdom of God.[3]

As the pilgrim people of God, the church lives in transition. Conscious of her heritage and merciful origin, she feels dissatisfied with her present situation and looks toward her future confirmation as God's own people, toward the complete fulfillment of her calling to the eternal glory of Jesus Christ (1 Pe. 5:10, 11).

> Only when we admit the correlative value of these three moments—the past of Israel, the present of the community and the future in glory—can we understand the existence and secret of the Church of Christ.[4]

BODY OF CHRIST

Second, the church is understood in Scripture as the body of Christ. The term "body," more than any other metaphor, expresses the spiritual and functional reality of the church. This reality is grounded on her corporate

---

3. Jürgen Moltmann, *Theology of Hope* (New York: Harper & Row, 1967), p. 325.

4. Blauw, *The Missionary Nature . . .* (First English edition (mimeographed) published under the title, *Main Lines of a Biblical Theology of Mission* (London: IMC/WCC-Department of Missionary Studies, 1960), p. 64).

unity. Corporate unity is what biblical theology calls corporate personality, that is, the presence of the many in the one.

> Christ is a "one" who includes within his resurrection-body "the many," i.e., a corporate personality, if that term is understood theologically rather than psychologically. In Hebraic thought "body" means "self," almost what we mean by "personality"; . . . It is this Hebraic view of what we call "personality," which lies behind the conception of the Church as the body of Christ. The individual Israelite was a member of Israel: the individual Christian is a member of Christ.[5]

The fact that the church is one has two implications. Since the many are incorporated into Christ, he must be understood as the fountain of their lives and unity. He gives energy to the body, uniting the diverse members around a single purpose. In addition to depending upon Christ for her daily life, the church also is subject to his authority. He is the head of the body, and thus the church is subject unconditionally to him.

The image of the church as the body of Christ is linked to her role as his bride. As such, the church has committed herself to him; she has pledged him her unconditional love; she waits for his return with expectant hope. In the meantime, she responds in obedience to his command and functions as his agent in the world.

> The Church is thus the means of Christ's work in the world; it is his hands and feet, his mouth and voice. As in his incarnate life, Christ had to have a body to proclaim his gospel and to do his work, so in his resurrection in this age he still needs a body to be the instrument of his gospel and of his work in the world.[6]

---

5. Alan Richardson, *An Introduction to the Theology of the New Testament* (New York: Harper, 1958), pp. 254, 255.
6. *Ibid.,* p. 256.

It is in this context that we need to understand the attributes of catholicity and apostolicity. According to Paul, the church is "the fullness of him who fills all in all" (Eph. 1:23). That is, she has been given to all mankind. In the church, the fullness of God's grace is offered to all humanity.[7] Any nationalistic, racist, or sectarian notion is categorically rejected. In Christ Jesus there is neither Jew nor Greek, slave nor free, male nor female (Gal. 3:28).

The catholicity of the church not only has a sociological dimension in that it includes all who respond to Christ's call no matter what the color of their skin, nationality, political ideology, economic status or educational background. The church is also catholic in that it permits men and women to be themselves in their anthropological fullness. That is, the church embraces people of all cultures. Then, through the redeeming grace of Christ, she enriches their respective cultures, gives greater depth to their talents and abilities, and restores them to fuller humanity.[8]

To say that the church is catholic is also to affirm the participation of that "great cloud of witness" (Heb. 12:1) in the life and ministry of the present church. That is, the church transcends the barriers of time, involving not only those who *now* confess Jesus Christ as Lord and Savior but also believers of all periods of history (Heb. 12:23).

Further, the church transcends the barriers of space. When the church acts in a given place, this is the action of the whole church. This is one reason why Christians the

---

7. Cf. Spanish version of *A Theological Reflection on the Work of Evangelism* (Geneva: Department of Evangelism and Mission of the World Council of Churches, n.d.), p. 17.

8. The restoration of man to fuller humanity is one of the meanings of the healings that are narrated in the Gospels. Jean-Jacques von Allmen points in this direction when he affirms that the gospel, through the acceptance of which man gains entrance into the church, restores men and women in their true humanity. In consequence, "they can be themselves in the church, thanks to salvation, restored to their [full] humanity, which paradigmatically, is proclaimed through the healings narrated in the Gospels." Jean-Jacques von Allmen, *El culto cristiano* (Salamanca: Ediciones Sígueme, 1968), p. 47.

world over must be concerned for one another—because what happens to one happens to all.

But the church is not only catholic but apostolic. That is, she is a "sent one." Her apostolicity stems from the fact that as the hands, feet, eyes, and mouth of Christ on earth, he has sent her to every geographical location, to every man and every structure of society. Under the guidance and power of the Holy Spirit, the church is to continue the task initiated by Jesus in his preaching ministry and fortified and confirmed in his redemptive work on the cross.[9] Consequently, the church cannot allow herself to

---

9. I base this affirmation on the fact that the mission of the church is *to the world* (cf. Mt. 28:18-20; Mk. 16:15; Lk. 24:45-49; Acts 1:8; Jn. 17:18; 20:21). I recognize that the term "world" means many things in Scripture. Nevertheless, biblical theology is clear about the close ties that exist between the world and man. As was pointed out in the last chapter, when the Bible, and particularly the New Testament, refers to the world in relation to God's mission it refers primarily to the world of man. (Cf. "Mundo y hombre en el evangelio de Juan," in H. Schlier, *Problemas exegéticos fundamentales en el Nuevo Testamento* (Madrid: Ediciones Fax, 1970), pp. 319-333; "El mundo; el dualismo joánico," in A. Wilkenhauser, *El evangelio según San Juan* (Barcelona: Editorial Herder, 1967), pp. 265-269).

Now, the world of man must be understood not only in the sense of persons, but also of places and structures. For man is a creature of time and space. Accordingly, he is spatially distributed through the different geographical regions of the earth. Since he is bound to a specific locality and is by nature a social being, his life in community leads him to establish relations with his fellow man in accordance with the values that govern his behavior. These values are at first biological and psychological in nature (they respond to man's struggle for survival). As he continues to cultivate his relations, the values that govern his behavior take on a social dimension. His relations also take concrete forms. They are slowly structured into an organized body. With time, these relations acquire a corporate "personality" which exercises a tremendous influence (in some cases, a *quasi* absolute control) over the individual's behavior.

These structures, together with the geographic regions of the earth, constitute, therefore, the stage of human life. Man lives in and acts through them. They shape and mold his life. This is why the church's mission to the world involves not only the act of going to the people that live in the different regions of the earth but also to the structures around which their existence revolves.

That the church has been sent by Christ to continue his work

be bound by geographical, social, economic, or political boundaries. As Christ's special agent, she has been sent forth to represent him in every sphere of human existence.[10] To speak of the church is to speak of a dynamic community, always in mobility. It is to speak of Christ's corporate presence in the world.

TEMPLE OF THE HOLY SPIRIT

The latter, however, must be understood in the light of the biblical concept of the church as the temple of the Holy Spirit. Among the many passages in the New Testament that deal with this concept, we must consider some closely.

The most obvious reference is found in the Pauline epistles, especially in the Corinthian correspondence. It is interesting to note how Paul uses both the concept of body and temple in his ecclesiological passages. In 1

---

in each region, to each man, and in each structure of the world can be deduced from the fact that in the great majority of figures and metaphors that Jesus used in the Gospels with respect to the role that the church ought to play in the world (salt, light, keys, bread, water, leaven, fire, etc.) the essential element is penetration. What else can these metaphors indicate but that the church has been called to make herself *present* in all the spheres of the world to give it flavor and to help preserve it from chaos; to let the light of the gospel shine in the dark places of this world; to open up the doors of life and hope with the liberating word of Christ to an alienated and dying world; to share the bread of life with the hungry masses; to give water to the thirsty; to leaven the earth with the gospel; and to proclaim in the midst of injustice and oppression the prophetic word of God which like fire burns and judges any kind of injustice or oppression?

10. Jesus said, "As the Father hath sent me, even so I send you" (Jn. 20:21). For his part, Paul affirmed that "we are ambassadors for Christ" (2 Cor. 5:20). An ambassador is a person sent as the representative of a government to a given country. The church is Christ's ambassador to the world. This means, at least, that wherever the church is, there Christ must be made present. As a good ambassador, the church must strive to make Christ's presence felt in every sphere of human existence.

Cor. 6:15 he speaks of Corinthian believers as members of Christ and in 6:19 affirms that they are the temple of the Spirit. We find the same thing in Ephesians where he relates the concept of body to edification which in turn is related to the concept of temple (cf. Eph. 2:14-22; 4:16). The same thing occurs in 1 Cor. 3:16. Here Paul refers to the church as the temple of the Holy Spirit after introducing the image of a building in construction (1 Cor. 3:9) in a passage that begins with an obvious reference to the concept of body (cf. 1 Cor. 3:1-5; 1:13). He again interpolates these three ideas in the liturgical passages of the epistle (chapters 11—14) when he refers to the edification of the body in the context of worship.[11]

These passages indicate that for Paul what makes the church the temple of the Holy Spirit is the fact that the Spirit indwells her. *And this is precisely what makes her the body of Christ.* The fact that she is in the process of edification indicates that she has not yet arrived at her consummation. Her position in Christ as his body and the temple of the Spirit is subject to her mission as Christ's collaborator (1 Cor. 3:9-15; Eph. 4:16). In other words, the church is both a reality and a missionary project. To bring her mission to a halt would be equivalent to affirming that the construction of the building has ended, that the perfect worship service to which the Book of Revelation and the eucharistic words of Jesus referred (Mt. 27: 29) is already taking place, that the church has arrived at full maturity. In short, it would be a denial of the reality of the present historical moment between Pentecost and the second coming; it would amount to affirming that the Kingdom of God has come in its full manifestation.

The second biblical reference that we must examine

---

11. In biblical thought liturgy is related to the concept of temple. See further the discussion on the cleansing of the temple (Jn. 2:13-22) and the concept of temple in 1 Pet. 2:5. (Cf. also those passages in the Pauline epistles where the apostle uses a liturgical terminology, which belongs to the concept of temple, to describe his apostolic activity—Rom. 15:16; Phil. 2:17; Rom. 12:1, among others.)

is the prophecy on the destruction of the temple which is imbedded in the section on the cleansing of the temple, especially the Johannine version (cf. Jn. 2:13-22). Both the prophecy and the context which surrounds it are important because they deal with the problem that early Christians faced: they had no holy place of worship, spacially located, which could be designated as *the place* where God in some special sense made himself present to his people.[12] This was a contrast to Judaism which had both the Jerusalem temple and the synagogues of the *diaspora* and which did consider them the house of Yahweh. Of course, for a short time there was considerable ambiguity among Jewish Christians with regard to both the temple and the synagogue. The New Testament makes clear that after the resurrection (Acts 2:46) the disciples continued to attend both places. This problem was solved with the destruction of the temple (A.D. 70) and the hostility of the Jews toward the early Christians when the latter visited the synagogues.[13]

The Johannine version of the prophecy on the destruction of the temple specifically states that Jesus took the place of the temple. Further, it reveals how this idea did not develop in the early church until after the resurrection (cf. Jn. 2:22). While in the synoptic version this saying of Jesus (cf. Mk. 13:1, 2; Mt. 24:1-3; Lk. 21:5, 6) alludes to his death and resurrection, in the Johannine the allusion is to the destruction of the temple. There is in John, nevertheless, a direct reference to Jesus' death and resurrection (2:19: "destroy" and "I will raise up"). Note the reference to Ps. 69 in 2:17: "His disciples remembered that it was written, 'Zeal for thy house will consume me.'" This brings to memory the unique role that the Jerusalem temple played in Hebrew theology—it was the symbol of the

---

12. Cf. Franklin W. Young, "The Theological Context of New Testament Worship," in *Worship in Scripture and Tradition* (New York: Oxford, 1963), p. 78.

13. Cf. the persecutions of Paul (Acts 14:1-5; 17:1-15, etc.) and other Christians.

presence of God in the midst of his people. The passage indicates that God's presence was manifested in the death and resurrection of Jesus. Hence the temple was not needed any longer. The resurrected Christ through his Spirit was now making God near. Jesus had himself become *the place* where God meets man.

This is verified by Jn. 4:20-24 where John records a dialogue between the Samaritan woman and Jesus. The Samaritan says:

> "Our fathers worshiped on this mountain; and you say that in Jerusalem is the place where men ought to worship." Jesus said to her, "Woman, believe me, the hour is coming when neither on this mountain nor in Jerusalem will you worship the Father . . . the hour is coming, and now is, when the true worshipers will worship the Father in spirit and in truth, for such the Father seeks to worship him. God is spirit, and those who worship him must worship in spirit and in truth."

In the Gospel of John, the expression "the hour" culminates in the death and resurrection of Jesus (cf. Jn. 13:1; 16:32). Hence John's affirmation that the truth behind these sayings will be known when the Holy Spirit comes (16:12-15). The true worshipers are those who worship in *spirit* and *truth*. True worship will take place after the fulfillment of Jesus' hour. Then man will be able to worship in spirit and truth because he will be able to encounter the risen Christ (the truth, Jn. 14:6) made present through his Spirit. Christ thus becomes the new temple of God, the place where God and man can meet each other through the Spirit.

If Christ has substituted for the Hebrew temple, how can Paul affirm that the church is the temple of God? We face this same problem in 1 Pe. 2:5 where the church, in an obvious reference to the Hebrew temple, is called a "spiritual house" whose members constitute a "royal priesthood" and ought therefore "to offer spiritual sacrifices."

The problem may be resolved if we bear in mind that

the Holy Spirit is himself the Spirit of Christ (Rom. 8:9; 2 Cor. 3:17). His function is to continue the work of Jesus (cf. Jn. 16:13-14; Acts 1:8). Consequently, the church may be considered the new temple of God because the Spirit of Christ indwells her and because she is his body. Wherever the Spirit is, there is Christ, and where he is, the church is also present. Insofar as the church is the body of Christ and the temple of the Holy Spirit, she is, in this *aeon*, the point of contact between God and the world. Through her life and ministry the world is made aware of the place where God can be found—in Jesus Christ.

This intimate, inseparable relation between the Spirit and the church is what makes the latter a holy community. As Brunner said,

> Therefore, because the Holy Spirit is the very life-breath of the Church, the Church participates in the special character of the holy . . . And so because it is itself the "temple of the Holy Spirit" it is in its very essence the sphere of the holy and needs no temple.[14]

The concept of holiness has to do with consecration, a setting apart for a specific task. To say that the church is holy is to speak of her servant character, for holiness is the sign of servanthood. The church is thus the servant whom God has set apart to be the instrument of the Spirit in his redemptive purpose for the world.

INSTITUTION

The church is not only spiritual or communal in nature but also institutional. That is, it has certain specific activities, rites, roles, goals, etc., which give it persistency and stability and which, therefore, distinguish her from other structures of society.

---

14. Brunner, *The Misunderstanding* . . . , p. 12.

Now I am well aware of Brunner's argument against an institutional concept of the church. His book *The Misunderstanding of the Church* is a frontal attack on the idea of the New Testament *ecclesia* as an institution. According to Brunner, the church "is a pure communion of persons entirely without institutional character."[15] He is right in emphasizing the communal aspect as the key to understanding the church's nature. This fellowship, however, does not exist in a vacuum. It takes place in concrete situations, and consequently, it takes different forms which give it an institutional character.

The latter is evident in Acts 2:46, where an atmosphere of "a pure communion of persons" has certain institutional characteristics: the celebration of the Eucharist, the ministry of the Word, the manifestation of a visible and continued fellowship. Other significant traits, such as the election and training of the twelve apostles (interestingly enough, the same number as the tribes of Israel) for the establishment of the church; the eucharistic words of Jesus (instituting the Lord's Supper as a permanent rite of the church); the command to go into the world and make disciples, baptizing them in the name of the Father, the Son, and the Holy Spirit; the different administrative forms that the churches take (with officers, rules of internal discipline, and, in some cases, universal implications) are clearly observed in New Testament theology.

In his small book, *Where in the World?*, Colin Williams defends the institutional character of the church in his treatment of the church's mission in the world. Quoting heavily from the "Report of the Theological Commission on Christ and the Church" (North American Section) at the Fourth World Conference on Faith and Order, he refutes Brunner's argument.

> The Scriptures also warn us against those who, claiming the Spirit's authority as an immediate possession, decry all institutional forms or channels . . . The work

---

15. Brunner, *The Misunderstanding* . . . , p. 17.

of the Spirit is notably marked by richness and variety
. . . But when all this is said, it remains true that in
his working the Spirit gives form. As in the Incarnation God binds himself to concrete manhood, so by the
Spirit in the Church he works in and through human
flesh and blood, words and acts, social and historical
structures. Any adequate view of the Church must give
proper attention to such social and historical structures![16]

The institutional character of the church is therefore
implicit in the theological and praxeological dimensions of
ecclesiology. It must be added that the organizational
forms taken by the church must be subject both to her
purpose and mission as well as to the leading of the Holy
Spirit. In other words, the church's institutional forms are
relative to the concrete situations in which the church
must live and carry out her ministry. Yet these forms are
under the judgment of the Word and must always strive for
consistency with the character of the church as the people
of God, the body of Christ, and the temple of the Holy Spirit.

In summary, what is the church? It is a multitude of
men and women from all walks of life, without distinction
of race, nationality, economic and educational background. It is a community gathered from every tribe,
tongue, and nation. It is a people called out of darkness
into God's marvelous light through the Holy Spirit, as a
result of God's revealed and redeeming grace in Jesus
Christ, to be God's own people, Christ's own body, and the
temple of the Holy Spirit in the concrete situations of their
everyday life. This is the root meaning of the term ecclesia:
"called out." But called for what? This is the subject of
the next chapter.

---

16. "Report of the Theological Commission on Christ and the
Church," Fourth World Conference on Faith and Order, July,
1963, pp. 26-30. Quoted by Colin Williams in Where in the
World? (New York: Department of Publication Services of the National Council of Churches of Christ, 1963), p. 55.

3/THE CHURCH'S CALLING*

The church is the gathering of the called ones (1 Cor. 1:9). She is the community of those who have been called out of darkness into God's marvelous light and who have responded in faith and obedience. What is the objective of this call?

THE PURPOSE OF THE CHURCH'S CALLING

THE CHURCH'S LITURGICAL PURPOSE. The primary objective of the church's call is the praise of the glory of

---

*This chapter also summarizes parts of chapter XII of my *Hacia una teologia de la evangelización.*

God's grace (Eph. 1:6). Worship is the church's *raison d'etre.* The New Testament is clear about the church's liturgical purpose. She has been called to offer constant liturgy to God. This call is implicitly contained in Paul's appeal to the Roman Christians:

> I appeal to you therefore, brethren, by the mercies of God, to present your bodies as a living sacrifice, holy and acceptable to God, which is your spiritual worship (Rom. 12:1; cf. 1 Pe. 2:5, 9, 10).

Worship is a natural, spontaneous expression of the redeemed. "Let the redeemed of the LORD say so," the Psalmist exhorts (Ps. 107:2, 3), while the twenty-four elders of Revelation sing:

> Worthy art thou to take the scroll and to open its seals, for thou wast slain and by thy blood didst ransom men for God from every tribe and tongue and people and nation, and hast made them a kingdom and priests to our God, and they shall reign on earth (Rev. 5:9, 10).

Thus the church has been elected in Christ to be a liturgical community. Worship is the purpose behind God's liberating action. This is the fundamental reason that Moses gives to Pharaoh for the liberation of the children of Israel: "Thus says the LORD, the God of Israel, 'Let my people go, that they may hold a feast to me in the wilderness' " (Ex. 5:1). This is also the task that will be performed day and night by those who have come out of the great tribulation. They "who have come out of the great tribulation" and who "have washed their robes and made them white in the blood of the Lamb", says the Book of Revelation, shall be "before the throne of God" worshiping him day and night (Rev. 7:14-15; 22:3). Consequently, worship is not a mere function of the church; it is her *ultimate* purpose.

THE CHURCH'S MISSIONARY PURPOSE. The church's election in Christ also has a missionary objective. As Peter says to the Christians of the *diaspora*, "But you are a chosen race, a royal priesthood, a holy nation, God's own people, that you may declare the wonderful deeds of him who called you out darkness into his marvelous light" (1 Pe. 2:9).

The term "mission" comes to us from the Latin *missio* which means "to send." Etymologically it is foreign to biblical thought, but as a concept it permeates salvation history from Genesis to Revelation.

In the New Testament, the idea of mission is imbedded in the verbs *apostello* and *pempo,* or their derivatives, *apostellein* and *pempein*. According to Karl H. Rengstorf, *apostello* appears some 135 times; *pempo,* about 80. Both verbs, says Rengstorf, may be translated "to send." *Pempo* points in the direction of "the sending as such, *i.e.,* the fact of sending, as in the transmission of an object or commission of the sending of a man," while *apostello* "is more sharply accentuated in relation to the consciousness of a goal or to effort towards its attainment."[1] This distinction cannot always be made. For example, both verbs appear interchangeably in Luke, while in John a sharp distinction is made between the sending of the Son by the Father (*pempein*) and the sending of the disciples by the Son (*apostellein*).[2] In spite of these differences, both words have a missiological character in the sense that both are used to refer to the Father's sending the Son and the Son's sending the disciples, both to fulfill God's redemptive purpose for humanity.

Hence the church's calling has a twofold objective: one, as we have seen, of an ultimate character, and another more transient, because it is limited to the church's action *in* history. The first is liturgical; the other, missionary. One is congruent with the church's role as "firstfruits" of

---

1. Karl Heinrich Rengstorf, *"Apostello,"* in *Theological Dictionary of the New Testament,* Vol. I, Gerhard Kittel (ed.), translated and edited by Geoffrey W. Bromiley (Grand Rapids: Eerdmans, 1969), p. 398; cf. p. 403.

2. *Ibid.,* pp. 403, 404.

the coming kingdom and the new man. As such, the church has been created for God's glory. Her missionary objective, on the other hand, has to do with her role as the community that serves the King. As such, she has been sent forth to participate in God's redemptive mission to the world: calling all mankind to the great feast, that perfect worship of which the Gospels and the Book of Revelation speak so eloquently (cf. Mt. 22:2ff.; Lk. 14:15ff.; Rev. 19:17ff.).

Accordingly, distinction must be made between the church's ultimate purpose (to glorify God) and her earthly mission (to be God's instrument by witnessing to Jesus Christ, proclaiming his gospel, and discipling all the peoples of the earth). At the same time, we must not lose sight of the fact that in spite of this distinction, worship and mission are interrelated. In the New Testament, mission is understood in liturgical terms, and worship is viewed as mission-oriented.

THE CHURCH'S WORSHIPING-MISSIONARY CALLING. That worship is oriented toward mission and that the church's missionary action can be legitimately understood in liturgical (sacramental) terms, may be clearly seen throughout the New Testament. Paul, for example, saw his own life as a "sacrifice" (2 Tim. 4:6), and his preaching ministry as a spiritual liturgy (Greek *latreuo ento pneumati mou*, Rom. 1:9) and "a libation" (Phil. 2:16, 17a). He considered the fruit of his apostleship (the Gentiles who were converted to Christ through his ministry) an "offering" (Rom. 15:16) and understood the prayers of his "fathers" as a liturgy (Greek *ho latreuo*, that is, I serve or I worship, 2 Tim. 1:3). As has been noted, he appeals to the Roman Christians, "by the mercies of God, to present" their "bodies as a living sacrifice, holy and acceptable to God," which was, according to him, their "spiritual worship" (Rom. 12:1). In Phil. 2:17b he calls the faith of Philippian believers a "sacrificial offering," and in 4:18 he describes the love offering that they had sent him through Epaphroditus as "a fragrant offering" and "a sacrifice acceptable and pleasing to God."

But the Pauline epistles are not the only New Testament books that use the sacramental language of the temple to describe the church's missionary action. Hebrews 9:14 speaks of the purification of the faithful's consciences from dead works through Christ's sacrifice. Such purification transforms the believers' dead works into living works and thus frees them to render a living worship to God. In 12:28 and 13:15, 16, the author exhorts believers to "offer to God [an] acceptable worship," sacrifices of praise that are well pleasing to God through deeds of mercy ("to do good and to share what you have"). This same thought occurs in James 1:26, 27 where true religion (Greek *threskeia*[3]), understood in its cultic dimension, is defined in horizontal terms as bridling the tongue in relation to one's neighbor, visiting orphans and widows in their affliction, and keeping "oneself unstained from the world."[4]

The Apostle Peter integrates the idea of worship into the concept of mission and relates the latter to the essence of the church. He describes the church as "a spiritual house" and "a holy priesthood" responsible for the offering of "spiritual sacrifices acceptable to God through Jesus Christ" (1 Pe. 2:5). In so describing the church, Peter is affirming that the church as a liturgical community is called to serve (or worship) God through the ministry of intercession for the needy. For the ideas of offering and sacrifices must be understood in Scripture in terms of sacrificial service.[5] Further, in emphasizing in 2:9 that the community of faith has been called out of darkness into God's marvelous light in order to proclaim his wonderful

---

3. For a serious treatment of the liturgical meaning of this word, see the following works:

K. L. Schmidt, "Threskeia," in TDNT, Vol. III, pp. 155ff.

Roberto Sartor Bressan, "Culto y compromiso social según la Epístola de Santiago," in *Revista Bíblica,* 34:143 (1972/1), 26.

4. For a serious exegesis of this part of Verse 27, see Rodolfo Obermüller, "¿Contaminación? En torno a una definición de la religión (Santiago 1:27)," in *Revista Bíblica,* 34:143 (1972/1), 13ff.

5. Cf., for example, Amos 5:21ff.; Is. 1:11-17; Jer. 6:20ff.; Hos. 6: 6; Mic. 6:6ff.; Jas. 1:26, 27; Heb. 13:15, 16, etc.

deeds, Peter is in fact affirming that the church's mission is in itself a great liturgy or spiritual sacrifice.

But the relation between the ultimate purpose of the church and her earthly mission does not consist merely in the fact that the Scripture conceives the church's mission as an act of worship, indeed probably the greatest worship that the church renders to God. This interrelation may be seen also in the fact that the church's worship on earth is oriented toward the fulfillment of her mission.

Here I feel we must distinguish between two inseparable worship events. The first may be considered the church's incarnational worship; it takes place in the concrete situation of the church's everyday life. The second is what we usually call Sunday worship, that is, the gathering on the Lord's day[6] of the faithful for praise, thanksgiving, adoration, confession, intercession, witness, exhortation, commemoration, dedication, and commission. Incarnational worship is more personal and indirect. It takes place primarily in the believer's everyday contact with his fellow man (although we must not forget that this kind of worship involves also the believer's devotional moments, his private prayers, Bible reading, etc.). Sunday worship is public and communal. Both are important. Without the one the other would be empty and meaningless.

Nevertheless, the church's communal worship plays a unique role in her everyday life and missionary action. It dramatizes and actualizes the past, witnesses to the present historical moment, and points to the distant future of both the church and the world.

Further, Sunday worship is the time when the members of the body, dispersed in mission throughout the structures and strata of the world, come together to give witness to their essential unity in mission. It dramatizes

---

6. For a good defense of Sunday as *the* day of the church's formal worship see the following works:

Oscar Cullman, *Early Christian Worship. Studies in Biblical Theology* No. 10 (London: SCM, 1951).

Jean-Jacques von Allmen, *El culto cristiano* (Salamanca: Sígueme, 1968), pp. 223ff.

the catholicity and apostolicity of the church. On the one hand, it emphasizes that what is taking place is no ordinary gathering, but the reunion of those "sanctified in Christ Jesus, called to be saints together with all those who in every place call on the name of our Lord Jesus Christ" (1 Cor. 1:2). On the other hand, it affirms the present moment of the church's history in that it does not call attention to itself but to the church's mission. This is why in the liturgical literature of the first four centuries worship was designated "church" and "mass."

The first of these terms (Greek *ecclesia*) is used in the Old Testament to translate the Hebrew concept of *kahal yahweh*. This concept designates the assembly of the people redeemed out of Egypt and confirmed as a "holy nation" at Sinai (Deut. 4:10).

We must understand the New Testament usage of *ecclesia* in this context. Far from using this word in a sociological or judicial sense (as a political assembly), the New Testament uses *ecclesia* as a liturgical term, *i.e.,* in reference to the assembly of the faithful coming together for worship.[7] This indicates that the church's worship is an assembly of Christ's redeemed community "gathered to meet the Lord," to commemorate, celebrate, and actualize his work and ministry, which is the core of the gospel, and to be herself "in and through this encounter."[8]

But the worship service is not only an assembly of the redeemed. It is also a gathering of those *sent* into the world. It is a sort of interlude, a celebration of God's past and future presence and action in their midst. Thus the origin of the word *mass*. For many, this term implies sacrifice, transubstantiation, Eucharist, etc. And while it is true that the term is both historically and theologically related to these concepts, nevertheless, the root meaning of the word is the Latin *missio,* meaning to send, or in the context of the worship service, dismissal in order to per-

---

7. Cf., 1 Cor. 11:18, 22; 12:4f., 12, 19, 23, 28, 33f.
8. Xavier León-Dufor, "Iglesia," in his *Vocabulario de teología bíblica* (Barcelona: Herder, 1967), pp. 357-358.

form a task.[9] This puts the worship service in the perspective of mission. In this respect it must be understood as a great missionary event, for it brings the faithful together to send them again into the world. In other words, worship discloses the church not only as a catholic and redeemed community, but also as an eschatological and missionary community.

DIMENSIONS OF THE CHURCH'S MISSIONARY CALLING

The church's calling to participate in God's mission has to do, therefore, with the command to go into the world and make disciples of all nations. This task, which in the New Testament is understood as a great liturgical event, has several dimensions. In 1 Peter these are defined in several liturgical-oriented functions. In a sense these dimensions could be considered worshiping functions since they have to do with the reality of worship as a kerygmatic, sacramental, and paradigmatic event. In another sense these functions have to do with the basic nature of the church. They verify the interrelatedness between the church's mission and her nature. As Blauw has said so eloquently:

> There is no other Church than the Church *sent* into the world, and there is no other mission than that of the Church of Christ.[10]

PROPHETIC. God has chosen the church to be preemi-

---

9. Cf. von Allmen, *El culto* . . . , p. 51. According to von Allmen, the term *misa* (English mass) comes from the low Latin *missa* which is a corruption of *missio* and which means literally "to send"; thus, dismissal to perform a task. In other words, "the last event . . . , the solemn dismissal to send the faithful again into the world (cf. Lk. 24:46-53) . . ." Von Allmen says that by the fourth century this term replaces all other designations for the public worship, thereby accentuating its *raison d'etre* "in a world which is not yet the kingdom." *Ibid.*

10. Blauw, *The Missionary Nature . . .* , p. 120.

nently a prophetic community. A prophet is one who announces and interprets God's mighty deeds in the unfolding of history. As a prophetic community the church exists to proclaim "the wonderful deeds of him who called [her] out of darkness into his marvelous light" (1 Pe. 2:9b). The fact that this purpose is introduced by the preposition "that" indicates that everything said previously is conditioned to the execution of this objective. In other words, the church's sovereign and merciful election to be the people of God is validated and fulfilled when she proclaims the mighty deeds of God. At the same time, the church can make this proclamation only *as* the people who have been set apart by God and for God. In this respect the church's proclamation is both an act of praise and thanksgiving as well as a testimony of her experience and merciful origin.

The Greek word *arete,* which in the Revised Standard Version is translated "deeds," can mean "a manifestation of divine power, a miracle"[11] or "praise."[12] No matter how one may translate it, the context points in the direction of God's mighty deeds, especially those that have to do with redemption. How else can one understand the call from darkness and the lovely names that are attributed to the church? Further, in Scripture the praises of or to God are provoked by his mighty acts. Thus both his creative work (cf. Ps. 33:1-7; 104:1-35; Is. 42:10-12, etc.) as well as the mercy which is clearly revealed in the election of his people (cf. Is. 43:21), provoke praise. To proclaim God's mighty deeds is to publicly pronounce a word of praise. It is to witness to the miracle which God in his mercy has performed in the community of faith, this miracle which constitutes the primary motive of the missionary enterprise.

It is interesting to note how the Gospels and the sermons of the primitive church revolved around the mighty

---

11. Cf. W. F. Arndt and F. W. Gingrich, *"Arete,"* in *A Greek-English Lexicon of the New Testament and Other Early Christian Literature* (Chicago: University of Chicago Press, 1957), p. 105.

12. Cf. the Spanish version of the *Jerusalem Bible,* translated from the French (Bilbao: Descleé de Brouwer, 1967), p. 1620.

works of Jesus. For John, the many "signs" that Jesus performed were the basis for his preaching and writings; these transcribed the verbal witness of his personal experience with the Master (cf. Jn. 20:30, 31; 1 Jn. 1:13). And while Luke was not an eyewitness of the ministry of Jesus, he too emphasized his powerful works (cf. Lk. 24:19, 46-48; Acts 1:1-5, 8). For Mark, the preaching of the gospel of the kingdom seems to have been intimately related to God's mighty deeds over the demonic powers (Mk. 1:14, 21-23; 3:13-15). In Matthew, however, perhaps better than in any other Gospel (although it must be admitted that Luke and John seem frequently to have the same concern), one can appreciate the effort of the primitive community in relating the mighty works of Jesus to the climactic moments of Israel. Peter based his preaching on what he had heard and seen (Acts 4:20), and Paul, starting from his Damascus experience, together with Stephen, tied the Christ-event to the history of Israel (Acts 7:2-3; 13:17-41; 26:1-29).

These and other references (especially in the epistles) seem to show that the proclamation of the deeds of God has to do preeminently with the Christ-event. But since the latter is God's *supreme* revelation (Heb. 1:1, 2), it is intrinsically related to the rest of God's acts in history, from creation to consummation. Consequently, the prophetic function of the church deals with the proclamation of the whole counsel of God (Acts 20:27).

This proclamation is the basis for God's call to the world to become part of the new humanity which he is creating in Christ. The fact that the phrase "that you may declare" is grammatically and contextually related to the expression "him who called you out of darkness" clearly indicates that the church's proclamation is the continuation of God's call.

> Just as God's sending of the Son continues in the sending of the Spirit and the sending of the community into the world (Jn. 20:21), so the calling of God continues in the proclamation of the Church.

This proclamation is of course nothing else but making known what this calling of God has amounted to.[13]

This call is the logical conclusion of the proclamation of the wonderful deeds of God. Since the Christ-event is God's deed par excellence, and since it represents the irruption of the kingdom of God in history (Mk. 1:15), the church's proclamation involves the announcement of a new order of life, of which the church is herself the firstfruits. There is thus an implicit call within this proclamation, a call to come out of the darkness, *i.e.,* out of the state of "alienation" into which all mankind has fallen (Rom. 3:10, 23; Eph. 2:1-3), into God's marvelous light. If "darkness" means "alienation," God's "light" means reconciliation and participation in the new order. This miracle takes place to the extent that men and women respond in faith and confess Jesus Christ as Lord and Savior (cf. 1 Pe. 2:7, 8). This is, in general terms, the message that the world needs to hear and that the church must preach.

PRIESTLY. Just as the church's election to be God's people carries the responsibility of witness and proclamation, so her character as both the temple of the Spirit and the body of Christ implies a priestly function. This is easily deduced from two fundamental facts. First, the temple, as we have noted, is linked in biblical theology to the idea of worship, and worship revolves around the concept of sacrificial offering. Second, the relation of the church with Christ links her necessarily to his functions as High Priest of the New Covenant. Let us consider these facts separately.

Biblical theology does not conceive of a temple without worship nor of worship without sacrificial offering. This is so clear that it is not necessary to go into detail. A quick look at the Old Testament convinces one that when its writers outlined their interpretation of history, they could

13. Blauw, *The Missionary Nature* . . . , p. 134.

not conceive of the religious life without sacrifice.[14]

This idea appears again in the New Testament, though the religious life (which in the New Testament becomes the Christian way of life) has a different character. It does not revolve around a holy place, spacially located, nor is it contingent on the old practice of animal sacrifices. It continues to be understood as a life of worship, but the latter is defined dynamically, *i.e.,* as an encounter of Christ with his church through the Holy Spirit (cf. Mt. 18:20; Jn. 9:20-26; Acts 6:13f.; 7:48ff.) and is based upon Jesus' one-time sacrifice of himself in behalf of all men (cf. Heb. 9:11ff.). Nevertheless, worship, as the highest expression of the religious life, recovers the concept of sacrificial offering (1) when the church is given the character of God's temple, (2) in the description of her mission in liturgical terms, and (3) especially, in her designation as a holy and royal priesthood (1 Pe. 2:5, 9; Rev. 1:6; 5:10; 20:6).

It must be emphasized that the church's priesthood does not exist apart from Christ's priesthood. For there is no other priesthood in the New Testament than Christ's (cf. Heb. 7:26ff.). His priesthood ended the old Aaronic priesthood in that he offered in time a once-and-for-all sacrifice (cf. Heb. 7:27; 9:12, 25-28; 10:10-14). Therefore, he is the mediator of the New Covenant (Heb. 7:24f.; 8:6-13; 10:12-18).

In spite of the fact that Christ's priesthood has a different origin and nature from that of the Old Testament Aaronic priesthood (since Christ's is of the order of Melchisedec—cf. Heb. 5:10; 7:1ff.), his priestly functions generally follow those of the Old Testament priesthood. In the Old Testament, the priest had a twofold function. First, he was a leader of worship. As such, his responsibility was to guard the ark of the covenant (a symbol of the presence of Yahweh) when there was no temple (1 Sam. 1-4; 2 Sam. 15:24-29); to receive the faithful in the house of Yahweh

---

14. Cf. Charles Heuret, "Sacrificios," in León-Dufor, *Vocabulario,* p. 729. (Cf. also Gen. 4:1-4; 8:20; 14:18; 15:9; Ex. 5:3; 18:12; Jer. 20:26; 1 Ki. 8:14; Ezra 3:1-6; Jon. 1:16; Is. 56:7; 66:20; Mal. 1:11, etc.).

(1 Sam. 1); to preside over the liturgies of the feasts (Lev. 23:11, 20); to officiate at the rites of consecration and purification—the royal anointment (1 Ki. 1:39; 2 Ki. 11:12), the purification of lepers (Lev. 14) or of women who had given birth (Lev. 12:6ff.); and especially to offer sacrifices. This last function was the priest's essential act. In it he appeared fully in his role of mediator. Thus he would offer to God the offerings of the faithful and would transmit to them the divine blessing.[15]

Second, in addition to his cultic functions, the Old Testament priest was considered a servant of the Word. It is true that in Israel the mediation of the Word of God was the province of the prophet. Yet the *prophetic* word, which was a living and existential message adapted to the concrete situations of everyday life, was one of two forms in which God's Word came to the people. The other form was imbedded in the oral and later in the written tradition. This form of God's Word was rooted

> in the great acts of sacred history and the clauses of the Sinaitic covenant. This sacred tradition crystallized, on the one hand, the narratives that made present the great memories of the past, and on the other, the law which got its meaning from them. The priests were the ministers of this word.[16]

As the servants of the Word in its traditional form, the priests were responsible in the liturgy of the feasts for the recitation to the faithful of the narratives which were the foundation of the faith (cf. Ex. 1—15; Josh. 2—6). They also proclaimed the law (Torah) in the renewal of the Covenant (Ex. 24:7; Deut. 27; Neh. 8). They were the ordinary interpreters of the law. When consulted by the faithful, they responded with practical instructions (Deut. 33:10; Jer. 18:18; Ezek. 44:23; Hag. 2:11ff.). Moreover, they exercised a judicial function (Deut. 17:8-13; Ex. 44:23f.) and were in

---

15. Cf. Agustin George, "Sacerdocio," in *Ibid.,* p. 724. Cf. also Ex. 24:4-8; 29:38-42; Deut. 33:10; Lev. 16.
16. *Ibid.*

charge of redacting the written law in the different codes, *e.g.*, Deuteronomy, the code of holiness (Lev. 17—26), the law of Ezekiel (40—48), the priestly legislation (Ex., Lev., Num.), and the final compilation of the Pentateuch (cf. Ezra 7:14-26; Neh. 8).[17]

We can see in Jesus this double function. He reveals himself a priest through the offering of his own sacrifice and the service of the Word. Thus he speaks of his death in sacrificial terms (Mk. 10:45; 14:24; cf. Is. 53; Ex. 12:7; 13:22f.; 24:8) and puts himself at the service of the law (Mt. 5:17f.).

The church is called upon to participate in these functions of Christ's priesthood. She is called to follow in his steps (1 Pe. 2:21ff.), bearing the cross (Mt. 16:24), drinking his cup (Mt. 26:22; 26:27), and "bearing abuse for him . . . outside the camp," *i.e.*, in the world (Heb. 13:12, 13). She is also called upon to mediate the word of forgiveness (Mt. 16:19; 18:18; Jn. 20:22, 23; 2 Cor. 5:18), proclaiming the gospel of the kingdom of God (Mk. 1:14, 15; Lk. 9:60; 10:1-16), and bearing witness to Jesus even unto death (Mt. 10:17-42).

In summary, the priestly function of the church has a liturgical, intercessory, and representative dimension. It is liturgical, inasmuch as the priestly functions are always linked to worship. So it does not matter whether one is dealing with the Sunday worship service or with the worship that takes place in the church's life and missionary action, the church is constantly involved in sacrificial action. This is what both the writer of Hebrews and the Apostle Peter mean by spiritual sacrifices of praise (cf. Heb. 13:15; 1 Pe. 2:5).

Such action is always oriented toward the other. Hence the church's priestly function has not only a liturgical but an intercessory character. Even when the High Priest had to offer a sacrifice for his own sins (Heb. 5:3), it was offered in order that he might be qualified to offer sacrifices on behalf of men (Heb. 5:1), since he himself was beset

---

17. *Ibid.*

with weaknesses (Heb. 5:2). With respect to the sacrifices that the church is called upon to offer, both Hebrews and James make quite clear that they have to be preeminently intercessory prayers and deeds of mercy (Heb. 13:6; Jas. 1:27). These sacrifices have to do with the church's intercession for the world, a function fulfilled through prayer and service. (This indicating the intimate relation that must exist between prayer and action. A praying church must also be a militant church.)

Third, the church's priestly function has a representative dimension. The church's worship is a substitute for the worship which the world, by virtue of creation, has been called upon to render to the Creator. The book of Genesis makes quite clear the liturgical calling of man (and of the rest of creation). In creation, God summoned the world to find self-fulfillment and peace by celebrating God and experiencing his rest through the leadership and worship of man (Gen. 1:1, 2; 4).

> But man through his sin has disoriented the world; he has deviated it from its true origin and has reduced the worship that should have been his to anxious sighings. God has denied this disturbance of the world and for this reason instituted in time the history of salvation—from the flood, which is the prefiguration of the end of the world, to the disappearance of the Egyptian army at the Red Sea, until the victory of Easter day and the coming of the Holy Spirit, going through all the ascendent and descendent stages of the chosen people, until the climactic point of the incarnation of the Son of God in Jesus of Nazareth.[18]

The worship service is thus a recapitulation of the history of salvation. For this reason it constitutes the moment and place where men find their primary objective as human beings (to glorify God) and discover their ultimate

---

18. Von Allmen, *El culto* . . . , p. 69.

purpose (to celebrate God's glory). Von Allmen reminds us that

> . . . the worship service is not the moment nor the place [where this discovery is made] on account of itself, but rather because of the world, substituting for it. It does what all of mankind and creation should do and is what all of mankind and creation should be. This is how the vicarious character of worship must be understood: it substitutes for the world because in Jesus Christ it can accomplish a task which it could not do on its own. Hence the church owes God and the world her worship in order to reveal to the latter the past that should have never been lost and the promised future.[19]

Through her worship the church acts as the representative of the world. The worship service is a reflex of the church's everyday activity in behalf of the world, *i.e.,* it celebrates and recapitulates the history which the church shares every day with the world. In other words, Sunday worship is a rehearsal of the incarnate worship that the church celebrates every day through the proclamation to the world, in word and deeds, of Jesus Christ as the hope of the world. This is why evangelism is a mediating action, and the proclamation of the gospel, one of the greatest services that the church renders to the world.

Therefore, the church ought to be concerned about the world, pray for it, and work toward its future, because she has been called out of darkness to participate in Christ's priesthood in the world. Like Jesus, she must have compassion for the multitudes (Mt. 9:27), "deal gently with the ignorant and wayward" (Heb. 5:2), and "go forth to him outside the camp, bearing abuse for him" (Heb. 13:13) on behalf of a lost and alienated world (cf. Phil. 2:7, 8; 1 Pe. 2:21ff.).

---

19. *Ibid.,* p. 70.

ROYAL. The church is also called to be a paradigmatic community, *i.e.,* a community that lives and demonstrates the liberating power of the gospel and the new possibilities available in Christ for a world oppressed and enslaved by demonic principalities and powers. This is why both 1 Pe. 2:9 and Rev. 1:6; 5:10 designate her as a *royal* priesthood. As the church participates in the priesthood of Christ, so she also participates in his kingship. This participation takes place on at least two levels.

In the first place, the church is firstfruits of the new man *i.e.,* the new humanity which God is creating in the person of the risen Christ (2 Cor. 5:7; Gal. 6:10; Eph. 2:2, 10, 15; 4:24). The resurrection of Christ and his subsequent exaltation over powers and principalities (Eph. 1:20, 21) have confirmed (1) his triumph over the cosmic rebellious principalities and powers (Col. 2:15; Eph. 4:8-10), (2) his victory through the cross over the death of the offspring of the first Adam, corrupted by sin (cf. Rom. 5:12f.; 8:3; 1 Cor. 15:21), and (3) the resurgence of a new race after the last Adam (1 Cor. 15:45). Since Christ himself is the last Adam and the firstborn of them that sleep (cf. 1 Cor. 15:20), he quickens those who come to him (cf. Eph. 2:5, 6; Col. 2:13), setting them with him in heavenly places (Eph. 2:6) and making them a kingdom of priests (Rev. 1:6; 5:10). Thus he considers himself "the ruler of the kings of the earth" (Rev. 1:5b), and those that have risen with him, co-participants (or rulers with him) in his kingdom (Rev. 20:6).

For the same reason, and as a result of Christ's triumph on the cross, the church has been given authority over the evil powers of this world (cf. Eph. 1:22, 23; Col. 2:9-15). As the body of Christ, the church is "the fullness of him who fills all in all" (Eph. 1:23b). That is, the church is an organism full of everything (life, authority, power, etc.) and which fills all in all (through her mission).[20]

---

20. Cf. V. Warnack, "Iglesia," in J. Bauer, *Diccionario de teología bíblica,* translated from the German (Barcelona: Herder, 1967), Col. 486, 487; Paul Lamarche, "Plenitud," in León-Dufor, *Vocabu-*

From this follow two important implications. The first has to do with the effect of the church's royalty upon her priesthood, or, as in the case of Christ, the reciprocity between priestly service and royal freedom. According to Blauw,

> The priestly serving of God is service in royal freedom; here priesthood and kingship interpenetrate reciprocally, as in Jesus Christ Himself. This royal freedom of the priestly service exists for the sake of witness in the world; yes, the life of the community as a royal priesthood is already a witness in itself. The proclamation of the marvelous deeds of God occurs not only by word and deed; it already takes place in the existence of the community.[21]

In other words, the church has been called to be, by the miracle of her own life, an exemplary community, *i.e.,* a model of what human society should be and is not. Without going into detail, let us consider the main attributes that should characterize human society.

In biblical thought, society is the obvious result of the creation of man. God created him in his own image (Gen. 1:26ff.) to live in community (Gen. 2:18ff.) and to have dominion over the earth, representing God before the rest of creation and acting as his viceroy (Gen. 1:28-30). Since his image was distorted by sin, since the race was divided (Gen. 11) and man lost his dignity and freedom as governor of the earth, God took it upon himself to recreate him by raising up a new race which would fulfill the vocation of mankind: a liberated, loving, and just society. The church, as the firstfruits of the new order, meets all of these qualities. She has been created in righteousness and holi-

---

lario . . . , pp. 619, 620; J. Schildenberger, "Plenitud," in Bauer, *Diccionario . . . ,* Col. 821-828; A. H. Van den Heuvel, *Estos rebeldes poderes,* translated from the English (Montevideo: Ediciones U.L.A.J.E., 1967), pp. 27-90.

21. Blauw, *The Missionary Nature . . . ,* p. 130.

ness; she is called upon to put on the new man (Eph. 4:
24). Further, she is a sign of peace (Eph. 2:15) and thus
ought to be "eager to maintain the unity of the Spirit in the
bond of peace" (Eph. 4:3), doing away with the divisions of
men (Gal. 3:27f.; Col. 3:10), living in love (Eph. 5:2; Rom.
13:8, 9; Gal. 5:14; 1 Jn.), and keeping herself firm in the
liberty of Christ, not allowing herself to be oppressed under any alien bondage (Gal. 5:1, 13; Jn. 8:32, 36; Rom. 8:
2, 21; 2 Cor. 3:17).

The royal function of the church consists, therefore,
at least in living the reality of the new order of life which
began with Jesus of Nazareth and which is moving toward
final consummation at the second coming. As I have said,
it is a paradigmatic activity, a living demonstration of the
freedom and dignity of the new man, and of the new possibilities in Jesus Christ for a world dominated and oppressed by demonic powers and principalities, full of hate
and injustice.

That the church participates in the kingship of Christ,
implies, second, that part of her missionary responsibility
is to unmask these demonic powers which resist God's
work and which were defeated at the cross (Eph. 3:9, 10).
As R. Schnackenburg says in his article on the kingdom of
God:

> To the church belongs the preaching and communi-
> cation of salvation to men (cf. Eph. 3:6-8), but also
> the unmasking of the powers in opposition to God
> (cf. Eph. 3:10). . . .[22]

Here it is necessary to make reference to an important fact in the preaching of Jesus. It deals with the mighty
deeds that accompanied his preaching (Mk. 1:39). These
consisted of the announcement of a new era (cf. Mk. 1:
14, 15) which had drawn near in the person of Jesus.
Hence the jubilant context of his preaching and the reason

---

22. R. Schnackenburg, "Reino de Dios," in Bauer, *Diccionario* . . . ,
col. 903.

why it is accompanied by signs and wonders (Mk. 1:29; Mt. 10:1; Lk. 9:1; 10:1ff.). We see the same idea implicit in the passages of the Great Commission, especially Mt. 28: 18 ("All power . . ."), Mk. 16:17, 18,[23] and Acts 1:8.

These and similar passages indicate that preaching is an eschatological event, a challenging announcement, and a mighty act in which the rebel powers of this world are put under judgment. Through preaching God intervenes in the life of men, leading them to renounce the kingdom of darkness, to change their allegiance to the kingdom of light, and to be liberated from the power of sin and death. As J. J. von Allmen has said:

> Contrary to what is so frequently believed, in preaching, something of interest to men occurs. Something happens to them. Preaching is an event that can be placed parallel to an exorcism: the demons are expelled and that which belongs to God is returned [to him] . . .[24]

As a royal community, the church is called not only to exercise a priestly ministry in royal freedom, but also to preach with the authority of Christ the Lord. This means at least that she cannot let her mission be paralyzed by threats from earthly and demonic powers. And likewise, that she is to serve with boldness and dedication even though it may appear as if she is wasting her time and energy. For

> God chose what is foolish in the world to shame the wise, God chose what is weak in the world to shame the strong, God chose what is low and despised in the world, even things that are not, to bring to nothing

---

23. This passage does not appear in the best manuscripts. Cf. A. Robert and A. Feuillet, *Introducción a la Biblia,* II, translated from the French by Alejandro Ros (Barcelona: Herder, 1970), pp. 223, 224.

24. von Allmen, *El culto . . . ,* p. 65.

things that are, so that no human being can boast in the presence of God (1 Cor. 1:27-29).

Thus we see how the threefold dimensions of the church's missionary calling converge. It is clear that though there are three dimensions, and consequently three different functions, *the mission is one.* The whole church is sent by Christ to the world to be *one* prophetic, priestly, and royal community through which the Spirit can continue to operate the miracle of the new creation.

4/THE CHURCH'S MESSAGE

Sum p. 82

In the last two chapters, it has been said that the church's missionary calling is oriented toward communication of the gospel of Jesus Christ to all the peoples of the earth. The church is God's messenger to the world. Her message is the gospel. It is required of an envoy so to understand and commit himself to the message he is sent to convey that he can transmit it with conviction and persuasiveness. If the church is to live up to her calling, she must understand and commit herself unconditionally to the message entrusted to her.

Our task in this chapter is to explore the biblical nature of the gospel in order to understand the depth of the commitment which the church is required to have as an instrument of God's mission. This may seem easy at first, but a quick look at the literature available suffices to convince us of the contrary. Especially since C. H. Dodd published his monumental work, *The Apostolic Preaching and Its Development*,[1] many scholars have dedicated hundreds of pages to the precise nature of the gospel. Many have followed Dodd's basic conclusions, adding footnotes here and there. Others have raised serious questions with regard to Dodd's approach and conclusions.[2]

All agree, however, that the gospel is basically and essentially a message of joy and gladness. It is good news—the most renowned news of history. This is why the first four books of the New Testament describe it as a glorious and powerful event accompanied by signs and wonders. "The blind receive their sight, and the lame walk, the lepers are cleansed, and the deaf hear, the dead are raised up, and the poor have the gospel preached to them" (Mt. 11:5).

THE GOSPEL AS THE FULFILLMENT OF THE OLD TESTAMENT HOPE

The gospel does not appear in the New Testament *tabula raza*. That is, it is not a New Testament creation. Rather the New Testament describes it as the fulfillment of the Old Testament hope. This is why it is first proclaimed to Israel (cf. Mt. 15:24; 12:1ff.; 10:6; 8:12; 12:32; 19:41ff.). It behooves us, therefore, to consider the essential elements of the messianic hope of the Old Testament.

AN ERA OF JUSTICE AND RIGHTEOUSNESS. In the first place, the Old Testament looked forward to an age of justice and righteousness. In the Old Testament, justice and

---

1. C. H. Dodd, *The Apostolic Preaching and Its Development* (Chicago: Willet, 1937).

2. For a good summary of the arguments pro and con see Michael Green, *Evangelism in the Early Church* (Grand Rapids: Eerdmans, 1970), pp. 60ff.

righteousness were considered basic to the success of society. Man was looked upon as needing to guide his conduct by God's standard and to be conscious of the rights of his neighbor. Man was neither allowed to take advantage of his neighbor nor to let himself be oppressed by him. To oppress one's neighbor amounted to usurping God's authority, for he was the author of life and consequently the only one who had authority to take a man's life. Likewise, to allow oneself to be oppressed or subjugated was to acknowledge someone else as God. Thus the Old Testament forbade idolatry—because idols were understood to be projections of the human personality, manifestations of man's attempt to be like God—and presented God as being on the side of the weak, the orphan, the widow, and the poor.

Now Israel was created as a model of a just and righteous society. God gave laws to guide her, teachers to explain the meaning of these laws, rulers to make sure that these laws were kept, and prophets to call attention to the people's deviation from God's standard and to remind them of their missionary responsibility to their neighbors as a "nation of priests" (Ex. 19:5).

Israel did not live up to her calling. She openly violated God's precepts, failed to live up to his standards and to fulfill her mission. God reminded her time and again that he expected her "to do justice" (Mic. 6:8; Amos 5:24; Jer. 22:3; Ezek. 45:9), but Israel followed her own plans and acted according to the stubbornness of her evil heart (Jer. 18:12).

Out of Israel's failure, the prophets envisioned a new age in which Yahweh's demand to "let justice roll down like waters, and righteousness like an ever flowing stream" (Amos 5:24) will become a reality, because he will make a new covenant with his people. He will put his law within them and will write it upon their hearts (Jer. 31:33). A law will go forth from Yahweh and his justice will enlighten the peoples of the earth (Is. 51:4; 42:4). Yahweh will accomplish this through the intervention of his servant who will establish "justice in the earth" (Is. 42:4; 11:1-12) and will "make many to be accounted righteous" (Is. 53:11) even by the outpouring of his soul unto death (Is. 53:12).

AN ERA OF PEACE. Together with the vision of an era of justice and righteousness, the Old Testament envisions the coming of an era of world peace. This vision is grounded on the peaceful character of God. Already in Judges 6:24 God is called *"Yahweh shalom"* (the LORD is peace). He is said to be the creator of *shalom* (Is. 45:7) and to delight in the *shalom* of his servants (Ps. 35:27). Hence he keeps in perfect peace the one whose mind is on him (Is. 26:3; cf. Ps. 4:9).

The Hebrew concept of *shalom* (peace) means "completeness," "soundness," "well-being." According to the French scholar, Xavier León-Dufor, the word *shalom*

> is derived from a root which, according to its usage, designates the fact of finding oneself intact, complete (Job 9:4), such as, for example, completing a house (1 Ki. 9:25), or the act of reestablishing things in their integrity into their original state . . . (Ex. 21:24) . . . (Ps. 50:14). Consequently, the biblical peace is not only a "covenant" which allows a quiet life, nor the "time of peace" as opposed to the "time of war" (Eccl. 3:8; Rev. 6:4). Rather it designates the well-being of the everyday life, the state of that man who lives in harmony with nature, with himself, with God. Concretely, it means blessing, rest, glory, riches, salvation, life.[3]

This is the idea behind the good tidings of peace in Is. 52:7; a time of universal salvation (Is. 2:2; 60:1ff.), harmony (Is. 11:6-9), justice and righteousness (Is. 11:3-5; 32:16, 17; Ps. 72:1ff.), deliverance from oppression (Ps. 72:12-14; Is. 52:10ff.), comfort and prosperity (Is. 66:12-14), worship (Is. 66:23), and holiness (Is. 62:12; Ezek. 37:23), "for the earth shall be full of the knowledge of the LORD as the

---

3. León-Dufor, *Vocabulario . . .* , pp. 582, 583.

waters cover the sea" (Is. 11:9). All of this will be wrought by the anointed of the Lord, the Prince of Peace (Is. 9:6), who himself will proclaim the message of glad tidings.

A HOPE MEDIATED THROUGH SUFFERING. This hope was mediated through the experience of suffering. Through the captivity, Israel recovered her lost eschatological perspective. She began to see Yahweh once again as her deliverer and to catch a glimpse of his coming salvation.

In no other passages is this more clearly revealed than in Isaiah's servant songs. They are addressed to a people who have passed through God's judgment. In their captivity they envision a new day of justice and peace. Israel will be healed from all her ills. She will rise up and experience God's coming salvation. Thus the comforting message of Isaiah:

Comfort, comfort ye my people,
    says your God.
Speak tenderly to Jerusalem,
    and cry to her
that her warfare is ended,
    that her iniquity is pardoned,
that she has received from the LORD's hand
    double for all her sins.

Awake, awake,
put on your strength, O Zion;
put on your beautiful garments . . .
Shake yourself from the dust, arise,
    O captive Jerusalem;
loose the bonds from your neck,
    O captive daughter of Zion.

For thus says the LORD: "You were
sold for nothing and you shall be
redeemed without money . . . in that day
they shall know that it is I who speak;
here am I."

How beautiful upon the mountains
  are the feet of him who brings good tidings,
who publishes peace, who brings good tidings of good,
  who publishes salvation,
  who says to Zion, "Your God reigns."

                             (Is. 40:1, 2; 52:1, 3, 6b, 7)

This vision, mediated through the experience of suffering, is itself imbedded in a context of vicarious suffering. The latter part of Is. 52 and the entire fifty-third chapter indicate without a shadow of doubt that justice and peace will come only at the price of suffering and death. The servant of Yahweh will be exalted only through his humiliation; he will bring peace by bearing the sins of many, by suffering oppression, chastisement, affliction, judgment, and death. He shall "make many to be accounted righteous" by bearing their iniquities. Israel will bear many children, she will "spread abroad to the right and to the left," her descendants will possess the nations (Is. 54:1, 3); her citizens will be to the nations Yahweh's priests and the ministers of God *through* the redemptive sacrifice of the servant of Yahweh (Is. 61:6).

THE GOSPEL AS FULFILLED
IN JESUS OF NAZARETH

We must understand the good news of the New Testament in the light of this hope. The gospel is the fulfillment of the Old Testament messianic hope. In the person of Jesus of Nazareth it announces the incarnation of the glad tidings of peace to the afflicted and the brokenhearted. Thus Jesus conceived of his earthly ministry in terms of his being Yahweh's anointed. He appropriated the commission to preach recorded in Isaiah 61 when he entered the synagogue at Nazareth and read:

"The Spirit of the Lord is upon me, because he has

anointed me to preach the gospel to the poor; he hath sent me to heal the brokenhearted, to preach deliverance to the captives, and recovering of sight to the blind, to set at liberty them that are bruised, to preach the acceptable year of the Lord."

And he closed the book . . . and sat down and the eyes of all in the synagogue were fixed on him. And he began to say to them, "Today this Scripture has been fulfilled in your hearing" (Lk. 4:18-21).

INAUGURATOR OF THE NEW AGE. In affirming categorically that in that very moment Isaiah's prophecy had been fulfilled, Jesus was saying that the new age had come with his preaching. "The acceptable year of the Lord" had arrived. This is confirmed by Mark who records Jesus' first sermon in Galilee. Mark says that

. . . after John was arrested, Jesus came into Galilee, preaching the gospel of God, and saying, "The time is fulfilled, and the kingdom of God is at hand; repent, and believe in the gospel" (Mk. 1:14, 15).

The word kingdom (Greek *basileia*) may mean (1) the exercise of sovereignty, a government; (2) the governed community; and (3) the place or territory where sovereignty is exercised.[4] In the context of Jesus' preaching it is specifically related to the arrival of a new age characterized by the sovereign reign of God in his Son. It deals with a new order of life. It is a decisive moment, the *kairos* (the appropriate time) of God, in which his sovereign will appears among men in a concrete, personal, yet cosmic form. It implies the formation of a new community and the exercise of God's sovereign rule over all principalities and powers. Hence, it is accompanied by signs and wonders (Mk. 1:27) and the call to repentance and faith (Mk. 1:15).

---

4. Cf. Oscar Cullman, *La fe y el culto en la iglesia primitiva,* translated from the French by D. Eloy Requena (Madrid: Studium, 1972), p. 35.

MANIFESTATION OF THE RIGHTEOUSNESS OF GOD. The kingdom which came near with Jesus was a kingdom of justice. In him God's righteousness was manifested. Through his life and work Jesus condemned the old era of law-and-condemnation by fulfilling God's righteousness, standing in the place of the weak and the downtrodden. In him the justice of God was fulfilled, because through his life and sacrifice he fulfilled the demands of the law and stood on the side of suffering humanity. Therefore, he can justify those who trust in him (cf. Rom. 3:21-26; 8:1-3). To enter the kingdom one must first be justified. The kingdom is a community of righteousness.

To say that the kingdom is a community of righteousness is not merely to affirm that it is made up of persons who themselves have been justified by Jesus Christ. It is also to affirm that it is a community of persons committed to the practice of justice. Jesus not only did justice on the cross by standing in the place of the weak and the poor (*i.e.,* on the side of sinful humanity). He continues to do justice by standing in the place of those who suffer. He continues to do justice to the weak by identifying himself with their suffering, and condemning all acts of injustice and oppression (cf. Mt. 25:34ff.). For this reason, the gospel is a message addressed to the poor, the brokenhearted, the blind, the bruised, and the captives. It is a message that protests against any iniquitous and unjust acts. Indeed the practice of justice and the condemnation of injustice are, according to James, the evidence par excellence of one's justification (cf. James 2:14ff.).

The kingdom constitutes, therefore, a new order that irrupts on the old. If the former is characterized in Scripture as the kingdom of light, righteousness, and life, the latter is described as the kingdom of darkness, unrighteousness, and death. The kingdom of God stands against the kingdom of Satan. And since the latter stands for what oppresses, dehumanizes, and enslaves man, the kingdom of God must stand for what humanizes, liberates, and enriches man.

REVELATION OF THE PEACE OF GOD. Since Jesus fulfilled with his life and sacrifice the righteousness of God, the new era he inaugurated must be understood also in terms of peace. Jesus was not only the manifestation of the righteousness of God but also of his peace. Through his sacrifice, *shalom* was revealed to all mankind.

> But now in Christ Jesus you who once were far off have been brought near in the blood of Christ. For he is our peace, who has made us both one, and has broken down the dividing wall of hostility, by abolishing in his flesh the law of commandments and ordinances, that he might create in himself one new man in place of the two, so making peace, and might reconcile us both to God in one body through the cross, thereby bringing the hostility to an end. And he came and preached peace to you who were far off and peace to those who were near; for through him we both have access in one Spirit to the Father (Eph. 2:13-18 RSV).

The messianic hope of an era of peace was thus fulfilled through the death of Christ. Through his death he abolished the power of sin and eliminated the one obstacle that had made impossible the manifestation of God's peace (cf. Is. 53:3-5). For sin leads to death and death represents the destruction of life (cf. 1 Cor. 15:22; Jas. 1:15). The price of peace was the destruction of sin and death; God's righteousness had to be vindicated (Is. 53:9ff.; Rom. 6:3; 2 Tim. 1:10; cf. Acts 2:23f.; 1 Cor. 2:7, 8).

CREATOR OF THE NEW MAN. This peace which Christ wrought through his death must be understood in terms of reconciliation. Reconciliation means, primarily, restoration to a previous position or the reestablishment of things to their original state. In the context of Ephesians and Colossians it also means transformation, creation, change. In Ephesians it refers to the creation of what Paul calls the "new man." As has been observed, the new man is the new humanity which God is creating in Christ to fulfill his purpose in creation, to be everything that God has wanted man to be, but also to enjoy the benefits he has wanted to bestow upon man.

In Colossians the term *reconciliation* encompasses "all things, whether on earth or in heaven" (Col. 1:20). In this chapter, the expression "all things" has at least two meanings. In verses 16 and 20 Paul alludes to all creation:

> in him all things were created, in heaven and on earth, visible and invisible, whether thrones or dominions or principalities or authorities . . . in him all the fullness of God was pleased to dwell, and through him to reconcile to himself all things, whether on earth or in heaven, making peace by the blood of his cross (Col. 1:16, 19-20 RSV).

All creation has been put under Christ's dominion. This is an *accomplished fact* (Eph. 1:22; Col. 2:15a). Nevertheless, not all creation has experienced Christ's reconciling transformation (Rom. 8:24ff.). The picture in Col. 2:15 is one of unwilling submission to Christ. In 1 Cor. 15:24ff., Paul points to the final destruction of every dominion, authority, and power. This seems to mean that the reconciliation of the whole cosmos does not mean harmonizing all things, but rather making them work in agreement with God's purpose. God's purpose in Christ in the present age is to have the great news of reconciliation shared with "every creature which is under heaven" (Col. 1:23). This must be fulfilled in order that the physical universe may be delivered out of the slavery of corruption into which it has fallen on account of man's sin (Rom. 8:20, 21).

In Col. 1:23 the term "reconciliation" refers specifically to man. But man, not in an individualistic sense, but in the light of the complexity of human society. For man is not an island in himself; he exists in a world of relationships, of groups, of social, economic, and political structures. As Ortega y Gasset used to say, "I am myself and my circumstances." Consequently, in this verse Paul speaks of the preaching of the gospel "to all of creation under the sky"[5]—in other words, the world of man understood holistically, man in the light of his whole situation, as a person who lives and acts in different structures. These structures have also been corrupted by sin and have alienated man from himself, his neighbor, and his purpose as a creature of God.

If the gospel is a reconciling message, it must be addressed not only to all persons but also to the particular situations that constitute the context of their daily interaction. The situations that shape the life and action of men and women must also be changed or transformed according to God's purpose, or the gospel will be robbed of its power and intent. For the gospel is a message with cosmic implications. Christ is Lord over all things (Eph. 1:22). His victory over sin and death reaches all spheres of human life. The good news of his triumph must be proclaimed in the political, economic, and social structures which are, admittedly, the results of man's interaction, but which acquire a corporate personality and themselves become agents of oppression. These too must be redeemed by the liberating power of the gospel.

At this point we must bear in mind the concepts of the church as a sign of reconciliation, the church as "firstfruits" of the "new man," and the biblical tension between the "now" and the "not yet." To say that the church is a sign of reconciliation is to say that she must herself be a reconciled community. As firstfruits of the new humanity, the church is a living example of the reconciliation of the whole cosmos (cf. Eph. 2:14ff.; Col. 1:20ff.). As such, she witnesses to the reconciling power of the gospel. Being herself a community of discordant elements, a body formed from the chaos of fallen humanity, her message is a living testimony of the light which shines in the darkness and which the darkness cannot overcome (Jn. 1:5). Thus she

---

5. Cf. *Jerusalem Bible* (Garden City, N.Y.: Doubleday & Co., 1966), p. 345 (New Testament section).

refuses to accept the chaos of fallen humanity as the ultimate word for human history. Positively, she proclaims God's good news of liberation, fulfillment, and victory over death. Negatively, she refuses to accept ignorance and poverty, starvation, hunger and malnutrition, exploitation, oppression and repression as a normal way of life.

The church's message involves a positive stand for all that seeks to make life fuller and more meaningful. The church takes this stand, among other things, by participating aggressively in the expansion of culture (understood in its wider sense as encompassing all of man's achievements) and by promoting the total well-being of man through her own life and example. The promotion of man's well-being must involve a more just society, a fuller life, and a deeper relationship with other human beings. To achieve this end, the church must dramatize and exemplify a genuine life of reconciliation by practicing love, justice, and peace in her own midst. Only a church which is a genuine community of love, peace, and righteousness can effectively promote the well-being of man. Only a church that lives the life of the kingdom can faithfully proclaim the good news of God's sovereign rule.

But note, the church is a *sign* of the kingdom, not the kingdom. She gives witness to the fact that the kingdom has come near, that justice, love, and peace have become already a living possibility, that salvation has been manifested already in Jesus Christ, and that the church is the "firstfruits" of the new humanity, which he is creating as the result of his saving work.

There is, however, a "not yet" linked to the gospel of the kingdom. The kingdom has come near, but it has not been fully revealed. God's grace has been manifested in Christ; God's universal judgment upon the nations has been postponed for a period of time known only to him. Justice, love, and peace have become a possibility, but man is still assailed by sin. The temptation to dominate others or to allow oneself to be dominated by others is still present. The struggle between light and darkness is still on.

Thus the gospel is also a message of bad news. God's word of salvation is a word of judgment and condemnation, and the church's commitment to peace, justice, and love is a living denunciation against injustice, selfishness, and alienation. This is also the reason why the church cannot commit herself *unconditionally* and *absolutely* to any human movement or any human being, no matter how committed either might be to the task of human liberation. For while the church must be totally committed to the humanization of man, she must also keep herself sufficiently free so as to raise her protest whenever any group or movement deviates from promoting man's well-being.

The gospel is, therefore, God's good news of salvation in Christ. It is a message incarnated in Jesus of Nazareth. It celebrates his triumph over sin and death. It confirms his authority over this world. It announces a new order of life based on the Old Testament hope of a just, peaceful, and loving world. But it is also a call to action. Thus it must be understood as *praxis.*

THE GOSPEL AS PRAXIS

By praxis is meant action based upon reflection, or the actualization of theory. To say that the gospel must be understood as praxis is to say that its truth must not only be analyzed and reflected upon, but fulfilled and actualized in concrete situations. It is to affirm that the gospel is a message about a living person who penetrates with power all of life's situations to help men and women in their deepest struggles.

THE BASIC SOURCE FOR THE PRAXIS OF THE GOSPEL. The basic source for the praxis of the gospel is the corpus of New Testament writings known as the Great Commission (Mt. 28:19-21; Mk. 16:15; Lk. 24:48; Jn. 20:21; Acts 1:8). These passages outline the content of the *evangel* (the life and ministry of Jesus Christ), its authority (the authority in heaven and on earth given him by the Father) and intent (to bring about the redemptive transformation of human society), and its praxeological character. That is, they give the theoretical foundations of the gospel and outline the dimensions of its praxis. The latter are expressed in verb forms and commands (Go ye . . . preach . . . disciple . . . witness). In a sense, they constitute the charter for the church's missionary action.

In the previous sections of this chapter we have considered the theoretical foundations of the gospel. It behooves us now to analyze its praxeological character.

THE PRAXEOLOGICAL CHARACTER OF THE GOSPEL

To proclaim. While Mark 16:9-20 does not appear in the oldest and most accurate manuscripts, the spirit of 16:15 (" 'Go into all the world and preach the gospel' ") can be found throughout the book (cf. Mk. 3:14; 6:7-13; 13:10, among others), the other synoptic Gospels (*e.g.*, Mt. 26:13; Lk. 9:2; 24:47, etc.), Acts (*e.g.*, Acts 16:10; 28:31) and the epistles (*e.g.*, 1 Cor. 1:17; Rom. 10:15; 2 Tim. 4:2). These passages have to do with the kerygmatic character of the gospel, *i.e.*, the gospel as news about a mighty event which must be announced; something which cannot be contained.

The verb "to proclaim" (Greek *kerusso*) comes from the *kerussein* root, meaning to proclaim like a herald.[6] In the New Testament, it is used mostly although not exclusively in reference to the *evangel*. It stands for the heralding of the gospel throughout the world. The term is first used in reference to the mission of John the Baptist (cf. Mk. 1:4). It is then applied to the mission of Jesus (cf. Mk. 1:14). Paul uses it frequently in reference to his own ministry (*e.g.*, 1 Cor. 1:17; 9:16b), and Luke applies it to the action of the entire church (*e.g.*, Acts 2:46; 5:42; 8:4; 9:35; 11:20).

It can thus be said that the early church understood the gospel as a message that had to be proclaimed

---

6. Cf. Michael Green, *Evangelism in the Early Church* (Grand Rapids: Eerdmans, 1970), p. 58.

throughout the entire world. In this proclamation, three elements stood out.[7]

First, the centrality of Jesus. The preaching of first-century Christians emphasized the early church's conviction that Jesus Christ

> was God's last word to man, the one who brought as much of God to us as we could appreciate in the only terms we could take it in, the terms of a human life; the one who in dying and rising again was manifestly vindicated in his claims and achievement.[8]

Second, it was oriented to the needs of the different types of people to whom the church addressed herself. Its emphasis varied from one situation to another. At Pentecost, for example, Peter emphasized the Hebraic background of the gospel, while at Athens Paul pointed to its supernatural and revelatory character. The Gospels themselves are an example of the early church's different presentations of Jesus' relevance to man's varied needs. For example, John carefully selected his material in order to produce faith in communities which were probably assailed by gnostic teachings.[9] Luke presented his material in accord with the needs of Theophilus. Mark most likely expressed Peter's approach to preaching,[10] while Matthew

---

7. Cf. *Ibid.,* p. 66.

8. *Ibid.,* p. 62.

9. Cf. José María Abreü, "Un enfoque político del Evangelio de Juan," unpublished thesis submitted to the faculty of the Seminario Bíblico Latinoamericano in partial fulfillment for the degree of Licenciado en Teología (San José, Costa Rica: SBL, 1972), pp. 6f.

10. This was the opinion of Papias. Cf. Eusebius, *H. E.* 339. Green seems to agree (and so do the modern Form Critics!). According to Papias, Mark

> was not himself an eyewitness of what he records, but was the interpreter of Peter. He wrote down what he remembered of Peter's preaching concerning what the Lord had said or done. He did so accurately, but not in order: Peter himself had composed his address in no chronological order, but *pros tas chreias,* in order to meet the needs of the audience.

Green, *Evangelism . . . ,* p. 64.

seemed to address the needs of Jewish Christians.[11]

Third, the early church's proclamation was decision-oriented. In other words, it called for a verdict.[12] It demanded a response. This is clear not only in the sermons recorded in the book of Acts, but also in the epistles (e.g., 2 Cor. 5:20b) and the Book of Revelation (e.g., Rev. 3:20).

The gospel is thus the message which the church has been commissioned to proclaim in such a way that Jesus Christ might be presented to the world in his fullness, as the Lord and Savior of creation. Such a presentation ought to be made in accordance with the varied needs of man. In other words, the preaching of the gospel must be issue- and situation-oriented. Yet it must not be simply information but full communication, i.e., it must seek to persuade the receiver of Christ's relevance and call him to change his course and turn in faith and obedience to Jesus Christ.

To disciple. In order for the gospel to transform man and positively affect his situation, it must be effectively taught. It must be interpreted in such a way to make it become incarnated in the life of those to whom it is presented. In other words, the gospel can become praxis to the extent that it is allowed to take root in the lives of men and women, and it can only take root in the process of effective discipleship.

To disciple someone is to establish a personal relation with the view of shaping his entire life. Discipling is not transmission of a body of knowledge; rather it involves introduction of material in such a way that the receiver can retain and incorporate it into his life.

To evangelize (or as we have called it here, to fulfill the gospel praxeologically) is to make men and women

---

11. For a more precise discussion on Matthew's purpose, see Green, *Ibid.*, p. 230 and notes 177, 178; also p. 79.

12. For an interesting analysis, though somewhat general, of the place of decision (calling for a verdict) in the mission of the church to the world, see Allen R. Tippett, *Verdict Theology in Missionary Theory* (Lincoln, Illinois: Lincoln Christian College Press).

disciples of Jesus Christ in their concrete historical situations. It is a conscious attempt so to relate man to Jesus Christ that the mind of Christ can be formed in him. It is thus a process of personal interaction where someone (the believer-evangelist, or corporately, the church) seeks to share the gospel with one or more persons (the unbeliever) in such a way that he not only understands and accepts it but also incorporates it into his life. He internalizes it, so that it may transform his lifestyle.

Understood thus, evangelization must have a twofold consequence: (1) it must produce a transfer of meanings and (2) must lead to an incorporation into Christ. Hence the command to go and "make disciples of all nations, baptizing them in the name of the Father and of the Son and of the Holy Spirit, teaching them to observe all that I have commanded you" (Mt. 28:19, 20). This leads us to a brief but important consideration of the doctrines of conversion and baptism, for when we speak of a transfer of meaning or a change of mind, we are referring to the biblical doctrine of conversion; and when we refer to the believer's incorporation into Christ we are speaking of baptism.

The gospel seeks preeminently to bring about a transformation in the lives of those who accept it. This change is what the Scriptures call conversion (Greek *metanoeia*). It implies at least two things: *repentance*, or a change of mind, and *faith* toward God. Effective discipling must lead to an about-face from wickedness and unrighteousness and a seeking after God through Jesus Christ our Lord (cf. Is. 55:6, 7[13]).[14]

This change must take place in the light of man's concrete historical situation. For man's sin takes place not in the abstract, but in concrete social situations. Accordingly, the call to repentance and faith must have direct

---

13. See also the following references in Acts 3:19, 26; 9:35; 11:21; 14:15; 15:3, 19; 26:18, 20.

14. For fuller discussion on the biblical concept of conversion, see Green, *Evangelism*, pp. 144ff.

relation to these situations. The gospel must confront men and women with the realities of their lives—their selfishness and irresponsibility; their ambition; their inferiority complexes; their tendency to oppress their neighbor and/or to "sell themselves" to their neighbor and allow him to oppress them. And not only must it confront them with their vital situation; it must call them to break with that situation and commit their lives unconditionally to Christ.

This commitment to Jesus Christ implies commitment to everything to which he is himself committed. José Míguez-Bonino makes this clear in an article on "The Present Crisis in Mission." He asks:

> What happens when somebody is converted to Christ? He must know that he is not going into some sort of secluded soul fellowship, but that he is called to obedience to the One who said, "The Spirit of the Lord is upon me, because he has anointed me to preach good news to the poor. He has sent me to proclaim release to the captives and recovering of sight to the blind, to set at liberty those who are oppressed, to proclaim the acceptable year of the Lord." This is the Christ of the Gospel and there is no other Christ to be converted to.[15]

This has not always been the case in the church's evangelizing enterprise. Instead of confronting men and women with their sin in concrete social situations, the church has often confronted them with their "abstract" sinfulness, leaving unaffected their sinful relations to their own life situations. Instead of confronting people with the demands of Christ, the church has accommodated the gospel to their way of thinking and living. By failing to confront them with the claims and demands of the gospel, by failing to call them to militant and responsible disciple-

15. José Míguez-Bonino, "The Present Crisis in Mission," quoted in E. M. Huenemann, "Evangelism and Renewal" (General Assembly Issue Paper No. 2, Ninth Convention of the National Council of the Churches of Christ, Dallas, Texas, December 3-8, 1972), p. 6.

ship, the church has preached what Dietrich Bonhoeffer rightly called "cheap grace."

The second consequence of effective discipling must be baptism. In the New Testament, baptism is understood as the mark of incorporation into Christ, into his body (cf. Rom. 6:3ff.; 1 Cor. 12:13). It is intimately related to conversion. It is the outward expression of conversion: a public act, a public profession of repentance from sin and faith in Jesus.

Throughout church history, baptism has been considered the sacrament of initiation. It is an outward witness to one's response in repentance, faith, and obedience to the gospel, signifying the believer's union with Christ and his entrance into the community of faith.

Effective discipling must therefore lead to incorporation into the church. For the new Christian, the church becomes a family in which he puts into practice his experience of reconciliation through fellowship and communion with his brethren. It is a school in which he grows and is trained for mission, a team with which he can function and serve.

Since the gospel demands change—turning to Christ in repentance and faith, transformation in one's way of thinking and acting, and positive commitment to new relationships, new lifestyle, values and world-view—it must be expounded with clarity and precision. This follows from Jesus' command to make disciples by teaching the peoples of the earth to observe all that he had commanded (Mt. 28:20a). While the term "command" implies a set of rules to be kept, in Scripture a command is more than a rule. It is a life principle, a revelation of God's will (cf. Deut. 6:1ff.). The emphasis is not on the commandment but on the *commander*. Thus, the law of God is a revelation of *his* righteousness and perfect will, or even a revelation of God himself. Accordingly, to observe Christ's commandments implies understanding of and commitment to Christ's way of life. Teaching his commandments implies interpretation of the meaning of Christ's self-disclosure. To expound the gospel is to interpret the meaning of Christ in the light of his own teachings. These are the teachings which the Spirit committed to the apostles (cf. Jn. 14:26; Eph. 2:20) and which the apostles faithfully transmitted to their disciples, urging them diligently to transmit them to other faithful men who would be able to teach others (1 Tim. 2:2; cf. 1 Tim. 6:20; 2 Tim. 1:8ff.; 4:1ff.).

One great tragedy in the church's evangelizing efforts has been the limited commitment of so many Christians to this truth. It has led to shallow evangelization, with little content and a gospel distorted beyond recognition. As I have pointed out elsewhere, the crisis of contemporary evangelization is not methodological but theological. Lacking sound theological foundation, the methods can't help but produce shallow results. When "the base is weak, the results are also weak, whether or not the best methods have been used in the process."[16]

Effective discipling must cope with the problem of resistance. There cannot be effective transference of meaning, a change of mind and lifestyle, without overcoming the obstacles which appear in the process of evangelization. Sin has affected the human personality in such a way that it has created roadblocks which obstruct the understanding, acceptance, internalization, and incorporation of the gospel (cf. Rom. 1:18ff.; 3:10ff.; 8:7, 8). Hence the relevance of Jesus' affirmation, "All authority in heaven and on earth has been given me," and the subsequent promise, "and lo, I am with you always, to the close of the age" (Mt. 28:18, 20).

The manifestation of the power of Jesus Christ and, consequently, God's decisive intervention in the process of evangelization become possible through the work of the Holy Spirit. Little wonder that he is referred to in the Gospel of John as the teacher (Jn. 14:26), the witness (Jn. 15:26), and the representative of Christ (Jn. 14:26). God himself in the person of the Spirit is the only one who can internalize

---

16. Orlando Costas, "Hacia una evangelización pertinente," in Costas (ed.), *Hacia una teología . . .* , p. 263.

the gospel in the unbeliever, guiding him to repentance and faith in Christ, putting him on the way to an effective and transformed lifestyle, incorporating him into the body, involving him (through the body) in effective witnessing; in short, leading him "to mature manhood [or womanhood], to the measure of the stature of the fullness of Christ" (Eph. 4:13).

To witness. The praxeological character of the gospel also includes bearing witness. What does it mean to bear witness to the gospel? Is it the same as proclaiming or teaching it? To bear witness obviously overlaps with proclamation and discipling, but to confuse it with either would lose some of its essential elements. To bear witness to Christ most likely leads one to proclaim and interpret Christ, but from a personal and therefore more profound perspective. It is at this point that the gospel manifests itself preeminently as praxis, *i.e.,* as an event that confronts man with his "ultimate concerns" (life, death, sin, guilt, forgiveness, justice, liberation, etc.) and that actualizes itself in man's concrete historical situation.

To bear witness is to affirm the truth. In the Old Testament, the concept of witness-bearing is tied to God's calling of a people to himself to affirm the reality of his mighty deeds to the nations of the earth (cf. Is. 42:6, 7; 43:10, 11; 44:8, among others). In the New Testament, it is used preeminently in reference to the gospel, as an affirmation of the reality of the gospel with a life-commitment even unto death.[17]

To evangelize is therefore not only to proclaim the gospel to all creation and to disciple effectively the peoples of the earth, but also to bear witness to the truth of the gospel. Such witnessing involves, first of all, testifying about the *reality* of the life of Jesus of Nazareth (cf. Acts 10:39; Lk. 1:2, and other passages). Far from being merely concerned with the Christ of faith (who reveals himself as the risen and cosmic Christ), as Rudolf Bultmann and his

---

17. For a brief but profound analysis of the New Testament concept of *marturia* (witness), see Green, *Evangelism . . . ,* pp. 70ff.

school would have us believe, the early church seems to have been quite involved in witnessing to the life and ministry of Jesus. Little wonder that she preserved the sayings of Jesus, first in the form of oral tradition and later in written form; that she saw the need for a canon of authorized writings to interpret his life and teachings; and that she incorporated these writings into her worship. In fact, so important were the life and ministry of our Lord to the early church that her worship services were rehearsals of the important periods of his life and ministry![18]

Second, witnessing to the truth of the gospel implies affirming the truth with regard to the work of Christ. This is precisely the meaning of Luke's version of the Great Commission.

> Then [Jesus] opened their minds to understand the scriptures, and said to them, "Thus it is written, that the Christ should suffer and on the third day rise from the dead, and that repentance and forgiveness of sins should be preached in his name to all nations, beginning from Jerusalem. You are witnesses of these things" (Lk. 24:44-48 RSV).

The "these things" of this passage are the basic facts about the Christ-event, namely, that Jesus came to suffer, that in the cross God's plan of salvation was fulfilled, that Christ rose from the dead, and that through his death and resurrection the forgiveness of sins is now a possibility to all who repent and put their trust in him. Elsewhere in the book of Acts, Luke records several statements in which the apostles bear witness to the reality of the work of Christ

---

18. As far back as the end of the first century, two great moments can be identified in the church's worship, namely, the Galilean (or the service of the Word), which actualized the public ministry of Jesus through the proclamation of the Word, and the Jerusalemite (or the Eucharistic service), which actualized his private ministry among the disciples through the celebration of the Eucharist. For a good summary of these two moments and sound bibliographical references, see the following works: von Allmen, *El culto . . . ;* Cullman, *Worship . . . ;* William D. Maxwell, *An Outline of Christian Worship.*

(cf. Acts 2:32; 3:15; 1:21, 22). These statements further corroborate the claims of Lk. 24:44-48.

Third, to bear witness to the truth of the gospel implies testifying to the veracity of God. For the gospel is the revelation of God (Rom. 1:1; 1 Cor. 1:1), and God is the ultimate reality of the universe. Consequently, to witness to the truth of the gospel is to affirm God as the ultimate reality of the universe.

But note, only they who have been with God, who have experienced him, can make such an affirmation. This is precisely the relevance of the incarnation:

> And the Word became flesh and dwelt among us, full of grace and *truth*. . . . For the law was given through Moses; grace and *truth* came through Jesus Christ. No one has even seen God; the only Son, who is in the bosom of the Father, he has made him known (Jn. 1: 14, 17, 18 RSV. Italics mine).

The incarnation of Christ means, among other things, that we have an authentic witness of the reality of God. He testifies of him with whom he has been and seen (cf. Jn. 18:37). He claims to be *the* truth because he is the ultimate revelation of truth (cf. Jn. 14:6; 3:11, 32, 33; 8:13ff.). Likewise the Spirit bears witness to the truth and is himself "the Spirit of truth" because he proceeds from the Father, represents, and makes present the incarnation of truth (Jn. 14:26; 15:26). And not only does the Spirit bear witness to the incarnation of truth, but the believer does also. He has been with Christ (cf. Jn. 15:27), *i.e.*, he has experienced him (Jn. 20:20, 29-31) and has received the Holy Spirit (Acts 1:8).

From this it follows that only those who have experienced what John calls "the new birth" (Jn. 3:3), *i.e.*, conversion, can bear witness to the truth of the gospel. For a witness must testify of what he knows. As R. K. Orchard has said:

> . . . the witness must be prepared to be cross-

examined, and should not expect the process of cross-examination to be always controlled by judges' rules. In principle, he must be prepared to stake his life on the truth of that to which he testifies.[19]

Only through a faith-encounter with Christ can men and women experience the truth. Only as they come to this knowledge are they qualified to bear witness to the truth of the gospel.

This knowledge of the truth places a tremendous burden on the believer. Since he has experienced the reality of God-in-history, he must interpret the manifestation-in-time of this reality. Hence to bear witness to Christ is not only to affirm what Christ has done for him, but also to interpret Christ's role in history—or conversely, to interpret history in the light of the Christ-event. This is precisely what the New Testament writers do throughout their writings: they bear witness to him as Lord of history and interpret history in the light of his work.

As a witness to the truth of the gospel, the Christian cannot be content simply with pointing to the historical facts of the life, ministry, and work of Christ. He must also interpret the meaning of Christ for the here-and-now. He must relate the Christ-event to all of life. Accordingly, the task of evangelization must not be understood as merely sharing one's personal experience with Christ. Of course it includes this, but it goes further. It involves testifying about the meaning of Christ to the history of mankind, or confronting the history of the nations with the meaning of the gospel. This in turn means confronting one's neighbors with the claims of Christ upon their lives, interpreting their particular history—the history of their family, community, country—in the light of the gospel.

In summary, the gospel is God's good news of salvation in Jesus Christ. It is a message that announces the inauguration of God's sovereign rule and the fulfillment of

---

19. R. K. Orchard, *Missions in a Time of Testing* (Philadelphia: Westminster Press, 1964), p. 80.

his redemptive purpose in history. It sets forth God's will for human society—to live in righteousness, peace, and love.

This message revolves around Jesus Christ. He is himself the good news, for he is the one who through his life and work inaugurated God's sovereign rule, revealed God's will, and made possible the fulfillment of that will.

The gospel is also a call. It not only proclaims God's good news, but calls men and women through repentance and faith in Christ to share in the wonderful things therein proclaimed. Those who respond enter into new life. They receive forgiveness of sins. They are justified and reconciled with God. They become part of God's church, firstfruits of the new humanity which God is creating through Christ, and a sign of the righteousness, love, and peace of God's kingdom.

Finally, the gospel is praxis. It demands not only intellectual commitment to its claims and demands but also practical and existential fulfillment of these demands. Such commitment calls, therefore, for the actualization of the gospel in everyday life, especially through what I have called its threefold praxeological character. To proclaim the gospel to all of creation, to disciple the peoples of the world, and to bear witness to Christ in the uttermost parts of the earth—this is what the church is to do in the light of her responsibility as God's messenger to the world. When the church does this, she engages in the task of evangelization and becomes not only the recipient of the evangel but the transmitter and channel through which the latter reaches its destination, namely, the world of man.

This is the church's message—the glad tidings prophesied by Isaiah and fulfilled in the person and work of Jesus of Nazareth. This is the message which the church has been commissioned to communicate to the world. To the extent that the church faithfully transmits this message to the world she will be faithful to her nature as God's peculiar people, the body of Christ, and the temple of the Holy Ghost, called to one prophetic, priestly, and royal mission.

GOD'S MISSION AND THE CHURCH'S GROWTH

5/THE IMPERATIVE OF CHURCH GROWTH

Study of the church's mission would be incomplete without inquiry into the phenomenology of her growth, for church growth is a natural and imperative trait of her missionary action. The purpose of the second part of our study is to consider the church's participation in God's mission in the light of the phenomenon of her growth. To begin with, let us analyze the imperative of this phenomenon for the life and mission of the church.

THE DYNAMIC NATURE OF CHURCH GROWTH

GROWTH AS A DYNAMIC PHENOMENON. "Growth" is a dynamic term. It is a word that suggests mobility. Literally it means increase, development, expansion, enlargement. It is thus an antonym of stagnation, inertia, sluggishness, static-ness.

Growth is also a relative term. Its precise meaning can only be understood in the light of its context. To say that something is growing is meaningless unless one explains how or in what sense it is growing. There are different kinds of growth: physical, emotional, intellectual, social, etc.

Growth is a complex phenomenon. It takes place at different levels and in different ways. It is multidimensional. Consequently, it cannot be appraised superficially, nor can it be understood apart from its concrete historical manifestations.

Growth can occur only where life exists; inanimate objects cannot experience growth. Life is a process, and since an organism is essentially a *living* body or a structure constituted to carry on the process of *life,* an organism that does not grow is in reality dead.

The death of an organism can take place at various levels and at different intervals. The life process can stop at one level but continue at another. But since one of the fundamental characteristics of an organism is the constant interaction of its parts, stagnation at one level will sooner or later affect the other levels until the entire organism comes to a halt.

CHURCH GROWTH AS A COMPLEX PHENOMENON. To speak of the growth of the church is also to refer to a complex phenomenon. As a life process, church growth must be seen as a corporate action, or as Alan R. Tippett has put it, "a body growing, a body of discrete but interacting parts."[1] The growth of this body takes place at various levels; it is multidimensional. This means that in order to appraise it meaningfully one must understand the

---

1. Alan R. Tippett, "A Resume of Church Growth Theology and Current Debate," a paper presented at the Fuller Theological Seminary Faculty Forum, March 16, 1970 (mimeographed), p. 3.

various levels at which it occurs and the various dimensions of the process itself.

How does the church grow? In what sense can we expect her to grow? Any study of church growth must address itself to these questions. The first question implies the necessity of observation and measurement. The second is more theoretical or theological. It deals with the *whatness* of church growth (a problem of definition which must be solved in part empirically—through the observational, scientific analysis of actual church growth situations—but which also must involve an understanding of the dynamics of the church). It also deals with the *why* of church growth (a problem of mission, and in the long run, of authority).

The first question is beyond the scope of this chapter since it is more empirical than theoretical. Our concern here is more theological than methodological.

As to the second question, our discussion has already touched on the dynamics of the church as a body, a temple, and a community sent into the world to make disciples for Christ. We have seen how inclusive this task is. It behooves us, therefore, at this time to define further this complex phenomenon. Beyond this, we will need to look at the biblical case and the theological rationale for church growth.

Obviously, our definitions of growth and of the church have given us a preview of our definition of church growth. What we need to do now is define the dimensions of this phenomenon. Let us, then, say that *church growth is that holistic expansion which can be expected spontaneously from the everyday action of the church functioning as a redemptive community.* Note the expression "holistic expansion" for it has been said that growth is multidimensional, that the church is a living organism, and that church growth is the growing of the body of Christ. In order for church growth to be holistic expansion it must encompass four major areas: the numerical, organic, conceptual, and incarnational.

By *numerical* expansion is understood the recruitment of persons for the kingdom of God by calling them to repentance and faith in Jesus Christ as Lord and Savior of their lives and their incorporation into a local community of persons which, having made a similar decision, worship, obey, and give witness, collectively and personally, to the world of God's redemptive action in Jesus Christ and his liberating power.

By *organic* expansion is meant the internal development of a local community of faith, *i.e.,* the system of relationships among its members—its form of government, financial structure, leadership, types of activities in which its time and resources are invested, etc.

By *conceptual* expansion is meant the degree of consciousness that a community of faith has with regard to its nature and mission to the world, *i.e.,* the image that the community has formed of herself, the depth of her reflection on the meaning of her faith in Christ (knowledge of Scripture, etc.), and her image of the world.

By *incarnational* growth is meant the degree of involvement of a community of faith in the life and problems of her social environment, *i.e.,* her participation in the afflictions of her world; her prophetic, intercessory, and liberating action in behalf of the weak and destitute; the intensity of her preaching to the poor, the brokenhearted, the captives, the blind, and the oppressed (Lk. 4:18-21).[2]

---

2. I first rehearsed this typology in a planning session of a small research project begun in March 1972 by members of the Institute of In-Depth Evangelism engaged in a training program at the Latin American Biblical Seminary from March to November 1972. The field work for the project was completed in December by three of the original members of the team. The project was oriented toward the study of the factors that are associated with the growth of Protestant churches in the Greater San José (Costa Rica) metro-

THE BIBLICAL CASE
FOR CHURCH GROWTH

In his book, *Church Growth and the Word of God,* Alan R. Tippett begins by affirming that "the evidence from Scripture for [church growth as a biblical concept] is *declarative, implicative, precedential,* or *cumulative.*" By declarative, Tippett means evidence that is based on direct, specific, categorical, or imperative statements. By implicative, he means "statements implied in the passages cited." He considers precedential evidence those passages in which God shows his approval of and sets his Spirit on a particular method. The fact that he once blessed it, says Tippett, indicates that it accords with his will at least for some situations. Finally, he designates as cumulative evidence "the quantitative assembly of scriptural statements that point in a single direction and reinforce each other." For example, passages that demonstrate God's love for man but which do not actually employ the word *love.*[3]

Tippett then shows how "the diffusion of the knowledge of salvation to the ends of the earth" permeates the whole of Scripture as both promise and action. He backs this statement with references to the various sections of the Old and New Testaments—the Psalms, prophets, Gospels, Acts, and epistles. According to Tippett,

> The whole Bible vibrates with expectancy—from the psalmist to the evangelist and apostle and the Lord himself. Of those engaged in the program of Christian mission today, obedience is surely required —but it is expected *obedience.* If the Bible still speaks to us, it surely speaks of the diffusion of the

---

politan area. It involved three basic surveys (of pastors, laymen, and community). An attempt was thus made to measure the growth of churches holistically.

3. Alan R. Tippett, *Church Growth and the Word of God* (Grand Rapids: Eerdmans, 1970), p. 9.

salvation experience, and the incorporation of the saved into a fellowship.[4]

Tippett goes on to state that "the New Testament . . . has a rich range of picturesque imagery that shows growth is to be expected—both physical, numerical growth from outside and spiritual, qualitative growth from within."[5] Let us examine the New Testament imagery showing that growth is to be expected in the church.[6]

THE NEW TESTAMENT IMAGERY FOR CHURCH GROWTH. Take for instance the life and ministry of Jesus, which is filled with growth metaphors. He calls several fishermen to follow him so that he can make them fishers of *men* (Mk. 1: 17). He compares the kingdom of heaven to a net which when thrown to the sea gathers fish of every kind (Mt. 13:47, 48). The world is a field white unto harvest (Jn. 4:35). His disciples are to pray that God might send laborers into his harvest (Mt. 9:38; Lk. 10:2), and then he sends *them* out to reap this harvest (Mt. 10:1-5). He sees himself as the vine and those he calls to himself as the branches (Jn. 15:5, 8). Consequently, they are *to bear fruit.* This fruit is conceived, in part, in terms of their service for the kingdom. They serve the kingdom by obeying the King's command and by recruiting people from the highways and hedges to the great coming banquet or feast (Lk. 14:21-24), by penetrating with the light of the world into the darkest places (Mt. 5:16; Jn. 8:12; 9:5).

Jesus views the growth of the new community not only quantitatively, *i.e.,* as the gathering in of the harvest, the fruit-bearing interaction between him and the community, and the incorporation of those who repent and believe into the life of the kingdom. The kingdom, he says, "is

---

4. *Ibid.,* pp. 11, 12.

5. *Ibid.,* p. 12.

6. In this section, I will follow quite closely the biblical data collected and classified by Tippett, with occasional variations here and there. Cf. *Ibid.,* pp. 12ff.

like a grain of mustard seed" (Mt. 13:31). It grows organically, from a very small seed to a large tree. Though it must cope with resistance (the seed falls sometimes by the wayside, on the rock, or among thorns), it experiences healthy growth when it falls into good soil (Lk. 8:5-8, 11-15; Mt. 13:1-8, 18-23; Mk. 4:1-9, 13-20).

Beyond the imagery linked to the life and ministry of Jesus, the New Testament presents other growing images of the church, especially in the Pauline epistles. Take, for example, Paul's concept of the church as a building growing into a holy temple (1 Cor. 3:9-11; Eph. 2:22) or his concept of the church as a family, growing by the "spirit of sonship" (Rom. 8:15; Eph. 1:5; cf. Eph. 4:14f.). Peter uses similar imagery. Christians are to grow unto salvation by drinking the pure spiritual milk (1 Pet. 2:2). They are further to build themselves, as living stones, into a spiritual house (1 Pet. 2:4ff.).

Perhaps one of the strongest images of church growth is suggested by the New Testament concept of stewardship, particularly the idea of fellow worker. In 1 Cor. 3:9 and again in 2 Cor. 6:1 Paul refers to the Christian as God's fellow worker (Greek *sunergoi*). In the first instance he uses the term to refer to the church as a field and a building. In the second, he uses it in relation to God's work of reconciliation. In chapter five, Paul speaks of the ministry of reconciliation which God has entrusted to the church. This ministry, he adds, makes the believer God's ambassador. It is this task which is imbedded in the "working together" of 6:1. ("Working together with him, then, we entreat you not to accept the grace of God in vain.")

The role of fellow worker implies tremendous privilege but also great responsibility. It suggests the idea of a responsible person whom God has brought in as junior partner and has given oversight of his work and from whom he expects a responsible rendering of accounts (cf. 1 Cor. 4:2). This is the idea behind the parables of the pounds (Lk. 19:11-28) and the talents (Mt. 25:14-30); and the figures of the vinedresser (Lk. 13:6-9), fishers of men (Mt. 4:19), harvesters (Jn. 4:35) and servants for the feast (Mt. 22:

8-10). Linked with the idea of a responsible partner are Paul's image of the soldier (Eph. 6:11-18; 2 Tim. 2:3, 4), the athlete (2 Tim. 2:5), and the farmer (2 Tim. 2:6); and Peter's concept of shepherding (1 Pet. 5:2-4; cf. Jn. 21:15-17).

Behind the idea of fellow worker lies not only the concept of responsibility but also of resources. God does not entrust us with a task without giving us adequate resources to fulfill it. In both the parables of the pounds and the talents the master gives the servants financial resources to invest for the kingdom. Paul speaks of the giving of gifts to the church "for the work of ministry, for building up the body of Christ" (Eph. 4:11, 12). We can assume that if God sees his co-workers as cultivators, builders, soldiers, fishermen, stewards, harvesters, and shepherds, surely he provides the resources for us to use in the expansion of the kingdom under the direction of his Spirit.[7]

NEW TESTAMENT EXAMPLES OF MISSION THAT LED TO CHURCH GROWTH. In addition to the New Testament imagery about growth, we see numerous examples of mission that led to the growth of the community of faith. These examples show that expansion of the community should be expected as a result of communicating the good news of the kingdom.

The first example is Jesus' own ministry. Mark links his first sermon (in Galilee) with the call of Simon, Andrew, James, and John (Mk. 1:14-20). Thus Jesus goes about preaching the gospel of the kingdom and forming a community of disciples (Mk. 3:13ff.). He trains them (Mk. 13: 13, 14; Mt. 5:1; Lk. 6:12ff.; Jn. 6:3) and commissions them to preach and to have authority to cast out demons (Mk. 3:14, 15). Finally he sends them to the ends of the earth "to make disciples of all nations" (Mt. 28:18).

Note that the formation of this community, which without doubt has numerical expansion in view, is limited to a few. At the end of his ministry Jesus had only 120 followers (Acts 1:15), yet there was growth. They grew in knowl-

---

7. Cf. *Ibid.*, p. 19.

edge, as the epilogues of Luke's and John's Gospels reveal (cf. Lk. 24:13ff.; Jn. 20:30—21:25).[8] They grew in their internal structure, as Acts 1 shows. And they seem to have grown in their involvement in ministry to the world, as the miraculous deeds they were authorized to perform (Mk. 6:7-13) and the horizontally-oriented signs (*e.g.,* the healings, the feeding of the five thousand, etc.) and the sayings of Jesus (*e.g.,* the parables of the Good Samaritan and the Judgment of the Nations) seem to indicate.

A second example of mission that led to community growth, and a corollary of the latter, is the case of the Holy Spirit's action in the early Jerusalem congregation. This was the community that grew out of the direct ministry of our Lord. In fact, it is here we can appreciate the interrelatedness of the different dimensions of growth. Though numerical growth was somewhat slow in the early community, and even though it may seem as if growth in knowledge had taken precedence over the number of persons who entered the fellowship of believers, yet we are told that in one day as many as 3,000 believed, were baptized, and incorporated into the church (cf. Acts 2:41). Henceforth numerical growth went on day after day. ("And the Lord added to their number day by day those who were being saved" Acts 2:47b.) But expansion was accompanied by growth in the apostolic teaching, in fellowship, worship, and service (Acts 2:42-45).

Of course, it is impossible to understand the tremendous expansion of the early Jerusalem church without the presence of the Holy Spirit. Jesus had ordered the disciples to remain in Jerusalem until the Spirit came (Acts 1:4, 8). It was thus the action of the Spirit through the apostles that brought about such fantastic growth.

---

8. The Gospel of John, especially, reveals growth in depth in relation to the disciples' understanding of their faith. Note, for instance, the two parentheses that appear throughout the book explaining that though they did not understand the meaning of a particular event or saying at the moment of its occurrence or utterance, they remembered and understood it after the resurrection (cf. Jn. 2:22; 12:16). Note also the reference to the Holy Spirit as teacher and witness (Jn. 14:26; 15:26; 16:7, 13).

In spite of the Pentecost experience, and even though Jesus had said that upon receiving the promise of the Spirit they would become his witnesses in Jerusalem, Judea, Samaria, and unto the uttermost parts of the earth (Acts 1:8), the Jerusalem congregation remained in the capital city, apparently without further interest in expanding its witness to the regions beyond. The Spirit had to wrestle with her. He caused the murmuring of Greek-speaking church members to lead to the election of seven men to serve as deacons, and moved one of them, Stephen, to preach the gospel everywhere among the Jews who had settled in Jerusalem from other parts of the world. He then let the preaching of Stephen end in tremendous persecution and used the flight of several church members from Jerusalem to diffuse the gospel in Judea, Galilee, and Samaria (Acts 9:31). After the call of Saul on the road to Damascus, the Spirit went to work on Peter through Cornelius and then used Peter to convince the reluctant congregation of Jerusalem of God's universal purpose. Toward the end of Acts 11, a nucleus of believers was reported in Antioch and probably in Phoenicia and Cyprus (Acts 11: 19). Especially at Antioch did the Word prosper greatly, so much so that Barnabas and Paul were commissioned by the Spirit through the church to minister the gospel to the Gentile world (Acts 13:2).

The Spirit's action in the early Jerusalem congregation led to mission, and mission to the growth of the church. As the church grew, she began to experience further the Spirit's ever-expanding action. The Pauline mission is the result of the expansion of the Jerusalem church. Mission thus led to the growth of the church, and the expansion of the church gave birth to a greater and deeper missionary movement.

It is beyond the scope of this book to go on recollecting how Paul and his colleagues went about from Antioch to Cyprus and southern Asia, back to Jerusalem, and to Europe, back again to Jerusalem and up to Rome preaching the gospel, discipling those who responded, through preaching, periodic visits, pastoral letters, and the sending of emissaries such as Timothy and Titus. It suffices to note that the Pauline mission marks the climax in the primitive community of the tremendous expansion which Jesus had begun with his disciples. Hence the Spirit, as the continuator of the mission of Christ, moved and acted sovereignly not only in the Jerusalem congregation but also in Paul's missionary efforts. In each case the concrete manifestation of the Spirit's presence was the conversion and discipling of persons, the expansion of their knowledge and commitment to Christ, and their growing involvement in the problems and agonies of man.

THE THEOLOGICAL RATIONALE FOR CHURCH GROWTH

In addition to the New Testament material, at least two theological reasons exist for affirming that mission must lead to church growth—or conversely, that church growth must be a reality in the life and missionary action of the church.

THE MISSION IS GIVEN BY GOD. First, mission must lead to church growth because the church has no other mission than God's mission to the world, and he always gives form to his action in history. This is indeed one of the leading themes of biblical theology. In the Old Testament, God reveals himself acting personally in history. His actions are concrete: he reveals himself as creator of the world and judge of the nations; he intervenes directly in the history of Israel, mercifully choosing her to be his treasured possession and delivering her from bondage, but also chastising her for her evil. In the New Testament, he reveals himself in the incarnation of the Son. The Son, in turn, becomes known through the Spirit, who gives birth to the church and acts in and through her in his mission to the world.

Since the church is caught up in the manifold and

dynamic mission of God, her mission to the world must take place in concrete historical situations. The New Testament warns us of the danger of an a-historical missionary endeavor. This is the input of the Johannine writings. A mission so spiritually minded that it does not manifest itself in the concrete situations of man is a "docetic" mission and thus sub-Christian. Christ, the model missionary, carried on his mission in and through his own flesh—he preached and taught to real human beings, he died on a cross, he rose again from the dead and ministered *in his body* to his disciples and he called them to go and disciple the *peoples* of the *earth.*

Mission must not only *take place* in concrete historical situations but must also *bear fruit* in these situations. God's action is always creative. Wherever he intervenes, something positive happens. This is why the New Testament takes a forward-looking, positive, expectant approach to mission. In mission, concrete results are to be expected. By results is meant transformation of lives, in-gathering of believers into worshiping communities, depth of understanding, stirring up the conscience about those things for which the gospel stands (justice and righteousness, love and peace), etc. These things should occur wherever the gospel is communicated, because the gospel is good news about a God of power and grace, whose will is that none should perish but that all should come to repentance and faith. Hence not only has he commissioned those who have responded to his call to go and share this message with others, but he has promised to be with them, acting decisively in their midst. Those who share it are to expect a miraculous operation.

THE GOSPEL IS COMMUNITY-ORIENTED. Second, mission must lead to church growth because the gospel is community-oriented. As has been observed, the gospel is the good news of the kingdom. One of the signs of the kingdom—perhaps the most evident—is the "community" of those who have committed themselves to the sovereign will of the King. If the proclamation of the gospel involves the calling of men and women to turn from their sins and commit their lives to God, their response to this call involves their incorporation into the life of the kingdom and hence into the community of the King. As McGavran has said, communities of believers "multiplying across the world in every nation demonstrate that a new era has begun. Like the Holy Spirit, they are an earnest of the triumphant reign of God, which in His good time He will bring in."[9]

This is not to say that the multiplication of congregations is in itself a sign of the kingdom. Rather it is the formation of *authentic* communities of faith that *live* the liberating power of the gospel in their concrete historical situations that demonstrate the life of the kingdom. Such congregations celebrate the gospel in the light of their culture and historical struggles, and engage themselves in liberating evangelistic activities through their lives, deeds, and verbal witness in such ways that the gospel becomes good news of salvation to others who are lost, oppressed, and alienated. The gospel becomes good news of salvation when the church, which is manifested through the aforementioned congregations, not only proclaims salvation as a future revelation (*eternal* life) but lives a liberated life. Or to put it in other terms, when salvation becomes in the church not only a promise but a reality and when the church acts not only as the prophet of the message of salvation but also as a paradigm of salvation.

In order for the church to be a paradigm of salvation, she must experience its fruit in her everyday life. In the New Testament, salvation has at least a threefold meaning: (1) liberation from the power of sin and death (Rom. 8:1, 2); (2) adoption into the family of God (Jn. 1:12; Rom. 8:16, 17, 29; Gal. 3:16, 26-29; 4:5b-7; 1 Jn. 2:1, 2); (3) participation in the reign of Christ (cf. Eph. 1:20ff.; 2:6; Rev. 1:5f.). These benefits of salvation disclose the church in three distinct but interconnected forms.

First of all, the experience of liberation from the power

---

9. Donald A. McGavran, *Understanding Church Growth* (Grand Rapids: Eerdmans, 1970), p. 17.

of sin and death makes the church appear as a *community of peace.* She must live a life of reconciliation and freedom. The concept of *shalom* (well-being, soundness, fullness of life, etc.) must become a reality in the church.[10]

Second, the fact that salvation means adoption into the family of God (or becoming the children of God) indicates that its experience must lead to incorporation into a fellowship of love. The church must be seen as a *koinonia,* a community which actualizes the love of God in her everyday life.

Third, salvation understood as participation in the kingship of Christ reveals the church as a *community of justice and righteousness,* because the kingdom of Christ is preeminently a kingdom of justice and righteousness. Thus to participate in his kingship is, among other things, to exercise equitable and fair judgment, or, to use an Old Testament expression, "to do justice" (Mic. 6:8).

It is in and through the community of faith that the Christian understands the meaning of and begins to reap the fruits of salvation. In this respect, the old phrase of the early church fathers, "No salvation outside the church," is a true affirmation. For it is in the life and mission of the church that forgiveness from sin, love, and hope are exercised. Further, the church is in itself the fruit of salvation because she is the family of God and the community of the King. She has not only experienced reconciliation and

---

10. At this point two remarks are in order. (1) The experience of *shalom* is possible through Christ who becomes "our peace" (Eph. 2:14ff.). This does not mean that only Christians can profit from its blessing. Obviously, when the church is able to bring about better living conditions in society, these benefit every member of society. But it does mean that for the Christian *shalom* is possible in and through Christ inasmuch as *shalom* comes as a gift of God and Christ is God's peace made flesh. (2) The church has the obligation to actualize God's *shalom* in her everyday life. If she cannot live a peaceful life with all of its implications, if she cannot provide the right conditions among her own for an authentic lifestyle she has no right to proclaim God's peace to the world. What a lesson for the church of the twentieth century who has often allowed her own to go unfed, to live in starvation and infrahuman conditions while her leaders have lived in luxury and wealth!

freedom but is through her very life a sign of reconciliation and freedom.

With such a community-oriented gospel, the church's participation in God's mission cannot but lead to church growth. It must bring about new believers, it must unite them in communities of worship, it must build them up in the faith, and it must guide them so to internalize Christ that he will become a living reality in their concrete human situations. Anything short of that weakens the comprehensiveness of God's mission, limits the power of the gospel, and contradicts the biblical imperative for the growth of the church.

6/THE CHURCH GROWTH MOVEMENT

Ever since Donald A. McGavran published his monumental *Bridges of God* in 1955, a missionary school of thought has developed, first around his research and writings, and more recently around the research and writings of other missiologists (Alan R. Tippett, Ralph D. Winter, C. Peter Wagner, Charles H. Kraft, Arthur Glasser, and their students), dedicated to the study and promotion of the growth of the Christian church among the peoples of the earth.[1] An Institute of Church Growth was founded in 1960 by McGavran at Eugene, Oregon. Several years later

---

1. The most up-to-date list of "church growth" students is found in the recently published *Festschrift* in honor of McGavran: Alan R. Tippett, ed., *God, Man and Church Growth* (Grand Rapids: Eerdmans, 1972), 460 pp.

it became part of the School of World Mission of Fuller Theological Seminary.

It is to the missionary activities stimulated by the missiological thought of these men that I refer when I speak of the Church Growth Movement. Behind this movement lies a missionary theory based upon the successful experience of J. Waskom Picket and Donald A. McGavran with people movements in India. This theory is constantly being reinforced by the research efforts of the faculty and student body of the Fuller School of World Mission and other allies throughout the world.

A missionary theory is basically an interpretation of mission. It analyzes the nature of mission, its chief ends, proposes a set of governing principles, and develops a strategy of missionary action. This is precisely what Donald A. McGavran and his colleagues have done through their theological, historical, and empirical analysis of church growth. Let us consider the essential elements of this theory in the light of their writings.

A THEOLOGICAL INTERPRETATION OF THE CHURCH AS A MISSIONARY COMMUNITY

Church growth theory must be understood first of all as a theology of the church's mission. Peter Wagner emphasizes this in his *Frontiers in Missionary Strategy*:

> Church growth is a very specialized field of theology. It concentrates on only one sub-point of the traditional theological encyclopedia, that of ecclesiology. Within ecclesiology, it narrows down even more to the field of missiology. . . .[2]

Tippett conceives of church growth theology in more

2. C. Peter Wagner, *Frontiers in Missionary Strategy* (Chicago: Moody Press, 1972), p. 40.

dynamic terms, as a "theology of the process of growing in the Lord." He adds that such a theology calls "for a clear doctrine of the Church," both in its nature and its role in space and time.[3]

THE "LOCUS" OF CHURCH GROWTH THEOLOGY. To say that church growth theory must be understood as a theology of the church's mission is to point to the church as the *locus* of its theological reflection, particularly the church in her outreach to the world. It is to see the church as a missionary community whose nature places her in the perspective of God's mission. Thus Tippett's emphasis on the church as a fellowship of believers and the body of Christ, *i.e.*, a people called out from the world and sent back into the world to communicate to the world the mind of Christ, his love, compassion, and word.[4] This fellowship and body is for McGavran a sign of God's reign. Quoting Cullman, he says,

> "The Church itself is an eschatological phenomenon . . . constituted by the Holy Spirit." It is part of the new order which began at the resurrection of Jesus Christ.[5]

Further, the church manifests itself in local congregations of believers. Hence, McGavran says, "Churches [or local congregations] multiplying across the world in every nation demonstrate that a new era has begun."[6]

MISSION AND EVANGELISM. From this, it follows that for church growth theorists the church's mission is preeminently oriented to the world. They vary, however, in their theological formulation of mission.

Tippett, for example, speaks of the church's "out-

---

3. Tippett, "Church Growth Theology . . . ," p. 13.
4. *Ibid.*
5. McGavran, *Understanding . . . ,* p. 17.
6. *Ibid.*

reaching ministries" in relation to the function of the body of Christ. He distinguishes between mission, service, and reconciliation. He states that

> In service we are meeting the bodily needs of man in all its multitudinous forms, man in his physical struggle for life. . . . The ministry of reconciliation deals with man in his mental turmoil, his psychological disturbances and his social discord. . . . But the nature of man is not confined to body and mind. He has also a soul and to this is directed the ministry of mission. The business of the missionary, at home or abroad, clerical or lay, is to bring people face to face with Christ, and if possible secure, by witness, by prayers, by vicarious suffering, a verdict for Christ.[7]

For McGavran, mission is much broader. He sees all three elements as part of the church's mission. He defines mission as "God's program for man." "It is not a man-initiated activity but *missio Dei,* the mission of God, who Himself remains in charge of it." As such, it is many sided ("Each aspect of it can be called mission"[8]) though he emphasizes the evangelistic character of mission. As he states in his response to J. C. Hoekendijk's article, "The Call to Evangelism,"

> A *chief* purpose of Christian mission is to proclaim Jesus Christ as divine and only Savior and persuade men to become His disciples and responsible members of His Church.[9]

In *Understanding Church Growth,* he shortens this affirmation while making it even more emphatic. "A chief and

---

7. Tippett, "Church Growth Theology . . . ," p. 13.

8. McGavran, *Understanding . . . ,* p. 31.

9. Donald A. McGavran, "Essential Evangelism—An Open Letter to Dr. Hoekendijk," in Donald A. McGavran (ed.), *Eye of the Storm* (Waco, Texas: Word, 1972), p. 56.

irreplaceable[10] purpose of mission is church *growth*[10]."[11]

Perhaps the most carefully formulated definition of mission among church growth theoreticians is proposed by C. Peter Wagner in *Frontiers in Missionary Strategy*:

> The mission of the church is so to incarnate itself in the world that the gospel of Christ is effectively communicated by word and deed toward the end that all men and women become faithful disciples of Christ and responsible members of His church.[12]

While each of these men formulate their definition of mission differently, they all see the church's task as having to do primarily with outreach and evangelism. Evangelism, in turn, is conceived of in terms of church growth. According to McGavran, "the aim of evangelism is the planting of churches."[13] Hence, he defines evangelism as

> seeking and saving sinners . . . finding lost children of God and bringing them rejoicing into the household of God . . . bringing lost men to the Savior . . . grafting multitudes of wild olive branches into the Divine Tree.[14]

Evangelism, however, does not aim at just any kind of church growth. According to church growth theory, three kinds of church growth are possible: biological, transfer, and conversion. McGavran defines each and carefully distinguishes them.

> Biological growth derives from those born into Christian families . . .
> Biological growth is good growth . . . Christians should, truly, bring up their children in the fear and

---

10. Italics mine.
11. McGavran, *Understanding . . .* , p. 32.
12. Wagner, *Frontiers . . .* , p. 134.
13. McGavran, "Essential Evangelism," p. 59.
14. *Ibid.,* p. 66.

admonition of the Lord. Yet this type of growth will never "bring the nations to faith and obedience," since the non-Christian part of the world's population is growing faster then the Christian and seems destined to continue to do so . . .

By transfer growth is meant the increase of certain congregations at the expense of others. Nazarenes or Anglicans move from the country to the city, or from over-populated areas to new lands the government is opening up. . . . Transfer growth is important. Every Church should follow up its members and conserve as many of them as possible. But transfer growth will never extend the Church, for unavoidably many are lost along the way.

The third kind is conversion growth, in which those outside the Church come to rest their faith intelligently on Jesus Christ and are baptized and "added to the Lord" in His Church. This is the only kind of growth by which the Good News of salvation can spread to earth's remotest bounds.[15]

CONVERSION IN CHURCH GROWTH THEOLOGY. The idea of conversion growth leads us to consider the uniqueness of conversion in church growth theory. Tippett, making maximum use of his anthropological background and experience with animists, defines conversion in terms of "power-encounter." With this expression he designates that encounter which must take place between God (who through the action of the Spirit of Christ claims man for himself) and demonic forces (which imprison man and want to keep him in a perpetual state of alienation and subjugation). According to Tippett, in an animist society,

When people take their fetishes within whom the fearful powers of the spirits have been contained, and now at a precise point of time voluntarily cast them on the fire or into the sea (a thing they had not thought

---

15. McGavran, *Understanding* . . . , pp. 87, 88.

possible before), and have done this in a new-found power of One who has power over all power . . . , so that suddenly they are free, they are new creatures and are prepared to put themselves under Christian instruction . . .[16]

For Tippett (and his colleagues), conversion must be understood in terms of decision-making. It may be described as a psychological process involving "a period of awareness, a point of realization, a period of decision-making, a precise point of encounter, and finally a period of incorporation."[17]

One of the most interesting aspects of church growth theology is the idea of group conversion. By this is meant the simultaneous conversion experience by the members of a given group of people as a result of a multi-individual decision. "Multi-individual," McGavran says,

> means that many people participate in the act. Each individual makes up his mind. He hears about Jesus Christ. He debates with himself and others whether it is good to become a Christian. He believes or does not believe. If he believes he joins those who are becoming Christians.[18]

Earlier, in *Bridges of God,* McGavran had gone deeper in his definition of group conversion. Then he said,

> It is important to note that the group decision is not the sum of separate individual decisions. The leader makes sure that his followers will follow. The followers make sure that they are not ahead of each other. Husbands sound out wives. Sons pledge their

---

16. Tippett, "Church Growth Theology . . . ," p. 21.

17. *Ibid.,* p. 22.

18. Donald A. McGavran, "People Movements," quoted by Malcolm Bradshaw, *Church Growth through Evangelism in Depth* (So. Pasadena: William Carey, 1968), p. 18.

fathers. "Will we as a group move if so-and-so does not come?" is a frequent question.

Peoples become Christians as a wave of decision for Christ sweeps through the group mind, involving many individual decisions but being far more than merely their sum. This may be called a chain reaction. Each decision sets off others and the sum total powerfully affects every individual. When conditions are right, not merely each sub-group, but the entire group concerned decides together.[19]

In 1955 McGavran saw group conversion as a *group-decision*, which of course involved individual decisions but which went beyond the idea of "the sum of separate individual decisions." Obviously a change has now taken place in his thought. By the time he wrote *Understanding Church Growth* (1968-69), he had substituted the concept of "group decision" for "multi-individual decision," as the following paragraph indicates:

There is no such thing as group conversion. A group has no body and no mind. It cannot decide. The phrase "group conversion" is simply an easy, inexact description of what really happens.[20]

This is not the place to delve into the causes for the change that has taken place in McGavran's thought nor to evaluate its soundness. From the looks of it, he has greatly influenced his colleagues and students.[21] Be that as it

---

19. Donald A. McGavran, *Bridges of God* (N.Y.: Friendship Press, 1955), p. 12.

20. Donald A. McGavran, "God's Will and Church Growth," quoted by Malcolm Bradshaw in *Evangelism . . . ,* p. 18. The material for this lecture as well as for the one previously cited from Bradshaw's book, is included in *Understanding Church Growth.*

21. Tippett follows the idea of multi-individual decisions (cf. *Growth and the Word . . . ,* pp. 31ff.). So do Wagner (cf. *Frontiers . . . ,* p. 104) and Bradshaw (cf. *Evangelism . . . ,* p. 18).

may, McGavran's "refined" concept of multi-individual decision still gives the concept of conversion a sociological orientation because it holds that conversion can and does take place in a group setting. In societies which revolve around group life, this becomes a tremendous possibility for the evangelization of entire communities, as will be observed shortly.

THE TWO STAGES OF CHRISTIANIZATION. The concept of multi-individual conversion must be understood in church growth theory in relation to what McGavran has called the two stages of Christianization. Following his understanding of Matthew's account of the Great Commission, McGavran distinguishes between "making disciples" and "teaching them." The first stage he calls "discipling"; the second, he designates "perfecting." He describes the first stage like this:

> Negatively, a people is discipled when the claim of polytheism, idolatry, fetishism or any other man-made religion on its corporate loyalty is eliminated. Positively, a people is discipled when its individuals feel united around Jesus Christ as Lord and Savior, believe themselves to be members of His Church, and realize that "our folk are Christians, our book is the Bible, and our house of worship is the church." Such a reorientation of the life of the social organism around the Lord Jesus Christ will be followed by ethical changes.[22]

The second stage—perfecting—he describes in terms of

> bringing about . . . an ethical change in the discipled group, an increasing achievement of a thoroughly Christian way of life for the community as a whole, and the conversion of the individuals making up each generation as they come to the age of decision. All

22. McGavran, *Bridges . . . ,* p. 14.

that great effort of the churches in old-established "Christian" civilizations, which deals with holy living and with social, racial and political justice is part of the process of perfecting. So also is all that prayer and labor which is dedicated to bringing millions of individuals, generation after generation, into a vital and personal relationship with Jesus Christ.[23]

Church growth theory, then, defines evangelism in terms of discipling and relates the latter to conversion. The stage of perfecting is more the province of Christian education. Both stages are essential to effective church growth. As Tippett says,

> . . . the fellowship cannot grow properly without the outside world in which to "work out its salvation in fear and trembling"; nor can the Body of Christ witness and serve and meet the needs of man without drawing on the resources of the fellowship. Church Growth theology would require the process of growing in the Lord to operate at both ends of this spectrum.[24]

Evangelism and Christian education, discipling and perfecting, conversion and nurture, quantitative and qualitative growth—these are two inseparable dimensions of the process of growing in the Lord. It is in the light of this process that church growth theory interprets the task of mission.

A SOCIOTHEOLOGICAL ANALYSIS OF THE PHENOMENON OF GROWTH IN CHRISTIAN COMMUNITIES

THE WORLD AS A CULTURAL MOSAIC. Church growth

---

23. *Ibid.,* p. 15.
24. McGavran, *Understanding . . . ,* p. 85.

theory is not only a theological interpretation of mission, but also a sociotheological analysis of the phenomenon of growth in Christian communities. For one thing, it sees the population of the earth as a vast mosaic of peoples. This mosaic is made up of different pieces which in church growth parlance are called "homogeneous units." These units represent the common characteristics that make a people. McGavran defines a homogeneous unit as "simply a section of society in which all the members have some characteristic in common."[25]

RAPID DIFFUSION OF IDEAS THROUGH GROUPS. Church growth theory sees the diffusion of ideas spreading more rapidly through groups than through individuals. There is likely to be more rapid growth in a "homogeneous unit" of society than in a heterogeneous unit. By a "homogeneous unit church" is meant "a church growing exclusively within one segment of society."[26] In The Dynamics of Church Growth, J. Waskom Picket explains why growth can spread more rapidly in groups than through individuals.

> There is abundant evidence on every continent that people are helped in coming to Christian faith and purpose and in living therein when friends, relatives, and associates share the experience with them and are hindered when they come alone, breaking with loved ones and neighbors . . .
>
> Normal people need one another in religion as in other aspects of life. All of us require social support to live the good life. The idea that the vital obligations of religion can be met only by individuals in private is more compatible with Hinduism and Buddhism than with Christianity, which is social in its essence. Congregational worship is at the center of Christian living. An individual cannot be in right relations with God and in wrong relations with people.

25. Tippett, "Church Growth Theology . . . , p. 12.
26. Bradshaw, Evangelism . . . , p. 16.

Jesus taught us to associate even our prayers for for-giveness with our practice of forgiveness.[27]

The concept of the rapid diffusion of ideas through groups is in church growth theory the result of careful observation of the phenomenon of "people movements." When a people make a joint decision for Christ without socially dislocating themselves and in full contact with their non-Christian relatives, "thus enabling other groups of that people, across the years, after suitable instruction, to come to similar decisions and form Christian churches made up exclusively of members of that people,"[28] a people movement can be said to be taking place. A chief (if not the most important) contribution of church growth theory to missiology is that it has made the church of the twentieth century aware of this phenomenon and has called attention to her responsibility before God to be not only on the lookout for its manifestations but also to take a responsible and active shepherding role toward a move-ment of multi-individual conversions when it begins to sweep through a given population. As McGavran has said,

> God has given the beginning of thousands of PMs to the church; but most of them have neither been recognized nor developed into mature churches. Many have died. Many have become static Christian en-claves. A few have swept through an entire population leaving congregations everywhere.[29]

DIMENSIONS OF CHURCH GROWTH. In addition to the concepts of the world as a great cultural mosaic and the diffusion of the gospel through groups, the analysis made

---

27. J. Waskom Picket, *The Dynamics of Church Growth* (Nash-ville: Abingdon, 1962), pp. 11, 12, 53.

28. McGavran, *Understanding . . . ,* pp. 297, 298.

29. Donald A. McGavran, "People Movements," in Stephen Neill, Gerald H. Anderson and John Goodwin (eds.), *Concise Dictionary of the Christian World Mission* (Nashville: Abingdon Press, 1971), p. 480.

by church growth theory of the phenomenon of growth includes a three-dimensional concept of the growth of Christian communities. We have already considered two dimensions of this concept, namely, the quantitative and the qualitative. The third dimension is organic. In his excellent study on *Solomon Islands Christianity,* Tippett defines each of them. Quantitative growth is basically conversion growth. Qualitative growth is the internal growth of the fellowship of Christians—sanctification, perfection, or simply growth in grace. Organic growth has to do with the emergence of a church "as the Church in a community, an indigenous body." Tippett says that

> organic growth cannot always be registered statistically, but it has a physical way of proving its reality. The changing organizational patterns of the church often reflect growth going on. The appointment of deacons in the early Church showed that the Church was growing.[30]

Even though church growth theorists insist that these three levels of growth must be seen as a unit, it is obvious that neither qualitative nor organic growth has the status of quantitative growth, *i.e.,* they are not as important as the in-gathering of new believers. This may be seen in the insistence of McGavran and his colleagues on measuring the qualitative growth by numerical growth. He maintains that "as soon as we separate quality from the deepest passion of our Lord—to seek and save the lost—it ceases to be Christian quality."[31] He adds that the church should engage in other tasks, but insists that

> Preaching good sermons, teaching illiterates to read, food supply, administering churches skillfully, apply-

---

30. Alan R. Tippett, *Solomon Islands Christianity* (London: Lutterworth Press, 1967), p. 31.

31. McGavran, *Understanding . . . ,* p. 52.

ing Christianity to all of life, using mass media of communication [etc.] . . .

should not take priority over discipling the nations.[32] Hence he calls on "those who prepare mission budgets and spend mission funds" to bear in mind "the ultimate goal to which God directs them,"[33] namely, "effective multiplication of churches in the receptive societies of the earth."[34]

Quantitative growth, according to Ralph Winter, is a reliable indication of qualities. It is "a 'necessary though not sufficient' evidence of faithfulness to God in evangelism."[35] To this we must add Tippett's affirmation to the effect that "conversion growth, especially when it takes place in large people-movements, requires the follow-up of quality growth." He concludes that "for church growth to be really effective, each of these dimensions of growth should be taking place together and interacting under the guidance and blessing of the Holy Spirit."[36] In other words, church growth, understood as the expansion of the church (in breadth and depth, width and height), must be a corporate process. Obviously, numerical expansion is of utmost importance, but in order for it to take place, it needs the depth of qualitative and organic growth. Consequently, organic and qualitative growth must lead to quantitative growth, and conversely, quantitative growth should be seen, generally speaking, as an indication of some form of organic and qualitative growth.

VALUE OF THE SOCIAL SCIENCES. In its sociotheological analysis of the phenomenon of religious growth, church

---

32. *Ibid.,* p. 49.

33. *Ibid.,* p. 50.

34. *Ibid.,* p. 49.

35. Ralph Winter, "Quality or Quantity?," in Donald A. McGavran (ed.), *Crucial Issues in Missions Tomorrow* (Chicago: Moody Press, 1972), pp. 179, 180.

36. Tippett, *Solomon Islands . . . ,* p. 32.

growth theoreticians see the need to use the insights and techniques of the social and behavioral sciences, especially anthrolopology, sociology, and statistics. In fact, a great number of church growth theorists are trained anthropologists. As Tippett has said of himself and his colleagues,

> Our specialized training is in the social sciences . . . We come to the Bible as men out of the human situation for whom the Bible is a working tool—a norm for faith and practice if you like. Our approach is problem-oriented and the answers we find have to work effectively out there in the cross-cultural world. We see biblically based theory that works in the world. Our methodology is experimental and any theory has to interpret the facts that are observed or collected in the world.[37]

In their inquiry into the phenomenon of church growth, these men see in anthropology a tool for understanding such things as the phenomena of culture and culture-change, the process of decision-making, the structure of leadership, and how to deal with the multitudinous cross-cultural situations with which the church must cope in her mission to the world.[38] Sociology helps them understand the nature of the human group and the behavior of man in society.[39] Man does not live alone; he lives in a world of relationships. If the church is to reach him, she must understand the phenomenon of his structured relationships. This is where the study of sociology can be extremely valuable. It helps us to understand not only the dynamic and complex nature of social structures but provides help-

---

37. Tippett, "Church Growth Theology . . . ," p. 1.

38. *Ibid.,* pp. 15, 21. See also, McGavran, *Understanding . . . ,* pp. 106ff.

39. Cf. Donald A. McGavran, "Homogeneous Populations and Church Growth," in Donald A. McGavran (ed.), *Church Growth and Christian Mission* (New York: Harper and Row, 1965), pp. 69ff.

ful insights about how the church is apt to grow in different segments of society.[40] Finally, statistics provide a most effective tool for measuring growth. According to McGavran, "The numerical approach is essential to understanding church growth."[41] This is so because factual data are needed to understand growth and decline. Such knowledge is essential in the process of evaluation, which in turn is important in planning for effective church growth.

A STRATEGY FOR THE GROWTH OF THE CHURCH

This leads to a third characteristic of church growth theory. Not only must it be understood as a theology of mission and a sociotheological discipline that studies the phenomenon of religious growth. It must also be seen as an optimistic strategy for the church's rapid expansion. The basis for this strategy is the success of people movements around the world; its essence can be summarized in at least five principles.

WITHOUT CROSSING CULTURAL BARRIERS. First, in discipling the peoples of the earth for Christ, one must bear in mind "that people who are highly conscious of solidarity with their society prefer to become Christians *without crossing cultural barriers*."[42] McGavran and his colleagues illustrate the importance of this principle from their wealth of experience. They give numerous examples of growing situations where people were not required to betray their own culture but could remain with their own kin. Hence, McGavran writes,

Church planters who enable men to become Chris-

---

40. Cf. McGavran, *Understanding . . .* , pp. 183ff.
41. *Ibid.*, p. 83.
42. Bradshaw, *Evangelism . . .* , p. 16.

tians without crossing such barriers are much more effective than those who place them in men's way.[43]

AWARENESS OF THE RESISTANCE-RECEPTIVITY AXIS. A second principle of church growth strategy has to do with what Wagner calls "the resistance-receptivity axis."[44] Some segments of society are more receptive than others. Church growth strategy emphasizes the importance of concentrating major evangelistic efforts in the receptive segments of society. This principle has several implications.

It implies, first, the necessity of relocating resources in order to take advantage of the receptiveness of a people toward the gospel. In other words, the church ought to concentrate its resources in those areas that are showing signs of growing receptivity to Christianity.[45]

Second, it implies conversely that the church ought to occupy lightly resistant areas. Concentrated effort in an area of hostility toward the gospel usually hardens people in their unbelief. This does not mean that Christians ought to withdraw from resistant areas. Rather, it means that they ought to exercise much patience and prayer. Since the Holy Spirit is the Lord of the harvest, it is he who must create responsiveness. Christians who face highly resistant populations should wait patiently and pray earnestly for the Spirit to move upon them and make them responsive. When he does, they should move in with all their energies and resources.

Third, the resistance-receptivity axis implies that priority should be given to what McGavran calls "strategic peoples." By this he means people who are strategically important for the rapid spread of the gospel to other people, such as, for instance, the chief of a tribe or a primitive society, an opinion leader in western society or an entire group.[46]

---

43. McGavran, *Understanding . . . ,* p. 200.
44. Wagner, *Frontiers . . . ,* p. 150f.
45. Cf. McGavran, *Bridges . . . ,* p. 109.
46. *Ibid.,* p. 114.

Fourth, it implies that attention should be given to growing situations in need of strength. Some churches experience tremendous growth through a given time but begin to weaken their position due to lack of depth in their internal structure.[47] Attention should be given to these churches, or they are bound to come to a dead end.[48]

CONCENTRATE ON CONGREGATIONAL MULTIPLICATION IN ESTABLISHED CHURCH SITUATIONS. Another principle of church growth strategy is the concentration on congregational multiplication in established church situations rather than in increasing the membership role of one local congregation. Wagner says that "the best way for a church to grow . . . is to be active in reproducing itself."[49] He warns that such an enterprise is bound to be costly. It will cost people, time, money, and identification, but the fruit it will produce will make the sacrifice worth while.[50]

---

47. In Chile, for example, we have a situation where churches have experienced a fantastic numerical and organic growth since 1909. Yet because attention has not been paid to other dimensions of growth (particularly conceptual and incarnational) these churches may be entering a period of stagnation. I base this affirmation on my personal observation as a staff member of an entity which is carrying out an intensive in-depth evangelism project in Santiago, Chile. What my colleagues and I have been able to observe in the last year and a half is that while in Chilean Pentecostal churches there is a tremendous flow of new believers, there is a growing number of people leaving the churches, especially young people of college age. Add to this the ideological challenges which the Christian church as a whole has faced in this rapidly changing society; the lack of a solid educational program in the churches; the fact that these churches, in spite of their tremendous success in the mobilization for witness of their constituencies, have not been able to penetrate the various social strata and structures of the country; and the tremendous internal tensions that characterize at the present moment several of the largest denominations (especially the Methodist Pentecostal Church and the Evangelical Pentecostal Church) and you have strong warning lights of stagnation.

48. Cf. Tippett, *Solomon Islands . . .* , p. 352; *Growth and the Word . . .* , pp. 68ff.

49. Wagner, *Frontiers . . .* , p. 188.

50. Cf. *Ibid.,* p. 191-193.

ENGAGE IN LAY TRAINING. Lay training is a fourth principle. McGavran points out that

> in any land, when laborers, mechanics, clerks, or truck drivers teach the Bible, lead in prayer, tell what God has done for them, or exhort the brethren, the Christian religion looks and sounds natural to ordinary men . . . No paid worker from the outside and certainly no missionary from abroad can know as much about a neighborhood as someone who has dozens of relatives and intimates all about him. True, on new ground the outsider has to start new expansions—no one else can—but the sooner he turns the churches over to local men the better.[51]

CARRY ON EXTENSIVE RESEARCH. Finally, church growth strategy emphasizes carrying out extensive research in church growth. The value of such endeavor lies in the fact that it can lead to the discovery of fertile soil and to the setting of realistic goals.[52] As Bradshaw says, ". . . an accurate understanding of the actual situation of the Church and its environment is half of the battle."[53] Hence McGavran suggests that missions should plow back 5 percent of their income into research.[54] Such an investment should lead in the long run to more effective evangelization of the earth's receptive populations.

A theological interpretation of the church as a missionary community, a sociotheological analysis of the phenomenon of growth in the Christian church, and a strategy for the growth of the church—this in general is the theory behind the Church Growth Movement. The merits of this movement lie mainly on the effect it has had on the missionary movement in general and on missionary theory in

51. McGavran, *Understanding* . . . , pp. 286, 287.

52. Cf. Wagner, *Frontiers* . . . , p. 191.

53. Bradshaw, *Evangelism* . . . , p. 34.

54. Donald A. McGavran, "Why Neglect Gospel-Ready Masses," *Christianity Today*, 10:769-771.

particular. Its weaknesses are imbedded in some of its theoretical assumptions. In the next chapter we shall critically evaluate the church growth school of thought, analyzing its unique contributions to contemporary missiology as well as its theoretical loopholes.

7/AN APPRAISAL OF CHURCH GROWTH THEORY

In dealing with the church's missionary imperative to-day one must not only understand the essential elements of church growth theory. The fact that dozens of mission-aries and Third World churchmen are flocking every year to study and engage in research at the Institute of Church Growth and the School of World Mission of Fuller Theo-logical Seminary; the fact that every year dozens of books and articles dealing with the church growth point of view are published both in North America and abroad; the fact that in 1968 the prestigious *International Review of Mission* dedicated an entire issue to the church growth debate; and that every time a major book on church growth theory is published, pro- and anti- voices are raised everywhere, all indicate that church growth theory is a most controversial issue in contemporary missiology. Thus it needs to be critically evaluated before it is accepted or rejected.

Missionary theories are never perfect; they need constant revamping. Because the growth of the church is an imperative task of mission, the church is responsible to study carefully and implement those principles which can contribute most to fulfilling her missionary responsibility. She must not only be sensitive to any critical appraisal of her missionary performance but must seek constantly to evaluate and improve those theories which emerge from within her own ranks, analyzing the nature of her mission, defining its objectives, outlining the governing principles that ought to guide her missionary endeavors, and developing a strategy for action.

The purpose of this chapter is to interact critically with the church growth theory expounded in the last chapter. By critical interaction I do not mean "negative criticism," but rather an analysis of the merits and liabilities of its theoretical formulation. I will also make a positive proposal for strengthening it and making it more effective. Let us consider first of all the importance of the Church Growth Movement.

CONTRIBUTIONS OF THE CHURCH GROWTH MOVEMENT TO CONTEMPORARY MISSIOLOGY

CHALLENGE TO THE MISSIONARY ENTERPRISE. One of the most important contributions of the Church Growth Movement to contemporary missiology is the way it has challenged the modern missionary enterprise. In a time of retrenchment, crisis, and confusion in the world missionary movement in general and in the theology of mission in particular, the Church Growth Movement has come out for a militant, optimistic, and forward-looking approach to the missionary enterprise. For one thing, it has taken a direct stand against the defeated, pessimistic attitude that has characterized so much missionary thinking in the last decades of the twentieth century. In the epilogue of *Understanding Church Growth,* McGavran challenges Christians everywhere to "lay down that defeatist attitude which keeps" them "convinced that the Church is not only at a standstill but in retreat."[1] He adds,

> Let us lay aside our contentment in changing a few aspects of non-Christian thinking for the better. Let us brush aside the cobwebs of opinion which obstruct our vision and lead us to believe that the morality and concern for others which rises from a Christian base may equally well rise from a non-Christian base.
>
> Let us face the fact that the world is open to belief in Christ as widespread as is our power to proclaim Him. The Church can move forward mightily. It is God's will that she do so. His power will bless us as we devote ourselves with heart, mind and will to the multiplying of churches from earth's one end to the other.[2]

This challenge has not gone unnoticed. James Scherer, in his review of *Understanding Church Growth,* says that the challenge of the book "to ecumenical missions is its claim to set forth a theologically irreproachable and scientifically tested norm for mission policy in a time of general crisis and confusion."[3] Later he comments on McGavran's performance in "lifting the fog" which according to him obscures the real causes that hinder church growth. Scherer says, "So rigorous is he in dispelling romantic notions and false theological rationalizations of

---

1. McGavran, *Understanding . . . ,* p. 370.

2. *Ibid.*

3. James A. Scherer, "The Life and Growth of Churches in Missions—A Review Article," *International Review of Mission,* Vol. LX: 237 (January, 1971), 126.

non-growth that he may be said to have de-mythologized the subject."[4]

More recently, the Church Growth Movement has found an unusual and important ally in Dean Kelley. In his book *Why Conservative Churches are Growing* Kelley, who is an executive with the National Council of Churches of Christ in the USA, reaffirms McGavran's thesis that the world is open to the Christian message and that the church can grow even in a country like the United States of America. Kelley says,

> Amid the current neglect and hostility toward organized religion in general, the conservative churches, holding to seemingly outmoded theology and making strict demands on their members, have equalled or surpassed in growth the yearly percentage increase in the nation's population. And while the mainline churches have tried to support the political and economic outcasts, it is the sectarian groups that have had most success in attracting new members from these very sectors of society.[5]

The challenge of the Church Growth Movement to the contemporary missionary enterprise has not only been manifested in its stand against the attitude of pessimism and defeat so common today in ecclesiastical circles but also in its challenge to churches and mission boards to justify their existence. Brushing aside shouts of "ecclesiastical triumphalism," "missionary imperialism," "numerolatry," and "ecclesiolatry," church growth theorists have landed a mounting attack on ecumenical as well as conservative missions for giving up on what they consider the number one priority of the missionary enterprise,[6] for using

---

4. *Ibid.,* p. 127.

5. Dean M. Kelley, *Why Conservative Churches Are Growing* (New York: Harper and Row, 1972), p. viii.

6. Cf. McGavran, "Essential Evangelism," in *Storm . . . ,* pp. 56ff.; Donald A. McGavran, "Will Uppsala Betray the Two Billion?" *Church Growth Bulletin,* Special Uppsala Issue (May, 1968);

the wrong strategy in mission,[7] and for justifying or covering up the failure of their missionary efforts by rationalizing both theologically and promotionally non-growing situations.[8]

Moreover, the Church Growth Movement has practically demolished the traditional mission station approach.[9] By announcing its death and propagating a more indigenous, people-oriented, and biblical missionary pattern, church growth theory has contributed to the indigenous church movement. By insisting on the training of lay personnel, by stressing group evangelization, and by emphasizing witnessing as part of the believer's way of life and not as the province of a professional evangelist or pastor, by defining evangelism in the perspective of the multiplication of local churches that will worship, teach, and exercise discipline in the light of their own particular circumstances, the Church Growth Movement has made a strong, if indirect, contribution to the formation of autochthonous churches with a message and lifestyle relevant to their economic, cultural, social, and political realities.

INSIGHT INTO CONVERSION, EVANGELISM, AND THE CHURCH. A second important contribution that the church growth school of thought has made to missiology is its fresh insight into conversion, evangelism, and the church.

Donald A. McGavran, "A Missionary Confession of Faith," *Calvin Theological Journal,* 7:2 (November, 1972), pp. 137ff.

7. Cf. Donald A. McGavran, "Wrong Strategy—The Real Crisis in Mission," in McGavran (ed.), *Storm . . . ,* pp. 97ff.

8. Cf. Wagner, *Frontiers . . . ,* p. 36, where he states:
. . . some evangelicals who are involved in good evangelistic and missionary activities but for one reason or another have been relatively static and fruitless, see McGavran as a threat because he so staunchly appeals to objective analysis in terms of measurable goals. In emotional-laden attempts to discredit the whole school of thought, some have even charged McGavran and his colleagues with "ecclesiolatry," "numerolatry," or some other form of idol worship.

9. Cf. McGavran, *Bridges . . . ,* pp. 64ff.; Picket, *Dynamics . . .* p. 54.

As I have said, the concept of multi-individual decisions gives a sociological orientation to the experience of conversion because it affirms that conversion, which depends on a personal act of faith in Christ, can take place in a group setting, where all the members of a given group (family, clan, tribe, or mutual interest group) participate in a similar experience with Christ after considering it together and deciding to turn to Christ at the same time.

This, of course, is contrary to the traditional North Atlantic (what McGavran calls *Eurican*) Protestant individualistic approach to conversion, which apparently has led to the questionable idea that the church is simply the sum total of those individuals who accept Christ as Lord and Savior, instead of the People of God, a *new humanity* which God is forming from *fallen humanity*. Further, the Eurican view has entertained the false notion that an individual decision for Christ, made against family opinion, is of a higher order than one which is made in consultation with the family.[10] This notion represents not only a distorted idea of God's evangelistic pattern (through groups, families, tribes, nations, etc.[11]) but a blurring of the unique role played by the family in society. For not only does the New Testament teach that the church is God's household, a reconstruction of the human family, but that a believer's family is sanctified by *his* faith in Christ (1 Cor. 7:14). This means, at the very least, that God's interest does not lie just in the salvation of individuals but in the transformation and enrichment of entire families.

The group approach to evangelism which the Church Growth Movement has propagated has given the church all over the world a new insight into evangelistic strategy.

---

10. Cf. McGavran, *Bridges . . . ,* p. 9.

11. This is exceedingly clear in the covenant relation of God with Israel. Abraham, for example, was called with his family (Gen. 12:1-2). In the New Testament the concept of household is extremely important. See, for example, the multiple references that the New Testament makes to entire households. Many of these references take place in an evangelistic setting (cf. Acts 10:1, 2ff.; 16:15, 31).

Even in societies where no tribes and clans exist, it is extremely valuable because there are always extended families, kinship groups, and webs of relationships. In fact, the homogeneous group becomes a reality even in a secularized society where people choose their friends on the basis of mutual interests. In such a setting, the idea of multi-individual conversions, of group evangelism, and homogeneous-unit churches is not only relevant but the most viable way to reach people for Christ.

STIMULATION OF THE STUDY OF MISSION. Third, the Church Growth Movement has greatly enhanced the field of missiology by stimulating the study of mission. The tremendous wave of research in missiology which has been sparked by the Institute of Church Growth is remarkable. The impressive research record of their missiological research center includes more than a hundred volumes covering such categories as church growth areas, national and denominational surveys, missionary methodologies, biblical and theological missionary principles, and "elenctics" (the science of bringing peoples of non-Christian religiosity to repentance and faith in Christ). The majority of these volumes either deal directly or are oriented to the Third World. These do not include, of course, the research done by members of the Faculty of the School of World Mission, who have published extensively and have engaged in research projects of their own.[12]

To the tremendous research performance that has characterized church growth theoreticians must be added the role which the William Carey Library, the Church Growth Bulletin, and the Church Growth Book Club have played in the dissemination of missiological research and writings throughout the world. This has sparked an interest in the publication of missiological material among several key publishing companies such as Eerdmans, Moody,

---

12. C. Peter Wagner, "Missiological Research in the Fuller Seminary School of World Mission," in *How Biblical Is the Church Growth Movement?* by J. Robertson McQuilkin, (Chicago: Moody Press, 1973), pp. 65-93.

Word, and Zondervan. Information on contemporary missiological issues is now being disseminated at a fantastic rate. Missiological classics such as Johannes Blauw, *The Missionary Nature of the Church,* and James Scherer, *Missionary, Go Home!,* which had gone out of print, have been made available once again. Important information on indigenous missionary movements in the Third World, which used to reach only the hands of those who had the privilege of extensive traveling, has become increasingly available to pastors, missionaries, and interested laymen the world over.

In a theological world in which the field of missiology had become an obscure appendix, the strong, forceful emphasis of the Church Growth Movement on the perennial responsibility of the church to the Great Commission has become a desperately needed corrective. In an ecclesiastical setting which had suffered in recent years from lack of commitment to the need of men and women for personal confrontation with Jesus Christ as Lord and Savior, the missiological endeavors of Donald A. McGavran and his colleagues have played an important prophetic role.

In 1970 and 1971 I wrote two papers criticizing (perhaps too harshly!) the theological and methodological thought of McGavran and his colleagues. I shared the second one with Alfred Krass, who serves as Consultant on Evangelism for the United Church of Christ Board for World Ministries. Even though he agreed with many of my criticisms, he defended McGavran's unique contribution to the missionary movement. In a written response, Krass commented:

> I sense that Mr. Costas does not recognize the historical dynamics here . . . McGavran has seen himself originally in terms of a counter-force to the "mainline" sending agencies, which have stressed devolution, handing over of initiative to the third world churches, and abdication from evangelistic responsibility in favor of health, education, and welfare-type work . . . As a member of a "mainline" agency, I feel

the need for McGavran's corrective on our heavily un-evangelical and pro-institutional involvements.[13]

I must admit that reading Krass's statement was a warming experience. In all fairness, it must be said that the statement should be applicable not only to McGavran but also to the other men who have collaborated with him in making the Church Growth Movement a significant trend in contemporary missiology.

THE PROBLEM WITH CHURCH GROWTH THEORY

The Church Growth Movement has not been without liabilities, which lie mainly in its theoretical formulations. Let us consider some of the problem areas that I have been able to detect in church growth theory.

SHALLOW HERMENEUTIC. One problem area with church growth theory is the fact that its theorists have not been able to come up with a sound hermeneutic for their theological endeavors. By this is meant that they have not contended in depth with the problem that arises out of the space-time difference between the biblical text and our historical situation.

In a sense the hermeneutical problem in church growth theory is rather ironic. For as has been observed, the Church Growth Movement has put a lot of emphasis on the cultural differences between the situations found in the biblical text and the varying situations in which the church must communicate the gospel. They believe in using the instrumentality of the social sciences to understand the strategic problems of mission today and to work out the tactics for a fruitful missionary strategy. It is not that

---

13. Alfred Krass, "Response to Orlando Costas' 'Postscript to the Theological and Methodological Thought of Donald McGavran,' " Unpublished statement (n.d.), p. 1.

church growth theorists are unaware of the time-space problem.

They have, however, interacted with the space-time difference only at the level of the tactico-strategic. They have failed to use the same scientific tools to interpret the text in the light of the many situations of contemporary man.[14] This has led to what appears to be at times a shallow treatment of the biblical text.

For example, in his chapter on "Church Growth and Theology," Arthur Glasser deals with the issue of authority. He rightly points to the fact that Scripture derives its authority from God himself who has disclosed himself through many and sundry ways, but especially in the incarnation of his Son. He then goes on to state (paraphrasing McGavran):

> What is it but derogation from God's authority, if we refuse to take plain biblical statements at their face value? The Bible is no purely human book, a miscellaneous collection of the best insights of man. Its several parts must be interpreted according to their context and coherent purpose, in reverent obedience to the Lord who speaks through them. Inasmuch as we trust Christ for our salvation, let us also trust Him for the information we need touching our performance of His mission.[15]

But is it enough to say that the several parts of the Bible "must be interpreted according to their context and

---

14. An attempt to do this is made in Charles H. Kraft, "Toward a Christian Ethnotheology," in Tippett, *God . . .* , pp. 109ff. In this chapter, Kraft proposes the development of a cross-discipline ("ethnotheology") "that takes both Christian theology and anthropology seriously while devoting itself to an interpretative approach to the study of God, man, and divine-human interaction" (p. 110). While this is a commendable proposal and a good start toward the correction of the above mentioned problem, it is insufficient because it limits itself to the variable of culture.

15. Arthur Glasser, "Church Growth and Theology . . . ," in *Ibid.,* p. 54.

coherent purpose"? What do we do with the textual critics, and particularly with the questions that have been
raised by "form criticism"? What do we do with the fact
that even in a simple biblical statement there may be several equally valid opinions about interpretation? How do
we know that the information *we* "see" in Scripture is
really the information which was meant to be conveyed?
How can we make sure that it hasn't been distorted by our
own "grid"? Isn't it a fact that in many ways our respective situations define how we interpret reality? Isn't it
then possible that our different thought-categories could
lead us to different interpretations of the text and thus to
different theological positions?

So the question is not so cut-and-dried. One may hold
to the authority of Scripture and yet be terribly wrong
about the meaning of a given passage. So it takes more
than obedience to the biblical text. It takes tireless effort
to understand it in "its context and coherent purpose."
Yet one cannot get to the context or purpose without interacting critically with the problems pointed out by those
who have worked with the text, nor without taking into account their interpretations. Moreover, one cannot understand the meaning of the text without critically interacting
with it from his own situation, which in turn calls for analysis of one's particular situation.

The question of interpretation is, therefore, not solved
simply by going to the text and accepting it just as it appears in our translated Bible or even as it appears in the
particular reprint available to us of the original. We must
apply the best possible tools of interpretation and take into
consideration the up-to-date findings of biblical scholarship. We must also analyze our situation, our symbols and
problems (cultural, social, economic, political, psychological, etc.), using the best tools of the social sciences and
interacting with their analysis of our situation. Thus we
must interpret the text in the light of our situation and our
situation in the light of the text.

Such an approach of course complicates the task of
theology. It necessitates an interaction simultaneously

with both the biblical text and the contemporary situation. At the same time it enhances our understanding of God's revelation and, consequently, the meaning of the church's missionary responsibility, because it helps us see the former from a closer perspective.

Thus, for example, when a person in an oppressive social system approaches a passage like Lk. 4:18, 19 in the light of his concrete situation, he is forced to look at such dyads as gospel and poverty, liberation and oppression, sight and blindness in terms of his own structured social, economic, and political problems. He is forced to confront the text with the question, what are the structural dimensions of these dyads? Conversely, the approach to *his* situation of oppression, injustice, and suffering in the light of the text would force him to ask, how does this particular situation appear in the light of the mission of Christ? In such a confrontation, the text is illumined by the situation (and thus its deeper, structural dimensions are more clearly understood) and, likewise, the text illumines the situation (by applying its own analysis and bringing out the hidden personal and existential dimensions of the problem).

QUESTIONABLE THEOLOGICAL "LOCUS." A second problem in the theological foundations of church growth theory has to do with its theological "locus." Mission, as McGavran has said, deals with God's redemptive program for man. Consequently, a theology of mission must be formulated in the light of God's redemptive purpose and the unfolding in history of that purpose; it cannot limit itself to a segment of the theological spectrum.

But this, precisely, has been one of the greatest weaknesses in the theological reflections associated with church growth theory. As Tippett has said, "Church growth does not cover the whole range of Christian theology."[16] Instead it has concentrated its efforts on ecclesiology.[17] By so doing, it has made the church the "locus" of its theo-

---

16. Tippett, "Church Growth Theology . . . ," p. 3.
17. Wagner, *Frontiers . . . ,* p. 38.

logical reflection. The outcome of this has been a theology of mission that revolves around the church instead of God's redemptive action in Christ (which is the basis for the existence of the church).

The problem with a church-centered theology, as church growth theology may tend to be, is that it militates against the "locus" of biblical theology: *Christ*. He is the foundation of our faith because he is God made flesh, the one who died for the sins of the world and rose again from the grave, thereby calling a people to himself and sending them back into the world to disciple for *him* the peoples of the earth. Accordingly, a theology of the church's missionary action must be Christ-centered or it will be a theology without foundation.

When church growth theorists affirm that the aim of evangelism is *the* multiplication of churches, they are advocating a theology that makes the church the end of God's mission. Granted that the gospel is community-oriented. The question is whether the community is the objective or a result (a necessary and imperative one) of the communication of the gospel. Or to put it in other terms, whether the community is an ultimate or a penultimate goal of God's mission.

Isn't the gospel the good news of the *kingdom?* Who is the center of the kingdom—Christ or the church? Who is the object of the kingdom—the community or the King? What is the aim of the kingdom—the exercise of Christ's righteous, peaceful, and loving reign in *heaven* and on *earth* in a restored and transformed universe, or the gathering of a community to him?

I'll admit that the gathering of a community to Christ is a living manifestation of his reign, a "firstfruits." I'll admit that in this respect the church is a temporary goal because it is a paradigm of what is to come. But can we go on to say that this is the aim of the kingdom? Doesn't the concept of kingdom include not only the government and the community of Christ, the King, but also the territory over which he exercises his sovereignty? What, then, does it mean to proclaim the good news of the kingdom? Doesn't it mean making it known in all of earth's domain? Doesn't it imply proclaiming the kingship of Christ in all the spheres of the world, including the high places in which the principalities, powers, and rulers of darkness dwell (cf. Eph. 6:12f.)? Doesn't this mean, in consequence, that there is more to mission than church planting?

God's redemptive mission has to do with the transformation of all of life in Christ Jesus. It is concerned with the church because the latter anticipates in her life and worship the fulfillment of this purpose. It points to the imperativeness of the church's growth as a sign of the expansion of God's kingdom and the fulfillment of his redemptive purpose in Christ Jesus. Yet its ultimate objective is not the church but the transformation of all of life. Its "locus" is Christ himself, the Lord and Savior of the world, he who will bring to completion God's purpose at the *eschaton*.

In order for a theology of mission soundly to reflect God's redemptive purpose and its unfolding in history, it must be Christ-centered. In other words, the "locus" of a theology of mission must be Christ and not the church. The Scripture has no room for an ecclesiological missiology, but it does have plenty of room for a Christological missiology!

Recently a forceful attempt has been made in church growth circles to correct this questionable "locus." In the volume already mentioned (published in honor of Donald A. McGavran), *God, Man and Church Growth,* an attempt is made to shift the "locus" from the church to God. The church is seen in the context of the two-foci, God's purpose and man's responsibility. Accordingly, the church is conceived of in terms of God's redemptive purpose in Christ and her growth as an obedient response to that purpose.

This is made particularly clear in Glasser's chapter, "Church Growth and Theology." Starting from the authority derived from God's self-disclosure, he goes on to focus his attention on God's sovereign will as revealed in his redemptive action in Jesus Christ. He thus sees the church in the light of God's purpose, as "an organism created and kept by Jesus Christ Himself," and a "divine-human society by which He does His work in the world."[18]

Yet when one reads statements like the following: "Nothing is more important but that the church grow,"[19] one cannot help wondering whether in fact the change in its theological "locus" is one of substance or of form. Even so, this essay, together with the overall approach of the book, marks a forward step in the theological foundations of church growth theory.

TRUNCATED CONCEPT OF MISSION. A third problem in church growth theory deals with the concept of mission that characterizes the writings of its proponents. We will not deal with the differences between Tippett's concept of "the church's out-reaching ministries" (service, reconciliation, and mission), McGavran's idea of mission as *"God's* program for man" with evangelism at the center, and Wagner's "3-P evangelism" (presence, proclamation, and

---

18. Glasser, ". . . Theology," in Tippett, *God . . . and Church . . . ,*" p. 60.

19. *Ibid.,* p. 61. This statement may be just a *lapsus lingua* (*i.e.,* a "slip of the tongue"), because in an also recently written essay, Glasser makes the following statement:

> The church is nothing less than "the missionary people of the kingdom of God." It does not establish the kingdom but bears witness to the fact that the kingdom has already been set up by its King. In all the New Testament there is "no brave talk of . . . ushering in his Kingdom—not so much as a syllable." Nor does the New Testament encourage Christians to identify their ecclesiastical structures with the kingdom. They dare not fall prey to the temptation to mark the advance of the kingdom merely in terms of institutional growth. Actually, only "the Church which is His Body" constitutes the people of the kingdom, but local congregations and denominations, still in this world, are not the kingdom. They are but mixtures of the true and the false, always under the judgment of God, always in need of spiritual renewal and the deepening of commitment to the missionary priority. This is not the age for ecclesiastical self-deification, but for the proclamation of the gospel of the kingdom. And it is the age in which Christians should never cease to pray: "Thy kingdom come!"—Arthur Glasser, "Salvation Today and the Kingdom," in Donald A. McGavran, (ed.), *Crucial Issues in Missions Tomorrow* (Chicago: Moody Press, 1972).

persuasion) definition of mission. Instead, we will zero in on the oneness and gospel-centeredness of mission.

If the gospel is the church's message; if her mission to the world involves proclaiming it, teaching it, and witnessing to it, then it is imperative that the church use all the means available to disseminate it. This means that the church's mission must be viewed in its wholeness and thus that (1) the incarnational witness (*i.e.,* the presence of Christians living for Christ in the world) should not be construed as a secondary means but as an essential part of the church's mission; (2) that the proclamation of the gospel should be understood as a form of social action (*i.e.,* service); and (3) that discipling should be conceived of in an ethical context.

In our discussion of the imperative of church growth, it was argued that since God's action in history always takes concrete form, the gospel should not only be proclaimed but bear fruit in concrete situations. It must lead to the expansion of the church. It must now be said that the gospel requires a concrete, incarnate witness. An un-incarnate witness is actually one of the worse forms of Christian heresy, because it militates against the historical character of Christianity.

The idea of incarnational witness is related to the concept of the non-verbal witness of Christians through their involvement in the concrete situations of life. For church growth theorists like Alan R. Tippett, however, "The idea of merely being in the world as a silent Christian presence is a far call from the Bible idea of witness as in the opening verses of John's letter, for example, or the use of the word in the gospel."[20] Elsewhere he adds:

. . . we frequently hear of missionary programs of good works, of social justice, of health and agriculture, being spoken of as witness. These forms of the Christian presence are certainly important and an essential part of Christian practice. Whether regarded

---

20. Tippett, "Church Growth Theology," p. 5.

as the "fruit" of the faith, or as works "worthy of repentance" they are part of the total Christian presence.
It may well be also that God uses this kind of service
to prepare the way for the Christian mission in which
man is confronted with the options of decision for
or against the gospel. That is, God may channel His
prevenient grace through the good works of the
Christian in the pagan situation . . . [But] It does not
follow that because one is there, even in the name of
Christ, that his witness is for Christ . . . And, in passing, it should be added that, although the New Testament does allow that the "works of Jesus" did testify
of him, by far the overwhelming balance of teaching
material speaks of witness in terms of something
actually vocal. It seems to me, as I try to see the
New Testament as a whole book, that it is saying as
from the Lord—"Go and tell what the Lord has done
for you, but see that what you do agrees with what
you say."[21]

These statements are important for several reasons.
(1) They show that for Tippett the idea of Christian presence is good, but as reinforcement of or preparation for a
"vocal" (verbal) witness. (2) They deny the validity of a
situational witness in itself. Thus the incarnation of Christ
is important because *it makes possible* God's personal
communication with man. It stands for God's adaptation to
our situation *in order* "to communicate with man."[22] Accordingly, for Tippett a non-verbal testimony is only important as a secondary frame of reference. It cannot convey in itself the gospel message.

Such a view is highly questionable for two basic reasons. The first has to do with John's emphasis, throughout his writings, on the historical character of Christianity.
He insists that the Word became flesh; that *as* the Father

---

21. Tippett, *Verdict Theology*, pp. 56, 57.
22. Charles H. Kraft, "Communicating the Supracultural Gospel to
Culture-Bound Man," (unpublished manuscript) p. 24.

has sent the Son, the Son has sent his disciples; and that his knowledge of the Word came not only by *hearing* and *seeing* with his own eyes, but by *touching* with his hands. This, too, is the rationale behind "the signs" recorded in John's Gospel. They reveal at least two things: (1) that concrete, albeit miraculous, deeds are a means by which people can come to faith in Christ; and (2) that worship must take a concrete historical form. This is the idea behind the tremendous sacramental theology of the fourth Gospel.

Therefore, far from being documents against "incarnational witness," John's writings seem to defend it. The concept of witness in John is always related to concrete action. The Son witnesses to the Father because he has seen him; his works give witness to the fact that he and the Father are one. The Spirit witnesses to the Son because he proceeds from him; he witnesses to the reality of the incarnation in and through the believers. The latter are, in turn, exhorted to witness to God's love by loving their neighbors.

Second, Tippett's view must be questioned in the light of the process of communication. When I read words like the ones quoted above, I get the impression that for him communication is primarily a verbal act. As an anthropologist he cannot help taking seriously the phenomenon of non-verbal communication. But as a theologian he gives me the impression of giving this phenomenon a secondary role in the communication of the gospel. We know, however, that communication is a total process, a mental, emotional, and social process by which concepts, attitudes, and experiences are shared with others. It deals with stimuli, reactions, replies, and behavior. It takes place at various levels and utilizes all the senses in accordance with the message, the level of operation, and the purpose.

Viewed from the perspective of communication, the gospel cannot be reduced to being merely a verbal message. For it has a dynamic nature and reaches people at the various levels of their existence. Many times it reaches people in verbal form. There are times, however, when the gospel is incarnated in a given situation and the Holy Spirit uses it to call people to repentance.

In my own opinion, Tippett not only does violence to biblical, especially Johannine, theology by pushing "incarnational witness" to the back seat as a secondary end or by boxing it within the concept of "prevenient grace."[23] He limits the theology of mission by reducing it to verbal action and discarding the validity of a Christian's non-verbal witness. The tragic consequences of such a perspective impose a limitation on the dynamic nature of the gospel and the redemptive action of the Holy Spirit, who we know *is* redemptively present in each Christian.

Of course, I do not mean to imply that since incarnational witness is an essential part of the church's mission there is no more need of proclamation, of verbally interpreting the meaning of the gospel, or calling people to repentance and faith. I do mean that incarnational witness may be thought of as a legitimate interpretation of the meaning of the gospel, and in some cases may even be used by the Holy Spirit to bring many to repentance and faith in Christ. This I think is what probably happened with the Philippian jailor (cf. Acts 16:28ff.). This, too, is the idea behind frequent testimonies to the effect that a person or a group, impressed by the life of a godly Christian, have come to them wanting to commit their lives to the same God who has changed their lives.

The church ought not only to see incarnational witness as an essential part of her mission, but conversely it ought to liberate the proclamation of the gospel from the notion that it merely fulfills a "spiritual" role in the life of man. Preaching has not only an evangelistic but a servicing function. By this I mean that its function is more than just proclaiming salvation in Christ and calling people to him. Preaching must also be seen in terms of social action because (theologically speaking) it aims at the total transformation of man. It thus calls man to turn from his sin and commit himself to a positive, others-oriented style of life.

---

23. Cf. *Ibid.*, p. 50.

The problem with church growth theory is that in its struggle against the horizontalization of mission, it has overly emphasized the vertical dimensions of preaching and has often bypassed the tremendous service that preaching renders to man and society (its demand for a life of righteousness, peace, and love).

The preaching of the gospel must not only be seen in its horizontal dimension. The act of discipling should also be seen in an ethical context, and not merely in terms of seeking a decision for Christ. McGavran's twofold stage of Christianization is, in my opinion, a rather limited way of analyzing a complex process. His treatment of Matthew's account of the Great Commission leaves much to be desired. To separate the "make disciples" of Mt. 28:19 from the parallel expression of vs. 20, "teaching them," is to force on the passage an interpretation contrary to the structure of the sentence that begins in verse 19. Further, it is to misunderstand the role of a disciple.

Both the "baptizing" and "teaching" clauses of verses 19 and 20 appear in parallel forms, as explanations of the "Go ye" clause of verse 19. Further, "baptizing" (baptízontes) and "teaching" (didáskontes) are two participles which are dependent on the main verb, "disciple ye" (matheūsate). They explain the nature of the command, integrating both functions to the process of disciple-making.

McGavran's exegesis leads him not only to misinterpret the intent of verses 19 and 20 but also the concept of a disciple.[24] A disciple is not merely one who receives and accepts a body of information. He is one who submits himself to the instruction of a teacher. Jesus called a group of men to be his disciples and taught them *for three years*. After his resurrection he continued to teach them through his Spirit.

To become a disciple of Christ is to enter into a learning relationship with him, a process that never ends. The beginning of this relationship is not without its demands.

---

24. See Karl Heinrich Rengstorf, *"matheūsate"* in Kittel and Friedrick, TDNT, Vol. IV, pp. 426ff., 441ff.

"If any man would come after me, let him deny himself and take up his cross and follow me" (Mt. 16:24). This calls for denial of oneself, unconditional submission to Christ, and *willingness* to undergo a series of radical ethical changes. To follow Jesus is more than joining his church (cf. Mt. 16:18); it is commitment to his cause even unto death.

To push the issue of ethical change to a post-conversion stage, as church growth theology does, is to limit the biblical understanding of conversion which calls for a turning from *sin* unto God, as well as to deny the didactic imperative of the Great Commission. For it is obvious that the presentation of the gospel requires the interpretation of the gospel, and this interpretation, if it is to mean anything, must be done in the light of man's life situation. This necessarily calls for the correlation of the gospel with man's ethical decisions, which is where sin is primarily manifested. How a people can come to a decision about Christ without some kind of reflection on their particular situation and Christ's demands upon their lives is beyond my understanding of the gospel! How Christ can enter into a person's life without his being convicted of his sin is beyond my understanding of repentance! And how a person can join Christ's church without knowing what the church is all about, without some kind of a conscious awareness of the miracle of the new life and without a sense of commitment to the "good life," is beyond my imagination!

Thus mission must be seen as a unitary whole. It cannot really permit a categorization of priorities such as church growth theorists have done. Service in Christ's name should be seen as a living demonstration of the gospel and thus as a witnessing event. Preaching should be seen not only in terms of church growth but of service. Discipling must be seen as an integrated process which involves the interpretation of the gospel in the light of man's life situation, leading men and women to experience basic ethical changes, incorporating them into the church, and shepherding them in such a way that they will continue to believe in Christ and act as responsible members of his church.

AMBIGUOUS CONCEPT OF MAN AND SIN. A fourth problem in the theology of the Church Growth Movement is in relation to the concept of man and society. There is an ambiguity in the treatment of man and society in the writings of men like Tippett and McGavran. On the one hand, they insist on the wholeness of man; on the other, they compartmentalize him. Tippett, for example, in his attempt to show how the church must minister to the whole man, sets up a tripartite conception of man: man as body, mind, and soul. The church should meet each area in her outreaching ministries. Thus she ministers to his body through her service, to his mind through the ministry of reconciliation, and to his soul through mission. We must ask whether such a concept of man is really biblical. It looks more like a phrenological approach to communication or a neoplatonic conception of man than like the biblical teaching of the nature of man.

McGavran's problem is not so much in his concept of man (although at times he comes close to Tippett's model) as with the nature of society. At times he emphasizes the interrelatedness of society. On other occasions he runs to the "society as the sum total of individuals" model.

In a sense, McGavran has moved backward in his concept of society since the publication of *Bridges of God.* In the last chapter, it was shown how in 1955 he took a strong stand against the "sum total of individuals" model for a group and how by 1968 he had moved to a more individualistic group concept. McGavran, perhaps without being consciously aware of it, has allowed himself to be influenced by the individualism that permeates conservative evangelical circles in North America. This has cost him a great deal of influence in circles which are more sociologically inclined, the mainline Protestant churches, for instance. Krass concludes that for some time McGavran

> has been out of real communication with the "mainline" agencies and one can attend meeting after meeting of those bodies without gathering that anyone really takes McGavran's thought seriously. In other

words, McGavran, a member of the Christian church, a "mainline" body, has ceased to figure prominently in the "mainline" dialogue, and has become effective mainly within the nonecumenical world.[25]

In his attempt to communicate effectively with the non-ecumenical world, McGavran has forfeited his earlier posture to the detriment of his cause. Thus a conflict can be observed in *Understanding Church Growth* between what we might call, for lack of a better expression, his functional-theological description of man and society (social change as the result of spiritual change in individuals[26]) and his theoretical-sociological description of man and society ("Men exist not as discrete individuals but as inter-connected members of some society . . . man is not an isolated unit but part of a whole . . ."[27]). This constitutes a tremendous loophole in his theology of mission and, therefore, in church growth theology.

ANTHROPOLOGICAL-FUNCTIONALISTIC SYNDROME. Finally, it seems to me that church growth theory suffers from an "anthropological-functionalistic syndrome." By this I mean, first of all, that church growth theory has overly depended on anthropology in its approach to research. Admittedly it has made plenty of use of statistics, but it has not delved very deeply into contemporary sociology and it has interacted very little with social psychology. Worst of all, it has hardly related to communication theory, a growing interdisciplinary field of study in which anthropology, sociology, and social psychology interact with other sciences such as linguistics, education, and speech around the phenomenon of communication.

In my judgment, this has inhibited church growth theory from an adequate reflection on the nature and theology of language. This in turn has led to what seems to me a

---

25. Krass, "Response," p. 1.
26. Cf. McGavran, *Understanding . . .* , pp. 17, 33, 59.
27. *Ibid.,* p. 183.

distorted concept of dialogue. According to Tippett, the dialogic approach to communication ought to be rejected because it is unbiblical (in that it does not aim for persuasion). An adequate confrontation with communication theory, however, would show how communication, to be effective, must be dialogic, *i.e.*, it must aim at a point of contact and is contingent upon effective feedback and responsible decision-making. Tippett and other church growth theorists see in dialogue a contradiction of the biblical concept of proclamation because it does not allow for a verdict.[28] Dialogue, however, does not necessarily block the possibility of calling for a verdict. It does, however, aim at a responsible decision based upon a meeting of minds, and thus opposes a pressured and manipulative decision-making process.

Both communication theory and biblical preaching agree that a message ought to be a two-way operation, involving give and take, question and answer, affirmation and response. That is how God addresses man (Is. 1:18). Analysis of the Old Testament prophetic literature, the Gospels, and Acts reveals that this was the style of Amos's, Jeremiah's, Ezekiel's, Jesus', Peter's, and Paul's preaching. Thus, awareness of communication theory helps in understanding God's pattern of communication. In the case of church growth theorists, such understanding would serve as a needed corrective toward their approach to dialogue.

Because church growth research has been mostly anthropological, it has interacted mostly with the variable of culture (at such levels as cross-cultural communication, leadership development, evangelistic strategy, etc.) and to a lesser degree with the psychology of conversion. It has not delved into the tremendous structural problems affecting the Third World—their poverty-stricken situation due to their economic domination by a few rich countries and national oligarchies; their state of oppression, repression, and injustice on account of political systems created by and oriented to the well-being of a small minority; the

---

28. Tippett, "Church Growth Theology . . . ," pp. 16, 17.

cultural, economic, political, and socially oppressive function of the technology of the affluent world, etc. What does the gospel have to say about this uneven, scandalous situation? Does the fact that the missionary enterprise has been linked in one way or another to the economic, political, cultural, technological, and social domination of the nonaffluent by the affluent world affect in any way her missionary action? How does all of this affect the planting of new churches? These and many other questions are hardly dealt with *in depth* in church growth circles. They seem to represent blind spots in the research endeavors of this movement.

The syndrome I am referring to in church growth theory has another manifestation, namely, its functionalistic approach to change. Both the anthropological orientation of church growth and the functionalistic social philosophy which permeate its approach to society make church growth theory appear as a functionalistic-anthropology characterized by a strategy-oriented approach to change.

By functionalism I mean the tendency to consider change from the perspective of what contributes or does not contribute to the stability of a given system. Translated into the church's mission in the contemporary world, functionalism means looking at the different social and cultural changes that are taking place in modern society from the perspective of what functions for our traditional conception of mission and what hinders it, instead of looking at change as a social phenomenon that brings about blessings and difficulties and to which the church must address herself in the formulation of her theology and in the fulfillment of her mission to the world.

For the Church Growth Movement, periods of rapid social changes are very important because people are usually more ready psychologically for conversion than in periods of social stability. This, of course, is a tremendous strategic missionary insight and a positive view of the phenomenon of change.

But why look at change just from this perspective? Doesn't the church also have a responsibility to look at society from the point of view of the expansion of the *ethical* qualities and demands of God's kingdom and not merely in terms of the growth of the church community?

This touches upon an issue which will be dealt with in future chapters, namely, do the signs of the kingdom appear only in the church or also in secular society? Without entering into the contemporary controversy, let me suggest that, given the fact that the kingdom is much larger than the church (for it involves not only the community but the territory over which the King exercises his authority), it does manifest its dynamic ethical qualities in the secular world. Thus the struggles for social justice and peace throughout the world *may be* signs of the presence of God's reign. These signs, of course, are not easily recognized by the world. The church, however, is called upon to interpret them to the world.

Consequently, the phenomenon of change and stability should not be merely looked upon in terms of evangelistic strategy. The church has a responsibility to reflect critically upon them in the light of the ethical qualities and demands of the kingdom. The question, then, should not only be, where are the responsive and resistant areas in a given society? (a very important question), but also, is the reality of the kingdom being disclosed more fully or is it being obscured by the social struggles in this society?

The tendency to consider change from the perspective of what contributes or does not contribute to the advance of the church has, in my opinion, kept the evangelical church from developing an adequate theology for such burning contemporary issues as urbanization, secularization, poverty, and revolution. It has inhibited her from interacting theologically with them. As a result, evangelicals have had (at least in our century) very little to say to the profound social, economic, and political struggles of our world. Accordingly, they have appeared to be unconcerned for the world's gut-issues; their faith is "a refuge" (to use the famous expression of Christian Lalive D'Epinay in his study of Chilean Pentecostalism) or an "opium" (to use the harder expression of Karl Marx).

Needless to say, if church growth, or for that matter any other missionary theory, wants to fulfill its missionary objective, it is going to have to interact theologically and sociologically (not merely strategically) with the phenomenon of change. Otherwise, it will not be able effectively to *penetrate* the social structures of our world with the gospel, nor intelligently to *discern* and *interpret* the signs of the kingdom in the secular structures of society, nor, consequently, to *contribute* to the expansion of God's reign in a heterogeneous and complex world.

In conclusion, church growth theory appears as an important and positive theory of mission. It has its liabilities. In this chapter I have pointed out a few. But it also has many advantages which have also been underlined in this and the previous chapter. It can be adapted to almost any situation. And as I have observed, its proponents are open to the strengthening of its weak points. In this respect, it is an open theory of mission. It behooves every one of us, therefore, as responsible churchmen, to utilize it as much as we can in our ministry and to strengthen it with our own valuable insights.

GOD'S
MISSION
AND THE
CHURCH'S
TENSIONS

8/MISSION AND CHURCH-MISSION RELATIONS

THE CHURCH-MISSION ISSUE

Study of the tensions arising from the church's involvement in mission is necessary for adequately understanding the paradoxical reality of the church's missionary vocation. For without such understanding, the gap between the "ideal" and the "real" cannot begin to be closed. Without a close look at the real church, which is a church in tension, the biblical model of the church (sound in biblical theology) cannot fulfill its critical, questioning, and corrective function.

One of the oldest tensions of the church is the relationship between the church in mission and the church out of mission. As Virgil Gerber has said,

> Church and mission have always been in tension. The missionary mandate which spawned the church

also spawned agencies for assisting the church in her mandate. In the course of history, churches produced missions. Missions produced churches. Their success produced tensions.[1]

THE ISSUE IN HISTORICAL PERSPECTIVE. In modern missionary circles, this has been and continues to be a red-hot issue. This was the issue behind the "three-self formula" propagated by Henry Venn and Rufus Anderson back in the nineteenth century.[2] It has been discussed at great length in missionary conferences, including Edinburgh (1910) and Willingen (1952). And it became the great passion of Roland Allen, as his writings so eloquently demonstrate.

In evangelical circles, the church-mission issue is just beginning to attract the attention of missionary leaders and theorists. For example, the Wheaton Conference on the Worldwide Mission of the Church (1966), while it had a study paper dealing with the problem, treated it rather generally and somewhat marginally. Not until 1971 did the Evangelical Foreign Missions Association (EFMA) and the International Foreign Mission Association (IFMA) directly attempt to deal with the problem. But this conference at Green Lake in 1971 barely scratched the surface.

CONTEMPORARY TRENDS. Three general trends can be identified in evangelical missionary circles with respect to the church-mission issue. Some, quite frankly, consider it unimportant. For them, the important thing today is whether the church is to take its task seriously, whether it is going to advance the gospel to the ends of the earth. Anything not directly related to this chief end of the church is of little value. In an editorial article which appeared in

---

1. Virgil Gerber, "Introduction," in C. Peter Wagner, *Church/Mission Tensions Today* (Chicago: Moody Press, 1972), p. 9.

2. For a fairly complete treatment of the "three-self formula," see Max Warren (ed.), *To Apply the Gospel*. Selections from the Writings of Henry Venn (Grand Rapids: Eerdmans, 1971).

the July 1971 issue of the *Church Growth Bulletin,* Donald A. McGavran took this position. Writing on the eve of the Green Lake church-mission relationships conference sponsored by the EFMA-IFMA, he said that "church-mission relationships have little importance in themselves. They are important chiefly if they enable effective discipling of men and *ethne* to take place."[3] This position is corroborated by Wagner in his "Mission and Church in Four Worlds" chapter in *Church/Mission Tensions Today.*[4]

Others consider the church-mission issue extremely important, but are aware of its extreme complexity. Quite frankly, they either do not know exactly what to do, or if they do, they feel incapable of doing anything substantial about it for personal and structural reasons. This I think was the trend represented at the Green Lake '71 conference. After outlining the main issues involved in the discussion and the objectives of the consultation (the third of which was "To develop guidelines which will help each mission to chart its own individual course of action in terms of changes which need to be made"[5]), Virgil Gerber, coordinator of GL '71, frankly admits that

> no one was under the illusion that a general consensus would emerge. The wide divergence of IFMA/EFMA missions in their church/mission relationships precluded any such consensus.[6]

Part of the reason for such a realistic approach to the consultation was that the problem was just too complex. So many issues were involved, theological and otherwise, that no easy answers and solutions were available. Paul Shea, a student delegate to the consultation, went a bit further in analyzing the cause for the apparent inde-

---

3. Donald A. McGavran, "Will Green Lake Betray the Two Billion?" *Church Growth Bulletin* (July, 1971), p. 152.
4. P. 227.
5. Gerber, "Introduction," in Wagner, *Church/Mission . . . ,* p. 14.
6. *Ibid.*

cisiveness of the participants. In his report, he expressed his appreciation for the desire of the participants "for *self-examination* and evaluation," but pointed out that "many came with definite, protective fences or circles around their existence." He goes on to say,

> . . . it was taken for granted, it seemed, that mission organizations must still exist, but with necessary changes. Perhaps a more radical examination was needed.[7]

Thus the question of complexity encompassed not only the grave theological and organizational issues at stake but also the tremendous personal and structural insecurity that then characterized (and continues to characterize) evangelical mission boards and missionaries.

Others, while recognizing the tremendous complexity of the problem, have nevertheless attempted to do something about it. The Latin America Mission, after years of trying to bridge the gap between the foreign mission board and the indigenous church, concluded that more drastic measures had to be taken. For years, the Mission had been characterized by the seriousness with which she had dealt with the concept of partnership in mission. This concept had been expressed throughout the different activities of all her ministries, but particularly through the policy of equal employment of Latin and North American personnel. Three years ago, the Board of Trustees and the General Directors had become increasingly aware of the need for more dramatic and radical steps. A consultation of the Board of Trustees in the USA and Canada, mission personnel, and Latin American pastors and lay leaders was called in January 1971 in San José, Costa Rica, to discuss in depth how the LAM could become a Latin *American* Mission and not just a Mission to Latin America (which is

---

7. Paul Shea, "For Student Delegates," in Virgil Gerber, *Missions in Creative Tension* (South Pasadena, Cal.: William Carey Library, 1971), p. 378.

what the name Latin America Mission implies). From these meetings emerged an autochthonous consortium of Latin American ministries which became known as the Community of Latin American Evangelical Ministries. Included in the consortium were the Latin America Mission of the USA and the Latin America Mission of Canada. What had been departments or ministries of the LAM now became autonomous bodies, and the parent organizations became sister organizations dedicated to the task of interpretation, recruitment of personnel, and financial development. The consortium also included two church bodies which were the outgrowth of the evangelistic endeavors of the Latin America Mission in Costa Rica and Colombia.

This action, of course, did not solve all the problems. In fact, it greatly increased tensions, especially among missionary personnel, as Horace L. Fenton, General Director of the LAM-USA, explains so clearly in his essay, "Latinizing the Latin America Mission."[8] Yet it represented a bold step toward indigeneity, a decisive search for a more biblical and relevant missionary structure in a world which is increasingly aware of its talents and responsibilities, and a courageous venture into the future of an emerging, autochthonous church.

The LAM is not the only one which has dared to take such steps. In the main-line denominations these kinds of steps have become by now routine. The most recent, and one of the most radical, has been the restructure of the United Presbyterian Church in the USA.[9] Also, many evangelical missions have nationalized their churches (or are in the process).[10] As far as I know, however, the LAM's restructure is the most radical.[11]

---

8. Cf. Horace L. Fenton, "Latinizing the Latin America Mission," in Wagner, Church/Mission . . . , pp. 156ff.

9. See Margrethe B. J. Brown, "Restructuring As a Response to a New Era in Mission," in International Review of Mission, LXI:244 (October, 1972), pp. 375ff.

10. Cf. "What's Happening in Church-Mission Relations?", in Gerber, Missions, pp. 223ff.

11. For another restructuring experiment closely akin to that of the

THE PROBLEM BEHIND THE ISSUE

The problem imbedded in the church-mission issue is extremely complex. It is at once historical, sociopolitical, theological, structural, and cultural in nature.

THE AMBIGUOUS ORIGIN OF THE MODERN MISSIONARY MOVEMENT. The problem stems in part from the ambiguous origin of the modern missionary movement, which originated as a result of the pietistic phenomenon. The Pietistic Movement grew basically as a reaction to the theological scholasticism of seventeenth-century Protestantism. It was a call to reformation of life. Arguing that the churches of the Reformation had become more interested in dogma than in the pious life, the Pietists began to emphasize regeneration, sanctification, and fellowship. They called the church to a spiritual renewal in which theology would be a means rather than an end and the true church would be conceived of in terms of a regenerated fellowship of believers who not only confessed the historic faith but lived it in the concrete situations of their everyday life.

Such emphasis on personal regeneration, on living the faith, and on the church as a fellowship of believers could not help but lead into one of the mightiest missionary movements the Christian church has ever known. Since the Pietists aimed at the reformation of the *life* of the church, and since not all of the church responded to their call to renewal, their pietistic endeavors led to the phenomenon of "the church within the church." This, in turn, led to the formation of missionary societies. The latter became the instrument for the many churches within the church which were mushrooming all over Protestant Europe to extend the Christian faith to the regions beyond. These

Latin American Community of Evangelical Ministries see chapter XI, where the model of the recently founded Evangelical Community for Apostolic Action (a by-product of the Paris Evangelical Missionary Society), as reported by Section III of the World Conference on Salvation Today, is discussed.

societies operated alongside the institutional church. Thus missionaries were sent by nonchurch organizations to plant the *church* in Africa, Asia, and the Americas.

Since mission had become the concern of a minority outside the official ecclesiastical structures, it became a sort of "nonchurch movement." Add to this the fact that in its early stages these societies sent as missionaries men and women who had a profound love for and dedication to Jesus Christ and who had caught up the vision of the regions beyond, but who were, nevertheless, theologically ill prepared. The result was a missionary enterprise with a lot of zeal but with a weak theological foundation. In consequence, it was a movement which in spite of its origin[12] carried on a missionary enterprise with little reflection on the nature and mission of the church.

The result of such an effort was clusters of believers with little church-consciousness. Accordingly, these newborn churches could not and did not develop adequate theological criteria for their life and ministry. They followed the only model available, namely, that of the foreign missionary, and in so doing, became strange communities in their own land, *i.e.,* foreign religious colonies.

The problem was not so much with copying the missionaries' church and ministerial model. It was with the *type* of model given them—a model that had very little theological depth, was imbedded in a foreign culture, and was not subject to critical reflection. The problem was that in giving them his ecclesiastical model, the missionary did not and could not give them a set of theological principles that could lead these churches to develop in time their own models.

THE SOCIOPOLITICAL CONTEXT OF THE CONTEMPORARY MISSIONARY ENTERPRISE. In addition to the ambiguous origin of the modern missionary movement, the

---

12. The Pietist Movement was born in the thought of well-educated men. In fact, its foci included such places as the universities of Leipzig and Halle.

problem imbedded in the church-mission issue stems from the sociopolitical context in which mission must take place today. This is a day of revolution, of profound social, political, and economic changes. The countries of the Third World, which heretofore had been not only the object of missionary activity but of colonization, imperialism, and exploitation, have been engaged in the last two decades in a struggle for justice, liberation, and fulfillment. The peoples of Asia, Africa, and Latin America, together with the poverty-stricken minorities of the North Atlantic world, are caught up in a process of political, economic, and cultural emergence. They are beginning to discover themselves in terms of their history, culture, and socioeconomic condition, as well as their unique political and economic possibilities.

This process of conscious awareness has found its way into the church, for she is part of society. When Christians in a missionary situation (and what Christian isn't caught up in a missionary situation?) personally and collectively discover a new (or rediscover their old) cultural frame of reference, they begin to correlate and differentiate from the cultural frame of reference given to them by the missionary establishment. This in turn leads to a questioning process. What does it mean to be an African, an Asian, a Latin American, or a Black-American Christian? This process is eventually bound to lead to the formation of authentic, indigenous ecclesiastical bodies, for it is obvious that a foreign-oriented and -directed body cannot cope with such an issue. This in turn will lead to the question, what is the role of the missionary society? And that question leads to the church-mission issue.

BIBLICAL THEOLOGY AND A MORE APOSTOLIC CONCEPT OF MISSION AND THE CHURCH. The problem behind this issue stems also, and especially, from the rediscovery of biblical theology and its recovery of a more apostolic concept of mission and the church. Viewed from the perspective of biblical theology, the church-mission issue is imbedded in several crucial theological questions, some of which have been discussed in preceding chapters. Let me enumerate some of these questions.

First, what is mission? Doesn't it have to do with God's concern and redemptive purpose for the world? Didn't Christ come to fulfill that purpose and wasn't the Holy Spirit sent to carry out what Christ set out to accomplish through his death and resurrection? But if the Holy Spirit was sent to continue Christ's redemptive mission, shouldn't we think of him as the extension of the incarnation and as the promoter and executor of God's mission in the present age? As the extension of the incarnation, shouldn't we think of him as desiring to make Christ real in concrete historical and cultural situations, to judge them, enrich them, and transform them for the glory of God and for his redemptive purpose?

Second, what is the church? Isn't it a social institution? As such, doesn't it need to be part of and identify with a given society? What is the relationship between the church and God's mission? Is the object of God's mission the church or the world? If it is the world, what is the church's function in that mission? If it is the church, how are we to understand the world in relation to God's mission? Is she to be construed as an end, as an instrument, or as both an instrument and a temporary goal of God's mission? What is the relation between church, kingdom, world, and mission?

Third, how ought we to understand a missionary society? As part of *the* church (an agency, a manifestation), as part of a particular church (*e.g.,* the German Church) or as a nonchurch agency which God uses to communicate the gospel to the peoples of the earth, but which is not a manifestation of the church and which ought not, therefore, to carry any churchly functions?

More recently, this question has led to another even more serious question. Ought mission boards to subordinate themselves to their ecclesiastical offspring, given their nonecclesiastical character? Are they to look upon themselves as a normal channel of the church, and thus permanent in character, or as an extraordinary channel which God raised for a specific purpose in a given period of history?

This last question is of extreme importance, given Ralph Winter's suggestion that foreign mission boards ought to plant not only churches but "younger missions."[13] It must be asked whether the task of mission boards as "extraordinary missionary channels" should be to reproduce themselves and thus institutionalize their extraordinary character, or whether they should not instead seek to transmit to their ecclesiastical offspring from the beginning the apostolic vision of the church and let the Spirit deal with them as to the precise form that this vision ought to take. Wouldn't missionary societies be running the risk of doing what the early Pietist missionaries did, namely, to take a concrete historical model and transplant it to a different situation and thus inhibit the Spirit from doing a new thing?

These are some of the questions imbedded in the rediscovery of biblical theology and, through it, in the recovery of the concept of the church as an apostolic community. Such a dynamic understanding of the church necessarily leads to a reappraisal of the traditional, often truncated concept of the church's nature and mission, and thus, to a creative tension between the church and the mission board.

A MATTER OF MISSIONARY STRATEGY. The church-mission issue is not only historical, sociopolitical, and theological in nature. It is also a matter of missionary strategy. To a certain extent it boils down to this: Can an unevangelized world, caught up in a process of political, social, economic, and cultural awakening, be effectively evangelized by a church that is not indigenous? Horace L. Fenton puts his finger on the sore spot when he says,

Foreignness is an increasing liability in the work of

---

13. Cf. Ralph Winter, "The Planting of Younger Missions," in Wagner, Church/Mission . . . , pp. 129ff.

the Lord, and our allegiance to the Great Commission may prove to be only lip service unless missions learn how to become more thoroughly rooted in the culture which they seek to serve.[14]

It is not simply a matter of nationalism vs. the church; not a question of getting people to understand what we want to convey to them; not merely an issue of nationalization in accordance with indigenous church principles. It is rather a question of following Christ's missionary strategy: he became flesh, dwelt among men, and met people at the point of their greatest need. It is a matter of letting the gospel take roots in the life, history, and culture of those whom we aim to evangelize. In short, it has to do both with (1) meeting the challenge of a world which is fed up with foreignness, imperialism, and colonization and is searching for life in terms of her own historical, cultural, social, economic, and political realities, and (2) a God who is the God of the living and who meets people in his Son, Jesus Christ, as he makes himself present to them through his Spirit in their own struggles, aspirations, failures, and achievements.

A QUESTION OF LEADERSHIP. The problem imbedded in the church-mission issue is also a question of leadership. All over the world, missionary societies are having to contend with an indigenous leadership which not only understands its own sociocultural context but also that of the missionary society. This new leadership is theologically quite sophisticated: not only can it distinguish what is indigenous and what is not, but also what is part of the gospel and what is not. In traveling around the world, one hears nationals here and there saying, "Give us the gospel, but don't give us your culture." It is this, perhaps more than anything else, that has opened up in missionary training centers the discipline of missionary anthropology.

---

14. Horace L. Fenton, "Latinizing . . . ," in *Ibid.,* pp. 147, 148.

A PROBLEM OF STRUCTURE. All that has been said boils down to a problem of structure. The church-mission issue revolves around the tension that arises over the particular form which the product of the missionary endeavor ought to take. Jack Shepherd points out that structures become

> sources of tensions in two special ways. On the one hand, they can become a medium in which wrongly motivated or mistaken ideas and concepts get fixed and then perpetuated. In such a case, good and well-intentioned people and efforts can be limited or impeded by the improper structures themselves. In another sense, structural limitations and defects resulting from failure to change and update can produce the kind of frustration and irritation that becomes corrosive and corrupting to those who are trying to work together within organizational relationships.[15]

In summary, the church-mission issue has to do with the new situation in which missionary societies and their ecclesiastical offspring find themselves. It deals with the way both churches and missionary societies treat each other, and especially, with their particular understanding of God's mission and their particular role in it. Finally, it has to do with the particular form which the church must take to be an indigenous, Christ-like community and to evangelize the world effectively.

TOWARD RELEVANT CRITERIA FOR A SOUND CHURCH-MISSION RELATIONSHIP POLICY

Having seen the complex nature of the problem behind the church-mission issue, it must be affirmed once more that easy solutions do not exist. Many alternatives have

---

15. Jack Shepherd, "Is the Church Really Necessary?" in *Ibid.*, p. 36.

been proposed, both theoretical and functional—from turning everything over to the national church, packing up and getting out, lock stock and barrel; to the Church Growth Movement's implied proposal that national churches should be burdened to get out to reach their communities for Christ, but if they don't, they should be let loose and the mission board ought to dedicate its energies and resources to evangelizing the unevangelized areas; to the creation of an international consortium of ministries, personnel, and resources that will enable the church to engage in mission in a profound and extended manner. Yet, interesting as all of these models are, the fact remains that there are almost as many structural alternatives as there are people. What is needed is not so much a knowledge of all the available alternatives, as the development of relevant and theologically sound criteria which will permit church and missionary societies to search for their own particular models.

THE FUNDAMENTAL STRUCTURES OF MISSION. In an interesting article Ralph D. Winter analyzes what he calls "the anatomy of the Christian mission."[16] He proposes that the search for a relevant and meaningful structure must involve first and foremost a clear idea of what the fundamental structures of mission are. He develops his thoughts around two terms which, according to him, have represented the two basic kinds of structures in mission: vertical structures and horizontal structures. Mission boards with vertical structures are basically denominational in character because their basis of support runs along a particular denomination. On the other hand, missionary societies are usually horizontal in their structures because they are nondenominational; their source of support stems from a mission-minded minority across many denominations.

---

16. Ralph D. Winter, "The Anatomy of the Christian Mission" in *Evangelical Missions Quarterly*, Vol. 5, No. 2, Winter 1969, pp. 74-89; reprinted in *The Warp and the Woof*, by Ralph D. Winter and R. Pierce Beaver (South Pasadena: William Carey Library, 1970), pp. 10-25.

Both types can engage in cross-fertilization, according to Winter. Thus, a vertical church structure at home can lead to a horizontal structure on the field; and vice versa, a basically horizontally-structured missionary society can develop a vertical structure on the field. A denomination engaged in interdenominational, nonecclesiastical mission in the field can be said to have an internal vertical structure and an external horizontal structure. Likewise, an interdenominational faith mission is usually horizontal at home, but if it engages in church planting in the field its external structure is vertical.

Winter suggests that both kinds of structure have advantages and disadvantages. The solution for the search of the most adequate missionary structure lies in understanding "the unique function, the advantages and disadvantages of each of these two kinds of structures."[17] Consequently, the issue of church-mission relationships ought to be tackled from a goal-oriented angle. An interdenominational faith mission or a denominational board engaged in a non-church planting ministry will need to develop a horizontal structure in the field. This usually is easier to handle because it may involve people from different denominations interested in the particular ministry of the missionary society. The situation is a bit more difficult in the case of mission boards caught up in church-planting situations. Should they be content with developing a vertical structure in the field (i.e., a denomination) or should they also engage in a horizontally structured mission (across the denomination it has founded, in a cooperative missionary enterprise elsewhere)? Winter raises some further questions:

> Should the founding of a new church in a given country ideally be the job of a foreign church or a horizontal-vertical mission like the Overseas Missionary Fellowship, which is both international and inter-ecclesiastical?

17. *Ibid.*

Another question is whether the final result of missions is merely a healthy national church without any infrastructure of horizontal organizations in that "mission land." That is, should we consider the mission task done when we have set up a viable denomination? Or, in the interest of the effective proclamation of the Gospel, do we need to make sure that not only in the US but also in the mission lands there are nationally-run, semi-autonomous, horizontal mission structures that will act as the shock troops of both home and foreign missions based in the country? [18]

In another article, Winter argues further for the necessity of mission "sodalities" (horizontal or para-ecclesiastical structures).[19] He points to the fact that "when in A.D. 596 Gregory the Great as the Bishop of Rome sent Augustine to England, it was the case of a diocesan *modality* calling upon a Benedictine *sodality* to do a certain job."[20] He then goes on to argue for the historical contingency of mission sodalities. He points out how throughout church history, voluntary societies (read "monastic orders" in the case of Catholicism) have been largely responsible for the planting of the church ("modalities" or vertical structures).

Winter argues from a historical as well as an anthropological perspective. "Modalities," he says, "are characteristically impotent apart from careful maintenance of consensus, whether they are civil or ecclesiastical structures."[21] It is harder for churches to spark a missionary movement than for a voluntary society. This is the reason why in Europe "the state churches have learned to live

---

18. *Ibid.*

19. Ralph Winter, "The Warp and the Woof of the Christian Movement," in *Ibid.*, pp. 52ff. (Reprinted from the *Evangelical Missions Quarterly*, July 1971.)

20. *Ibid.*, p. 57.

21. *Ibid.*, p. 60.

with at least some mission sodalities."[22] For as the tradition of a church gets older, and the constituency gets larger and more complicated, it becomes inevitable "that a single . . . board" will not be able by itself to "fully express the vision and energy of the whole constituency."[23] Thus, while churches strive for unity and wholeness,[24] they cannot produce the kind of diversity and heterogeneity that a human group needs. Consequently, horizontal church structures are essential in order to preserve "the wholesome *diversity* of the human community" just as vertical church structures are needed to preserve "the wholesome *unity* of the human community."[25]

Winter is right in pointing out the unique and essential role of horizontal structures in the history of the missionary movement from the West. If it had not been for these "shock troops" the gospel would not have reached as far as it has. The Holy Spirit has used "mission sodalities" to advance the gospel as a mighty wind. Voluntary societies have provided the necessary outlet for the energies of millions of Christians. They have helped preserve "the wholesome diversity" of the body of Christ.

But can we establish a universal generalization out of a historical particularity? Doesn't the existence of missionary societies apart from church bodies represent in reality God's judgment upon the church? Wouldn't they signify God's permissive rather than his perfect will?

There is no ground in the New Testament for a concept of mission apart from the church, just as there is no concept of the church apart from mission. This does not mean that the biblical concept of the church leaves no ground for wholesome diversity. On the contrary, the church is both a heterogeneous and a homogeneous organism.

---

22. *Ibid.*

23. *Ibid.*

24. "The glory of the church, even the local church, is that it patiently endeavors to foster balanced, redemptive community across the whole span of ages, the differences in sex, even differences in station in life." *Ibid.*, p. 54.

25. *Ibid.*, p. 55.

It expresses its unity in the interconnection of its various parts *in mission*.

This means, at least, that while there are natural sodalities and modalities within the church, these must function integratively—not apart from each other. Rather than separating church and mission, modalities and sodalities, the two must work together as one. In other words, the church *must* aim at wholesome unifying diversity *in* mission. When the church gets so bogged down with the preservation of unity that she fails to give adequate expression to her missionary responsibility; when in her missionary endeavor she fails to make adequate room for the legitimate expression of God's multiple gifts, mission sodalities emerge spontaneously. Such a phenomenon, however, ought not to be seen as representing God's perfect will. Rather it is something God permits on account of the church's failure and that represents his judgment upon her.

Mission sodalities should, therefore, be *church* sodalities. The biblico-theological model of the church does not allow for a missionary structure apart from the church. Sodalities ought to function structurally apart from modalities only when the church loses sight of her missionary responsibility and fails to acknowledge the diverse gifts which the Spirit bestows upon her to fulfill the multiple dimensions of the missionary mandate.

This places tremendous responsibility upon independent missionary societies. For if they exist only because the church has failed to do its job, then they should continue to function *only* as long as the church does not recognize her responsibility and fails to make adequate provision for the particular end to which the para-structure has come about. Whenever a missionary society makes her temporal character an end, she forfeits her right to exist as a legitimate expression of God's mission.

Of course, the situation gets complicated by the offspring of the missionary societies. There are on the one hand hundreds of churches that they have planted around the world. There are on the other hand hundreds of para-structures that have emerged after the model of the foreign missionary society or for the same reason that brought the latter into being. What, therefore, ought these churches and para-ecclesiastical structures to do? Should they merge? In addition, what ought to be the role of the foreign missionary society? Should it continue to perpetuate itself through the continuation of existing para-ecclesiastical organizations or the formation of new ones in order to plant the church across the multiple groups and cultures where the gospel has yet to penetrate?

As has been noted, according to Winter, missionary societies ought not only to plant churches but younger missions. He sees "the planting of younger missions" as a necessity for the advance of the gospel. He feels that if we are to reach the hundreds of millions that are still outside the boundaries of Christianity, specialized mission structures are needed to penetrate the different cultures within which these men and women are to be found. Further, with the tremendous population explosion around the world, it is clear that the Great Commission will not be fulfilled "unless it can become fashionable for the younger churches to establish younger missions."[26]

> God has allowed a gorgeous diversity among the butterflies, the leaves, the flowers, and the human families of mankind. If He does not intend to reduce the number of butterflies and flowers to a single model, He may not intend to eliminate all the ethnic, racial and linguistic differences in the world today. If He doesn't, then there is (and always will be) a powerful case for special mission organizations to facilitate the inter-cultural contact and to provide the lifeblood that will enable the whole body to flourish through interdependence, rather than to languish in fragmented isolation or to be stultified in a monotonous uniformity.[27]

26. Winter, "The Planting . . . ," in Church/Mission . . . , p. 139.
27. Ibid., p. 141.

I see three basic problems with Winter's approach. (1) It militates against the historico-universal character of the church. (2) It makes a universal generalization out of a historical particularity. (3) It makes a theological principle out of a missiological failure.

It has been said that the church is not only a divine, future-oriented community but also a human organism. As such, it is a historical reality; it must express itself in concrete historical situations. In other words, the church must always be an indigenous community. It must grow, function, live in relationship with a concrete historico-cultural situation. Indigeneity, far from being an external phenomenon, is a natural process. A church cannot be indigenized; she must be indigeneous, *i.e.,* she cannot *be made* to be herself; she must *be* herself. Indigeneity is a relative term for it has to do with a specific cultural and historical situation. Either a church is related to her particular situation or she is not. She cannot be forced from the outside. She must herself become attached to that situation through her life and ministry.

However, the church is not only a historical but a universal reality. She must always be understood in a historico-universal context. Thus she must transcend historico-cultural barriers while expressing herself in cultural categories. In Christ there is neither Jew nor Greek, slave nor free, male nor female (Gal. 3:28). The church has just as much responsibility for expressing herself in concrete historico-cultural situations (*i.e.,* she is just as responsible for the expression of her *distinctiveness* in cultural categories) as for giving concrete witness to her unity in Christ.

To make the planting of "missions" a specific task of the foreign missionary society is to perpetuate the particular problems that the foreign missionary society has had in her church planting endeavor and the serious consequences which the daughter churches have had to bear. The foreign missionary society has suffered, generally speaking, from the aforementioned paradoxical corollaries: she has been somewhat detached from the specific context of her endeavor (*i.e.,* a-historical) and she has functioned within a foreign frame of reference. Her church-planting endeavors have been greatly limited. Her daughter churches have struggled in many instances (and many find themselves still caught up in this struggle) to discover their historical character as Christ's church in a given situation. Some have also discovered their universal character, *i.e.*, their interrelatedness to the total body of Christ. A good number of them, however, have either suffered from "provincial myopia" (*i.e.*, they are so nationalistic or denominationally oriented that the church of Christ begins and ends with them) or from the other-worldly syndrome (*i.e.*, the notion that the church is purely "a spiritual" organism which does not need to interact with a concrete cultural and historical situation).

Further, sodalities, even when they exist apart from modalities, cannot be fabricated from the outside. They emerge naturally and spontaneously as part of concrete historical situations. To build into the purpose of a foreign missionary structure the creation of national sodalities is to transplant the particular historical situation that brought the former into being and to militate against the historico-universal character of the church and, consequently, of the missionary enterprise.

But even when the historical circumstances require the existence of horizontal missionary structures apart from church bodies, these have to contend with their own temporal character and with the theological principle of a united, diversified church in mission. To insist on the perpetual reproduction of missionary societies is to build into the church's nature (which beyond any psychological, anthropological, or sociological consideration must be understood theologically) a structural abnormality that results from missiological failure. Worse yet, such a proposal militates against the imperative of a wholesome, unified, and diversified international and cross-cultural witness, which is a chief and irreplaceable objective of the church.

VISION OF THE CHURCH IN MISSION. We need to go beyond the structural dichotomy of church and mission.

We need more than mere understanding of what the fundamental structures of mission are. We need a comprehensive vision of the church *in* mission. We need to see the church as a catholic, missionary, and Spirit-filled community.

If the church, as Jesus prayed in Jn. 17:21, ought to express her unity in mission so that the world might believe; and if the Spirit endows the church through his many gifts, then the missionary enterprise must not be understood in terms of sending and receiving church bodies. Rather it ought to be understood in terms of a dynamic, worldwide, Spirit-filled, church partnership *in* mission. This is the idea behind the 1954 suggestion of the International Missionary Council:

> The urgent need for further strengthening the international and interdenominational character of the missionary movement has been expressed . . . in pleas for an increase in the sending of missionaries by younger churches and the sending of international and interdenominational teams for specific tasks in certain places. The emergence of churches in all parts of the world thus provides a God-given opportunity to broaden the base of the missionary movement, thereby demonstrating in new ways the character of the universal church, and meeting the threat to the mission of the church posed in certain forms of contemporary nationalism.[28]

This is precisely what the Latin American Community of Evangelical Ministries is attempting to do. It represents a structural attempt to bridge the gap between church and

---

28. Quoted in James A. Scherer, *Missionary, Go Home!* (Englewood Cliffs, N.J.: Prentice Hall, 1964), pp. 139, 140. This recommendation was carried out into a structural reality when in 1961, at the New Delhi Assembly, the International Missionary Council formally merged with the World Council of Churches. One wonders sometimes, however, whether the WCC has not been guilty at times of quenching the energies of sodalities and thus concentrating so much on preserving the unity of its member churches (which in

mission, based upon the conviction that the Church of Jesus Christ is much bigger than a sending body or a particular national church; that the mission is from God and that we as his people participate in it in accordance with the personal and collective gifts that the Holy Spirit bestows upon all of us. It is a small attempt to call all sides, vertical and horizontal entities, national and international, to become involved in God's mission strategically and resourcefully in an international consortium of ministries oriented toward the evangelization of an entire continent. By integrating para-ecclesiastical service and evangelistic agencies with a theological institution and two ecclesiastical bodies (the Asociación de Iglesias Bíblicas del Caribe in Colombia and the Asociación de Iglesias Bíblicas in Costa Rica), the Community has become one of the most relevant experiments in missionary circles today.

Vision of the church as a catholic, missionary, and Spirit-filled community could lead churches, national para-ecclesiastical entities, mission boards, and their supporting churches to develop a sound policy for their interrelationships. For it could help them overcome the structural, leadership, strategic, sociopolitical, theological, and historical barrier—which has constituted the real problem behind the church-mission issue—and put them both on the road to the fulfillment of what should be their one supreme goal, namely, that of a united and diversified, international and cross-cultural missionary outreach. Such a vision demands a venture in faith, unconditional commitment to the Lord of the church who calls her into a life of obedient service, and willingness to work diligently toward a united and diversified witness in the six continents.

---

some cases simply means keeping "happy" the ecclesiastical "hierarchy") than in fulfilling the Great Commission. Even so, the merger of the IMC and the WCC and the subsequent creation of the Commission and Division of World Mission and Evangelism represents an effort to eliminate the ideas of sending and receiving churches and to substitute for it the more theologically correct churches in mission.

9/MISSION AND THE LIBERATION OF MAN

Section 1/ The Problem in Historico- Theological Perspective

THE NATURE OF THE PROBLEM

Another important issue in contemporary missiology is the question of humanization as an integral part of the missionary enterprise. Of course, mission has always had a humanizing quality. The church has always considered the improvement of life a legitimate and necessary offspring of mission. The contribution of the missionary movement to social reform, health, education, welfare, relief, technology, and development is well known.

The controversy stems from what Peter Beyerhaus has called "a completely new understanding of mission."[1] In classical missiology the aforementioned endeavors have

---

1. Peter Beyerhaus, *Missions: Which Way? Humanization or Redemption* (Grand Rapids: Zondervan, 1971), p. 33.

been considered "fruits," "by-products," or "secondary objectives" to the "chief" objective of mission (*i.e.*, the proclamation of the gospel and the planting of the church among the peoples of the earth). Today they are understood in some circles as intrinsic elements of the church's witness to the gospel. Further, they are considered ways by which the good news of salvation comes to contemporary man.

It is in this context that we encounter the concept of the liberation of man as an intrinsic part of the church's mission to the world and as one of the strategic manifestations of God's saving action today. Salvation, it is said, has a liberating dimension. We live in a world where man is seen holistically and not in dichotomies (soul and body, mind and spirit, material and spiritual, etc.). We live in a period of history where our understanding of life has been enriched by the efforts of the social sciences; where biblical scholarship has uncovered new dimensions in the biblical concepts of man, sin, salvation, the church, and the world; where the opportunities and challenges of world history were never greater for the cause of world mission. In such a moment, the good news of salvation, it is said, must emphasize those dimensions which will cope with the challenges or needs of the day, which will speak to the issues of the moment, which will take advantage of the new light, the new tools, and the new opportunities that have opened up to the church for witness.

Salvation must, thus, be seen against the backdrop of man's many situations. Sin must be conceived of not only in terms of man's personal, transcendent and vertical relationships, but also, and especially, in terms of his horizontal and structured interrelationships. In this respect, the good news of salvation must particularly take into account the bondage of so many people to oppressive principalities and powers. It must set forth the liberating action of the sovereign God not only of persons in their internal conflicts but also of people who suffer under the yoke of economic exploitation and social, political, and cultural oppression.

Hence to make known God's good news of salvation is

not only to proclaim verbally what God has already done in Jesus of Nazareth, but to discover what he is doing today in behalf of those who suffer under the bondage of the demonic. It is to act decisively, in partnership with God, on behalf of the oppressed and afflicted. Salvation is therefore understood as liberation *from* oppression and despair *for* hope and freedom. Hope and freedom are in turn understood in terms of God's new creation. To be saved, among other things, is to be set free in order to be human; to be able to stir up one's present by the future of a new world and a new humanity.

This concept of mission and salvation has, of course, enraged many conservative evangelicals. Complaining that such a missiology distorts the classical theology of mission, they have mounted a frontal attack against any missiology that seeks to integrate personal and corporate salvation at the expense of the former. Ecumenical missiologists,[2] while trying to give conservative evangelicals a fair hearing in their respective publications and mission conferences, have nevertheless resisted almost any suggestion to tone down a bit their emphasis on humanization, or at least to come forth equally strongly for such traditional concepts as repentance, conversion, proclamation, and church growth. The result has been further polarization of an already divided church.

UPPSALA AND THE RENEWAL IN MISSION REPORT

The issue seems to have emerged at the Fourth General Assembly of the World Council of Churches held in Uppsala, Sweden, July 4-20, 1968. As Arthur Glasser has said,

In many ways the Fourth Assembly of the World Council of Churches, held in Uppsala in 1968, marked

---

2. That is, missiologists who are related to the World Council of Churches.

a watershed in relations between conservative Evangelicals and liberals . . . The focus of their polarization was the essence of the gospel and its relation to the urgent task of human development. Conservative Evangelicals will not readily forget how they were politely and effectively contained in their efforts to modify Section II: *Renewal in Mission,* which appalled them with its secularized gospel and reduction of the mission of the church to social and political activism.[3]

These are rather strong words which transmit a lot of hard feeling. Note how Glasser attributes the difference to opposing views of "the essence of the gospel and its relation to the urgent task of human development." He then goes on to accuse the drafters of the Section II Report of coming out for a "secularized gospel" and of reducing "the mission of the church to social and political activism." Such a charge demands close analysis of the Renewal in Mission Report.

The Report is divided into three parts. The first deals with the mandate for mission; the second with the contemporary opportunities for mission; and the third with the necessary freedom for mission.

The first part is rather dialectical. While it has a definite anthropological starting point ("We belong to a new humanity that cries passionately and articulately for a full human life."[4]), the first paragraph concludes, nevertheless, with Jesus Christ as the new man. The same trend may be observed in the second paragraph: it begins with men searching for their true identity and ends with their crying for the Triune God. Man's universal sonship is affirmed only to be balanced by man's refusal to live up to that responsibility.

---

3. Arthur Glasser, "Salvation Today and the Kingdom," in McGavran, . . . *Missions Tomorrow,* p. 33.

4. Norman Goodall, ed., *The Uppsala Report 1968* (Geneva: World Council of Churches, 1968), p. 27.

The dialectic character of the first part is accompanied by an atmosphere of theological ambiguity. On the one hand, the new manhood is conceived of both as a goal and a gift, and thus, as requiring a response of faith. On the other hand, man's response to Jesus is said not often to appear "as a religious choice at all. Yet it is a new birth. It sets a pattern of dying and rising which will continually be repeated."[5] What kind of a new birth is this, which does not come as a result of a religious response? Can man die to self and rise with Christ without commitment to the person of Jesus Christ?

The ambiguous character of part one leaves the reader of the document with a sense of incompleteness. It says so much and yet leaves so much unsaid. It is so profound and yet so shallow. It attempts to be so concrete and yet winds up being so theoretical.

Yet as ambiguous as the first part may appear to be, parts two and three seem to alarm evangelicals more. For it is in these sections that the Report illustrates specifically and concretely what is meant by the affirmations of part one. These "for instances" are alarming not merely for what they say but for what they do not say.

Parts two and three reflect the conclusions of the study authorized at the Third Assembly of the World Council of Churches, held in New Delhi, India, for a comprehensive study on "The Missionary Structure of the Congregation," to be carried out in the years between the New Delhi (1961) and the Uppsala (1968) Assembly.[6] The results of this study were published in Thomas Wiser's, *Planning for Mission*,[7] and the official report, *The Church for Others and the Church for the World*.[8] Perhaps the most important conclusion reached by the study (if one could sum-

---

5. *Ibid.,* p. 28.

6. Visser W. A. 'T Hooft, ed., *The New Delhi Report* (London: SCM, 1961), pp. 189-190.

7. Thomas Wiser, ed., *Planning for Mission* (London: Lutterworth, 1966).

8. *The Church for Others and the Church for the World: A Quest*

marize such a comprehensive project) was the fact "that the congregation is not the only structure of mission available to the Church for her witness in the world."[9] Consequently, the Uppsala Assembly authorized the initiation of

> a new study which is closely linked with the former study and pursues the same methodology. The area of study would, however, be different. It would not be concerned with the local congregation and its involvement in mission, but with the appropriate participation of Christians in the *institutions*[10] of society.[11]

It is in the light of this latter decision that we must consider part two of the Report on Renewal in Mission. Beginning with the very biblical affirmation that the Church in mission is the Church for others, the Report goes on to "describe a few priority situations for mission today."

a) *Centers of power . . .*

b) *Revolutionary movements . . .*

c) *The University everywhere . . .*

d) *Rapid urbanization and industrialization . . .*

e) *Suburbia, rural areas . . .*

f) *Relations between developed and developing countries . . .*

g) *The churches as an arena for mission . . .*[12]

This last "priority" situation is particularly interesting, not only for the place it occupies in the list, but also for the commentary that accompanies it. The report says:

---

for Structures for Missionary Congregations (Geneva: World Council of Churches, 1967).

9. Goodall, . . . *Uppsala* . . . , p. 200.

10. Italics mine.

11. *Ibid.,* p. 201.

12. *Ibid.,* pp. 30, 31.

The words of proclamation are doubted when the church's own life fails to embody the marks of the new humanity. The church is rightly concerned for the world's hundreds of millions who do not know the Gospel of Christ. It is constantly sent out to them in witness and service. But that concern becomes suspect when the church is preoccupied with its own numerical and institutional strength. It is called to be the servant body of Christ given to and for the world.[13]

Granted that the churches as they appear in their self-centeredness, in their lack of involvement in God's mission, in their failure to embody the servant spirit of Christ, are arenas for mission. But shouldn't this be at the top of priorities? When their house is in disorder, shouldn't Christians straighten it out before trying to straighten their neighbors? Why aren't other equally important missionary situations included in the list, *e.g.,* people movements to Christ and people everywhere who find themselves in despair, meaninglessness, and anxiety?

This part of the Report concludes with a list of criteria for evaluating missionary principles.[14]

—do they place the church alongside the poor, the defenseless, the abused, the forgotten, the bored?
—do they allow Christians to enter the concerns of others to accept their issues and their structures as vehicles of involvement?
—are they the best situations for discerning with other men the signs of the times, and for moving

---

13. *Ibid.*

14. According to Peter Beyerhaus, the intention behind this list was "to replace the old idea of ethnic and religious mission fields, which tend to be localized in the southern hemisphere, with a new historical-theological understanding of the special opportunities for missionary activity within present political-social events." . . . *Which Way? . . .* , p. 39.

with history towards the coming of the new human-ity?[15]

Once again it must be asked, wouldn't it be a legitimate criterion for evaluating missionary priorities, whether people are finding meaning in life through a faith encounter with Christ? Isn't the formation of new congregations committed to the new order of life, *i.e.,* the kingdom of God with all its implications (love, peace, and justice), a legitimate criterion for evaluating missionary priorities? Obviously evangelicals had every reason to be enraged at the apparent bias of the drafters of the Report against traditional yet liberating missionary concepts such as repentance, conversion, and church growth.

Similar comments could be made about the third part of the Report, "Freedom for Mission." So much in it needed to be said; yet so much was left unsaid which should have been said and which the drafters—from the looks of the floor discussion[16]—purposely left out. That the churches must be set free from obsolete structures to be true missionary communities cannot be disputed.[17] That the churches must reexamine "the variety of tasks to which the people are called in their ministry in the world . . ." and "the whole scope and purpose of theological education";[18] that "we must find new and effective ways in which the Gospel can be proclaimed today and understood in . . . all areas of life . . .";[19] and that mission should be understood in terms of an international partnership in which the resources of the whole church—men, money, and expertise—are made available to the whole church:[20] such ideas are all too readily accepted by conscientious, biblically and mission-oriented Christians everywhere. But

---

15. Goodall, *Uppsala . . .* , p. 32.
16. Cf. *Ibid.,* p. 25ff.
17. Cf. Paragraph 1 of Part II, *Ibid.,* p. 33.
18. Cf. Paragraphs 2 and 3, *Ibid.*
19. *Ibid.,* p. 34.
20. Cf. *Ibid.,* p. 35.

equally strong is the evangelicals' contention that the churches must be set free to make known to the non-Christian world the distinctiveness of the Christian faith and thereby invite them in all humility, love, and persuasiveness to a faith commitment to Jesus Christ.

And this was precisely the contention of evangelicals in the floor discussion that preceded the adoption of the Report by the Assembly. The strongest criticism came from J. R. W. Stott of the Church of England, who complained that "he did not see in the report any concern for the spiritual hunger of man comparable to that which had been expressed regarding physical hunger and poverty."[21] Kenneth Grubb, also of the Church of England, said that he would like "to have added to section I, sub-section 2 the proclamation that there is no other name than that of Jesus Christ given under heaven amongst men whereby we must be saved."[22] Even Professor Rudolf Obermüller, of the Evangelical Church of the River Plate, who is far from being a "theological conservative," said that "he missed from the draft the emphasis on the biblical basis of mission that had appeared in the original document."[23]

In the light of the discussion, the Assembly agreed to refer the draft back to the Section for revision.

At a later session Metropolitan Lakdasa De Mel presented the revised report. There had been much discussion about the theological aspect of the document, he said. The section had felt that proclamation was only relevant if it took into account the deep longings of men today: the genius of the Gospel was that it spoke to these longings. The main drive of the document lay in *parts two and three*[24] which were

---

21. "Discussion of the Report on Renewal in Mission," in *Ibid.*, p. 25.

22. *Ibid.*

23. *Ibid.*

24. Italics are mine.

commended to the churches for serious study and action.[25]

And action they did get—from evangelicals all over the world!

EVANGELICALS AND THE RENEWAL IN MISSION REPORT

Prior to the Uppsala Assembly, Donald A. McGavran had challenged the delegates with a provoking article in the *Church Growth Bulletin.* Posing the question, "Will Uppsala Betray the Two Billion?" he anticipated the evangelicals' subsequent criticism of the World Council of Churches position as reflected in the Section II Report vis-à-vis the evangelization of the world. Asking whether Uppsala would set a course of action which would substitute "ashes for bread," fixing "the attention of Christians on temporary palliatives instead of eternal remedies," and thus leaving the two billion—an obvious reference to the "Decree on the Missionary Activity of the Church" of Vatican II[26]—"in their sin and in their darkness, chained by false and inadequate ideas of God and men,"[27] McGavran set the pace for the subsequent initial reaction of J. R. W. Stott at the Assembly:

> The World Council confesses that Jesus is Lord. The Lord sends his Church to preach the Good News and make disciples. I do not see the Assembly very eager to obey its Lord's command. The Lord Jesus Christ wept over the city which had rejected

25. *Ibid.,* p. 27.

26. Cf. "Decree on the Missionary Activity of the Church," *The Documents of Vatican II,* Walter M. Abbott, S. J., ed. (N.Y.: Guild Press, 1966), p. 597.

27. Donald A. McGavran, "Will Uppsala Betray the Two Billion?" *Church Growth Bulletin,* IV:5 (May, 1968), p. 1.

him. I do not see this Assembly weeping similar tears.[28]

Following the Assembly, Stott further clarified his criticism of the Report in two articles in the *Church of England Newspaper*[29] and the *Church Growth Bulletin.* In the latter, he stated:

Section II is a hotchpotch, a compromise document, a variegated patchwork quilt sewn together out of bits and pieces contributed by delegates and advisers whose convictions were in fundamental disagreement . . . Mind you, the final version of Section II might have been a lot worse than in the end it was. As a result of pressure from evangelicals (usually misnamed "traditionalists" and then regarded with the appropriate contumely), a number of important additions were made . . . Nevertheless, it must be confessed with shame and sorrow that these are rather isolated concessions to evangelical pressure. The document as a whole not only expresses no coherent theology of mission but is actually self-contradictory . . . As the work of Section II progressed (was it progress?) there was a tragic failure to come to grips with the issue. Ecumenicals and evangelicals (if one may thus categorize the two main viewpoints) sparred with one another, and contrived to get included in the final draft some expression of their basic convictions. But there was no real meeting of minds, no genuine dialogue, no apparent willingness to listen and understand as well as speak and instruct.[30]

28. Goodall, *Uppsala . . . ,* p. 26.
29. J. R. W. Stott, "Why I was Disturbed," *Church of England Newspaper* (August 23, 1968), quoted by Beyerhaus, . . . *Which Way? . . . ,* p. 40.
30. J. R. W. Stott, "Does Section Two Provide Sufficient Emphasis on World Evangelism?" *Church Growth Bulletin,* V:2 (Nov., 1968), pp. 38, 39.

In the same number of the *Church Growth Bulletin,* David A. Hubbard charged that while evangelicals "shared the concern expressed by the voting delegates toward the abused and afflicted, the poor and oppressed of the world, their attempt to see both evangelism and social concern as essential, unchanging, binding obligations upon the church in every age was not always reciprocated."[31] Hubbard, who went to Uppsala as an evangelical "adviser," added: "To be honest, I found myself baffled as to why we had to work so hard in a Christian assembly to agree on things that are so basic Christian affirmations."[32]

Writing in the spring of 1969, Arthur Glasser, in an evaluation of the evangelical stance in the Ecumenical Movement from New Delhi to Uppsala, commented that in the Uppsala Assembly, particularly in the Report on Renewal in Mission,

> little or nothing was said to remind a world in confusion, darkness, and spiritual need that the church of Jesus Christ has been entrusted by God with a more than adequate answer to its deep and wrenching problems. Evangelicals listened in vain for a clear word about either a living Christ who came to save His people from their sin, or an eleventh hour warning of judgment to come. "Nothing expresses the insecurity and anxiety of human existence more profoundly than the fact that the fear of extinction and the fear of judgment are compounded in the fear of death" (Niebuhr). And yet, Uppsala was virtually silent about the relevance of Christ's Gospel to these universal fears![33]

Not all evangelicals reacted negatively to the Uppsala

---

31. David A. Hubbard, "The Theology of Section Two," in *Ibid.,* p. 41.

32. *Ibid.*

33. Arthur Glasser, "What Has Been the Evangelical Stance, New Delhi to Uppsala," *Evangelical Missions Quarterly,* V:3 (Spring, 1969), p. 145.

Report of Section II. Paul Rees, particularly, in an editorial in *World Vision Magazine,* wrote of the "common effort" of such diverse groups as Roman Catholic, Anglicans, and Free Churchman that forced, at least in part, the members of the Committee of Section II to change "the mood, the language, and the thrust" of the Report. For him it was a victory achieved "from within" in a "conglomerate" such as the World Council of Churches.[34]

Rees's claim may be in part substantiated by references to evangelicals in the report of the Central Committee of the WCC and the recommendation of one of the Assembly's committees. In the Report of the Central Committee, Franklyn Clark Fry stated that the latter had striven assiduously "over the past six years" to increase its "contacts with the deeply committed and fervently Christian brethren at the other end of the spectrum,"[35] an obvious reference to the evangelicals. This effort was further corroborated by the Assembly's adoption of the following recommendation.

> The member churches of the World Council, which have already experienced something of the mutual correction and edification which is made possible by our common membership in the Council, need also the contribution of the evangelical churches and desire to share with them in such ways as may be found mutually acceptable, in practical tasks of service and witness. It is our hope that all who share together the Scriptural and Trinitarian faith in Jesus Christ as God and Saviour may thus be enabled both to work together and to build one another up in the common faith . . . In view of the fact that there is in the membership of several member churches a considerable body of those who would accept the name "conservative-evangelical" whose theological convic-

---

34. Paul S. Rees, "Influencing a Conglomerate," *World Vision Magazine,* 12:9 (October, 1968), p. 47.

35. Goodall, *Uppsala . . . ,* p. 280.

tion, spiritual experience, and missionary zeal might well find more vital expression in the life of the World Council of Churches, this Assembly hopes that these member churches will give serious thought to this matter, and will seek ways by which this witness may be more adequately represented in the life of the Council.[36]

Rees, who had criticized the original draft in the July 1968 issue of *World Vision Magazine* for its theological vagueness and lack of evangelistic urgency, in the aforementioned editorial, witnessed to the improvement of the final draft of the Report as a result of the pressure exerted, in part, by evangelicals. Recognizing all the liabilities of a "denominational" conglomerate such as the World Council of Churches, particularly its diverse, contradictory elements of tradition and theology, he celebrated the influence, albeit small, of evangelicals on the final draft of the Report, given the fact "that the World Council is one of the immense and shaping facts of life in this second half of the twentieth century."[37] He lamented, however, that

> out of zeal to get a much clearer statement on the central substance of the Gospel [evangelicals] may have left on some persons the impression that we are not sufficiently alive and aroused to the concern about *people* that should go hand in hand with concern for *doctrine*. After all, a socially insensitive orthodoxy is far more of a contradiction of the New Testament than most of us who call ourselves evangelicals are ready to admit.[38]

Rees's positive reaction, balanced as it may seem, was

---

36. As quoted in Glasser, "Evangelical Stance," p. 130. I have searched for this recommendation in the official Report of Uppsala (but have not been able to find it).

37. Rees, "Influencing . . . ," p. 47.

38. *Ibid.*

a lonely evangelical exception. Everywhere, at least in the North Atlantic world, the reactions of evangelicals were rather negative.

THE FRANKFURT DECLARATION

Perhaps one of the strongest reactions to the Report came from a group of conservative theologians in Germany who were greatly disturbed with the new trends in the Ecumenical Movement's missiology. Under the leadership of Peter Beyerhaus of the University of Tübingen, the group of fifteen[39] adopted a declaration on the Fundamental Crisis in Christian Missions at Frankfurt on March 4, 1970.[40]

The text of the Frankfurt Declaration begins with a preamble setting forth the church's mandate for mission. Its starting point is "the sacred privilege and irrevocable obligation of the church of Jesus Christ to participate in the mission of the triune God. . . ."[41] Based upon this

---

39. It must be made clear, however, that only thirteen of the fifteen who originally signed the statement are in reality professional theologians. Of the other two, one is a professor of mathematics, although a very well theologically informed layman, and the other, a churchman. Among the thirteen, three are former missionaries.

40. It is interesting to note the similarity between the style of this declaration and that of an earlier historic document in the German Church, namely, the Barmen Declaration, adopted by representatives of the Reformed and Lutheran traditions in May 1934 as a protest against the Third Reich and *German* Christianity. The latter is preceded by an introductory statement, followed by six principles of faith. Each principle or article is divided into three parts: a Scripture text, an affirmation of the theological truth imbedded in the text, followed by the refutation of a false teaching of the German Evangelical Church. Obviously, Beyerhaus, *et al.* sees a similarity between the Barmen Declaration and the Frankfurt Declaration, the latter being a response to the missionary crisis in the Ecumenical Movement, and especially, in the German Church. Thus the issue to which it is addressed is in the mind of Beyerhaus, *et al.* closely akin to the crisis which the church faced in Nazi Germany in the 1930's.

41. Beyerhaus, . . . *Which Way?* . . . , p. 111.

conviction, the Declaration goes on to point to the fundamental crisis in "organized Christian world mission," namely, "the displacement of their primary tasks by means of an insidious falsification of their motives and goals."[42] Out of deep concern for the "inner decay" of contemporary Christian missions, the original fifteen decided to make this Declaration to the following people: (1) "All Christians who know themselves through the belief in salvation through Jesus Christ" to be responsible for the work of mission; (2) "Leaders of churches and congregations"; (3) "All missionary societies and their coordinating agencies, which are especially called, according to their spiritual tradition, to oversee the true goals of missionary activity."[43]

Three requests are made to the addressees: (1) To test the theses set forth in the Declaration on the basis of their biblical undergirding and to determine the accuracy of their description with respect to errors and modes of operation in churches, missions, and the Ecumenical Movement. (2) Sign it, if they agree with it. (3) Join in their own sphere of influence with the authors "both repentant and resolved to insist upon" the seven missionary principles set forth in the body of the document.[44]

These principles, entitled "Seven Indispensable Basic Elements of Mission," are structured in this manner: They are preceded by one or more Scripture passages. This is followed by a section which sets forth the principle in the form of an affirmation, followed by a third section on opposition and rejection of a particular "distorted" principle or practice in the contemporary missionary movement.

Following the request of the subscribers, let us analyze the seven principles set forth in the Declaration. Since the Declaration is not exegetical but theological and affirmative, rather than consider the various passages used in its

42. *Ibid.,* p. 112.
43. *Ibid.,* p. 112, 113.
44. *Ibid.*

support, let us concentrate on the affirmations themselves, both negative and positive.

1. *Principle one* deals with the foundation, goals, tasks, and content of the proclamation of Christian mission. All these find their basis in the Lordship of Jesus Christ "and his saving acts as they are reported by the witness of the apostles and early Christianity in the New Testament."[45] Consequently, the writers express their opposition to "the current tendency to determine the nature and task of mission by sociopolitical analyses of our time and from the demands of the non-Christian world."[46] They further deny the relativity of the gospel, affirming that the latter is "normative and given once for all."[47]

So far so good. The problem comes with the following sentences:

> The situation of encounter contributes only new aspects in the *application*[48] of the Gospel. The surrender of the Bible as our primary frame of reference leads to the shapelessness of mission and a confusion of the task of mission with a general idea of responsibility for the world.[49]

This statement raises several important questions in my mind. For one thing, doesn't one run the risk of losing the dynamic and transcendent nature of the gospel which, while admittedly grounded on a historic event, speaks nevertheless to all situations and all levels and is thus ever becoming contemporaneous? After all, the gospel is not merely good news about a past event. It is this, of course, but it is also good news about a living Person who is himself acting redemptively through his Spirit in the here-and-now. Accordingly, the situation of encounter is more than a revelation of the ways by which the gospel may be ap-

---

45. *Ibid.*
46. *Ibid.*
47. *Ibid.*
48. Italics mine.
49. *Ibid.*

plied. Since the gospel speaks to man's concrete situation—which is always a situation of sin—the situation of encounter reveals more than "new aspects in the application of the gospel." It reveals new dimensions of the gospel. It enhances our understanding of the gospel. It helps us to see things that heretofore we have not seen. To deny this is to negate the biblical affirmation that now we know in part (cf. 1 Cor. 13:12) and the promise that the Spirit will guide us into all truth (cf. Jn. 16:13). It is to deny the Spirit's creative action in the world.

Granted that the gospel is "a given," but it is also a promise. To say that it is grounded on the resurrection of Christ is to affirm that it is a message about the future. Now this future is not unidimensional and static; rather, it is complicated and dynamic. While it involves a final event, the future proclaimed by Christianity is nevertheless open-ended (no one knows the hour nor the day when Christ will return). It is both a far and a near future. It is constantly dropping glimpses which not only feed our hope but also uncover new dimensions of the once-and-for-allness of Calvary.

Thus, the Spirit's action in the world consists not only of convincing people of their respective situations of sin but also of opening the eyes of the church to *understand* the gospel in the light of these situations. The gospel is good news of God's reign which has rushed in a new order of life. Can we in our feeble, limited, and imperfect minds understand all the dimensions of the new order? Of course not! The Holy Spirit many times uses our encounter with people to help us understand the meaning of the gospel in their particular context.

The situation of encounter is, therefore, important because sin manifests itself in many and sundry ways. It is further important because man is a changing creature. If the gospel is truly eternally contemporaneous, it must speak concretely to each new situation. This, I repeat, is not a mere question of application. It is a matter of the nature of the gospel itself, which confronts man in his own courtyard, speaks to his concrete need, and reveals God's saving power in redeeming him, first and foremost, from his own situation of sin.

The problem with this particular section of the Frankfurt Declaration is its metaphysical presupposition, namely, that there is a difference between the "essence" of the gospel and its "application." Consequently, it sees the Bible as the "primary frame of reference," and implicitly, the situation of encounter as a secondary one. Yet even the Bible itself doesn't follow this paradigm. It sees man's concrete situations as relevant for the understanding of God's miraculous intervention in history in the person of Jesus of Nazareth. How else can we understand the incarnation if we do not see it as a serious attempt on God's part to meet man in his own particular situation? The fact that Jesus was born a Jew is not coincidence. God was in this act speaking concretely to a given people in a particular setting. The same Scripture which portrays an effort on the part of Matthew to describe Jesus as a Jew, records another effort to present him as a man interested in everyday human problems (Luke), a dynamic, all-powerful person (Mark), and the incarnation of truth (John). The same may be said of Paul's use of the Athenian situation to unfold the meaning of the gospel. Surely in each of these cases the situation of encounter is not a secondary frame of reference but a primary one. This is so because the God who acts in Jesus of Nazareth is the same God who is active in all creation, thereby bringing both his redemptive act in Jesus Christ and the situation of man into vital encounter.

To affirm, therefore, that the situation of encounter constitutes a primary frame of reference for our understanding of the gospel is not to surrender the Bible as a primary frame of reference, nor to deny, as the Frankfurt Declaration seems to imply, the normativeness of the gospel, nor to confuse the task of mission. It does mean that each generation must go to the Bible and the gospel with its particular situation if it is to understand to the fullest all the dimensions of God's redemptive mission in its midst. To refuse to do this is to short-change God, to limit our own understanding of God's economy, and ultimately, to prove ourselves unfaithful stewards.

2. *Principle two* deals with the goal of mission. The text affirms that the supreme end of mission is twofold: "the *glorification* of the one *God* throughout the entire world and the proclamation of the lordship of Jesus Christ, his Son."[50] This is followed by a rejection of "the assertion that mission today is no longer so concerned with the disclosure of God as with the manifestation of a new man and the extension of a new humanity into all social realms."[51] Hence *humanization* is rejected as a primary goal of mission and considered, instead, to be "a product" of the new birth and an "indirect result of the Christian proclamation in its power to perform a leavening activity in the course of world history."[52]

As in the case of principle one, the problem with principle two is not so much with the affirmative part as with the negative one. For example, "the assertion that mission today is no longer so concerned with the disclosure of God as with the manifestation of a new man" is a caricature of the Renewal in Mission Report. As has been observed, the Report does describe God's mission "as the gift of a new creation," and thus as the manifestation of the new man, but it explicitly affirms that the latter is "a radical renewal of the old [creation] and the invitation to men to grow up into their full humanity *in the new man,*[53] Jesus Christ."[54] Obviously, this statement categorically links the new humanity to Jesus Christ. The Report says that mission today is concerned with the disclosure of the God who acted in Jesus Christ to bring about a new humanity. At no time does it express lack of concern for the disclosure of God. Neither does it come out for a "new man" totally unrelated to Jesus Christ himself.

---

50. *Ibid.*
51. *Ibid.*
52. *Ibid.*
53. Italics mine.
54. Goodall, *Uppsala . . . ,* p. 28.

Further, the distinction that the Declaration makes between the goal and the by-product of mission is highly questionable. Granted that the ultimate purpose of the church is the glorification of God and that the proclamation of the Lordship of Jesus Christ is unquestionably "a chief end of mission," as McGavran has emphasized.[55] But the proclamation of Christ is not an end in itself. It has a specific objective. It is true that in her proclamation the church glorifies God, but it is not *merely* the fact of the proclamation that glorifies God, but rather the fact that through this proclamation men and women come to the saving knowledge of Christ. This saving knowledge is the means by which the miracle of the new creation takes place. *One of the dimensions* of the new creation is its humanizing quality. To be in Christ is to be part of a new humanity.

Humanization, understood in its biblical perspective, is not a mere indirect result of Christ's saving action. It is at the heart of Christ's redemptive activity, for Christ came to recreate fallen humanity. Hence the new birth is not simply a spiritual, internal operation. It is a complete about-face, in which man is totally transformed, reoriented, to such a degree that though he continues to be assailed by sin, he is given the power to overcome it. Otherwise, how are we to understand all those New Testament passages that deal with experiencing the power of Christ's resurrection and of the Holy Spirit?

The question of humanization becomes, therefore, a matter of responsibility, of living lives worthy of the Christian vocation, of being consistent with the claims of the gospel. Rather than its being a fruit, the New Testament considers this a test or the evidence par excellence of one's salvation, as James so clearly demonstrates. Salvation means, among other things, transformation from a self-centered life to an others-centered life. It means total commitment to a life of service. To place this dimension of God's saving action in the realm of the indirect results of

---

55. McGavran, "Essential Evangelism . . . ," p. 56.

the gospel is to create an illicit dichotomy and to militate against the wholeness of the gospel.

It is true that "a one-sided outreach of missionary interest toward man and his society [can lead] to atheism."[56] But it is equally true that a one-sided missionary interest in the transcendence of God, which reduces man to a secondary role, is a form of gnosticism (a theological school of thought which the New Testament writers condemn as one of the worst forms of Christian heresy because it fails to take seriously the reality of the incarnation). If Christianity is grounded in any one specific truth it is in this: the fact that God became man. Henceforth, God must be seen as being pro-man because his Son became one like us. To deny this is to deny the heart of the gospel and, consequently, the thrust of the Christian world mission.

3. *Principle three* is concerned with Christ as the basis, content, and authority of the Christian mission. It challenges "all non-Christians, who belong to God on the basis of creation, to believe in him and be baptized in his name . . ."[57] It opposes

> the false teaching (which is spreading in the ecumenical movement since the Third General Assembly of the World Council of Churches in New Delhi) that Christ himself is anonymously so evident in world religions, historical changes, and revolutions that man can encounter him and find salvation in him without the direct news of the Gospel.[58]

This affirmation contains an obvious reference to statements that have been put out by groups and persons related to the World Council with regard to the Christian

---

56. *Ibid.*, p. 115. I have changed the "leads" which appears in the text for "can lead" for obvious reasons. There are some, as will be shown in the next chapter, who may be described as taking a one-sided outreach of missionary interest toward man but who definitely remain firm in their belief in God.

57. *Ibid.*

58. *Ibid.*

faith and non-Christian religions. Most of the statements that would verify the Declaration's direct assertion are in reality unofficial documents of the conciliar movement. The official documents use a much more careful language. Take, for example, the Report of the Witness Section in New Delhi. It affirms "that God has not left himself without witness even among men who do not yet know Christ . . ." It states "that the reconciliation wrought through Christ embraces all creation and the whole of mankind" and "that this great truth has deep implications when we go out to meet men of other faiths." But it frankly admits that "there are differences of opinions" among Christians when they "attempt to define the relation and response of such men to the activity of God amongst them."[59]

The same can be observed in the official report of Section I ("The Witness of Christians to Men of Other Faiths") at the meeting of the Commission on World Mission and Evangelism in Mexico City in 1963. The report asserts that "in the world of other faiths there are some who are secret believers, avoiding for various reasons membership in the visible Body of Christ." But it goes on to qualify this by noting: "Nevertheless, to be a Christian necessarily involves being brought by Christ into the visible, witnessing community of faith."[60]

And finally, from paragraph six of the Renewal in Mission Report:

> The meeting with men of other faiths or of no faith must lead to dialogue. A Christian's dialogue with another implies neither a denial of the uniqueness of Christ, nor any loss of his own commitment to Christ, but rather that a genuinely Christian approach to others must be human, personal, relevant, and humble. In dialogue we share our common humanity, its dignity and fallenness, and express our common

---

59. 'T Hooft, *New Delhi*, p. 81.

60. Donald K. Orchard, ed., *Witness in Six Continents* (London: Edinburgh House Press, 1964), p. 145.

concern for that humanity. It opens the possibility of sharing in new forms of community and common service. Each meets and challenges the other; witnessing from the depths of his existence to the ultimate concerns that come to expression in word and action. As Christians we believe that Christ speaks in this dialogue, revealing himself to those who do not know him and correcting the limited and distorted knowledge of those who do.[61]

As can be observed, these statements are very carefully worded. Does this mean that the Frankfurt Declaration's assertion in principle three is false? No, it simply means that it is not directly evident in the *official* documents of the World Council of Churches. Even in the second part of the Renewal in Mission Report, which speaks about opportunities for mission today, a statement equivalent to the assertion of the Frankfurt Declaration cannot be found. Neither can one find support for the second rejection of principle three:

We likewise reject the unbiblical limitation of the person and work of Jesus to his humanity and ethical example. In such an idea the uniqueness of Christ and the Gospel is abandoned in favor of a humanitarian principle which others might also find in other religions and ideologies.[62]

As I have observed in my analysis of the Renewal in Mission Report, the final draft adopted by the Assembly leaves much to be desired, not so much for what it says, but for what it does not say. The same can be said of many of the missiological statements of the World Council, from New Delhi to the most recently held World Conference on Salvation Today. However, none of the official documents that I have seen live up to the negative assertion of

---

61. Goodall, *Uppsala . . .* , p. 29.
62. Beyerhaus, *. . . Which Way? . . .* , p. 115.

principle three of the Frankfurt Declaration. This looks more like a straw man than a description of the official position of the World Council of Churches.

4. *Principle four* defines mission in terms of *"the witness and presentation of eternal salvation* performed in the name of Jesus Christ by his church . . . by means of preaching, the sacraments, and service."[63] Further, it states that this salvation is due to the sacrifice of Christ, "which occurred once and for all and for all mankind."[64] Salvation is appropriated to individuals "through proclamation, which calls for decision, and through baptism, which places the believer in the service of love."[65] The document then goes on to voice its opposition to neo-universalism or "the idea that in the crucifixion and resurrection of Jesus Christ all men of all times are already born and already have peace with him, irrespective of their knowledge of the historical saving activity of God or belief in it."[66]

As an evangelical, I agree with the signers of this declaration in their opposition to neo-universalism. My problem is with the primacy of proclamation, and this understood verbally, in the conversion experience. Doesn't even Scripture attribute to the Lord's Supper a preaching function? "For as often as you eat this bread and drink the cup, you proclaim (*katangellete*) the Lord's death until he comes" (1 Cor. 1:26). Isn't service a legitimate form of witness? And doesn't the opening statement of 1 John come out for the possibility of three different channels of communicating the message of eternal life? ("That . . . which we have heard, which we have seen with our eyes, which we have looked upon and touched with our hands, concerning the way of life" 1 Jn. 1:1). Further, isn't there in Scripture a tension between proclamation and service? Indeed, the two need each other: preaching is empty without service and service is meaningless without preaching.

---

63. *Ibid.,* p. 116.
64. *Ibid.*
65. *Ibid.*
66. *Ibid.*

Salvation comes to man as the church proclaims in word *and* deed the good news. A distinction of priorities between word and deed is neither theologically sound nor communicatively correct. For the process of communication involves the totality of one's personality: words and gestures, intellect and emotions, *logos, pathos,* and *ethos.* While salvation is appropriated as men and women respond in faith to the gospel and are baptized, the gospel itself comes to them through the church's verbal proclamation as well as through her sacramental witness and servicing testimony.

5. *Principle five* deals with the place of the church in the missionary enterprise. According to the Declaration, "The primary visible task of mission is to call out the messianic, saved community from among all people." Therefore, mission "should lead everywhere to the establishment of the Church of Jesus Christ . . ."[67] The church, wherever planted, "exhibits a new defined reality as salt and light in its social environment."[68] These authors see the church as distinct from the world. They oppose the view that the church "is simply a part of the world."[69] They go on record as opposing a corollary of the latter view, namely, the idea that salvation has *only* a this-worldly dimension, "according to which the Church and the world together share in the future, purely social, reconciliation of all mankind."[70]

Note the positive orientation toward church growth. There is, however, in this principle a tendency toward conceiving of the church as an ultimate instead of a penultimate goal of mission. Such a perspective reduces all other dimensions of the task of mission to secondary roles, an idea which has been and will continue to be questioned in this volume.

6. *The sixth principle* again emphasizes the univer-

---

67. *Ibid.,* p. 117.
68. *Ibid.*
69. *Ibid.*
70. *Ibid.*

sality of the gospel. It states that the offer of salvation is directed to all men who are outside a direct relationship with Christ. It rejects the notion that the way of salvation—apart from Christ—can also be found in non-Christian religions; that a silent witness "among the adherents to the world religions and a give-and-take dialogue with them are substitutes for a proclamation of the Gospel which aims at conversion"; and that "the borrowing of Christian ideas, hopes, and social procedures . . . can make the world religions and ideologies substitutes for the Church of Jesus Christ."[71]

Once again I am disappointed with the text of the Declaration. My problem does not lie with what it affirms but with what it rejects and the way it rejects it. Specifically, the concepts of "Christian presence" and "dialogue" with the non-Christian religions are refuted on the grounds that they are said to be substitutes for a proclamation of the gospel, which aims at conversion. Yet the Renewal in Mission Report specifically denies that dialogue replaces proclamation. It says:

> Dialogue and proclamation are not the same. The one complements the other in a total witness. But sometimes Christians are not able to engage either in open dialogue or proclamation. Witness is then a silent one of living the Christian life and suffering for Christ.[72]

This statement is further corroborated by the aforementioned Witness to Men of Other Faiths Report of the Commission on World Mission and Evangelism meeting in Mexico.

> In the dialogue with a man of another faith, however, we must be aware that he as an individual cannot be separated from the religion and community

71. *Ibid.*, p. 118.
72. Goodall, *Uppsala . . .* , p. 29.

which dominates him in all his thoughts and deeds. A dialogue cannot therefore be carried on without a thorough *confrontation*[73] with his full religious system.[74]

From the looks of these documents the basis for the Frankfurt Declaration's rejection of both the concepts of Christian presence and dialogue with the non-Christian religions is ill founded, at least in the official circles of the World Council of Churches. I have no doubt that functionally and in nonconciliar statements one does find such views held by many who call themselves Christians. Yet in reference to the conciliar movement, it must be said that Frankfurt once more sets up a straw man.

7. *Principle seven* is by far the most extensive. It begins with a chronological definition of mission ("mission is the decisive, continuous activity of God among men between the time of the resurrection and second coming of Jesus Christ"[75]). It then goes on to declare several eschatological events related to the task of world mission: the end of the time of the Gentiles, the climactic conflict (under the leadership of the Antichrist) between the church and the world, the second coming of Christ, the last conflict between Christ and Satan (Armageddon), and the establishment of the messianic kingdom.

From this eschatological declaration, the original subscribers to the Declaration go on to make a threefold refutation, namely, (1) "The idea that the eschatological expectation of the New Testament has been falsified by Christ's delay in returning and is therefore to be given up"; (2) "The enthusiastic and utopian ideology" of the progression of history toward a new, just, and peaceful world community; and (3) "The identification of messianic salvation with progress, development, and social change."[76]

---

73. Italics mine.
74. Orchard, *Witness* . . . , p. 146.
75. Beyerhaus, . . . *Which Way?* . . . , p. 119.
76. *Ibid.*

They also affirm, however, "the determined advocacy of justice and peace by all churches . . . that developmental aid is a timely realization of the divine demand for mercy and justice as well as of the command of Jesus, 'Love thy neighbor.' "[77] Yet, the latter are seen only as "an important accompaniment and authentication of mission." They affirm further "the humanizing results of conversion as signs of the coming messianic peace."[78] But they are careful to explain that even so "all of our social achievements and partial successes in politics are restricted by the eschatological 'not yet' of the coming kingdom and the not yet annihilated power of sin, death, and the devil, who still is the 'prince of this world.' "[79] The priorities of missionary service are thus established by the aforementioned.

This last principle describes fully the one fundamental problem with this document, namely, its negativistic and polemic style. The concept of the kingdom, which is so crucial in the issue under discussion, is not introduced until the end and then only in its "not yet" dimension. In fact, the drafters of this Declaration are silent about the equally valid "now" of the kingdom.

Their failure to consider the present dimensions of the kingdom leads them to a very objectionable stance vis-à-vis the church's responsibility to the world. One can understand a Christian's reservation with *absolutely* identifying messianic salvation with progress, development, and social change. But it is a gross theological error to refuse to grant that Christ, as Lord of history, is active in the conflicts of history; that in fact, salvation, understood in part as participation in the life of the kingdom, involves active commitment toward world peace, understood in the broadest terms—as *shalom*—and equally strong commitment to the struggles for justice.[80]

---

77. *Ibid.*
78. *Ibid.*
79. *Ibid.*
80. Here I must take issue with Beyerhaus in . . . *Which Way?* . . . , pp. 35, 36, who in a parenthetical note states, in refuting the

It is true that the adopters of this document do take a position in favor of the church's advocacy of justice and peace. But by refusing to relate this to messianic salvation they push the latter to an other-worldly category, thereby limiting the scope of redemption. For the fact of the matter is that Christ came to give *life,* and to give it abundantly, and this life has not only a personal but a collective, social quality. It not only has a future dimension but a present one as well.

The question is not whether "efforts to aid develop-

---

usage of *shalom* in ecumenical missiology, that
the New Testament concept of peace [*eirene*] is deliberately avoided because *shalom* more adequately expresses the fuller, *i.e.,* the this-world-oriented, view. *Eirene,* however, characterizes man's new relationship to God which is based on a reconciliation in Christ. This reconciliation can be received only by faith.

Beyerhaus seems to give the impression that the New Testament concept of *eirene* is limited to man's vertical relation with God. We know, however, that *eirene* is the term used in the LXX to translate *shalom* and that it carries over the usage of *shalom* both in the Old Testament as well as in Rabbinic literature. Foerster, in his article in the *Theological Dictionary of the New Testament,* states that in spite of the fact that the main sense of the Greek word *eirene* "is a state of rest," its usage in the LXX links it to the concept of *shalom,* which "contains the thought of well-being or salvation." Accordingly,
Since . . . the LXX uses [*eirene*] for almost all the [*shalom*] passages in the OT, it is natural that the content of the Heb. term should have penetrated into the Greek.

Further on, Foerster adds that there are three conceptions in the use of *eirene* in the New Testament:
a. peace as a feeling of peace and rest; b. peace as a state of reconciliation with God; and c. peace as the salvation of the whole man in an ultimate eschatological sense. All three possibilities are present, but the last is the basis. This confirms the link with OT and Rabbinic usage.

With regard to the last possibility, he states further, that
On the basis of OT and Rabbinic usage [*eirene*] . . . acquires a most profound and comprehensive significance. It indicates the eschatological salvation of the whole man which is already present as the power of God. It denotes the state of the [*kaine ktisis* = new creation] as the state of definite fulfillment. In this sense salvation has been revealed in the resurrection of Jesus. (Woerner Foerster, *"Eirene,"* in Kittel, *Theological Dictionary of the New Testament,* Vol. II, pp. 406, 412, 415.)

ment and revolutionary involvement in the places of tension in society are seen as *the*[81] contemporary forms of Christian mission,"[82] but whether these are places where the gospel can be dramatically demonstrated. Or to put it in other terms, whether participation in the contemporary struggles for justice can be regarded as legitimate manifestations (glimpses, if you wish) of salvation.

As an evangelical I must take sides with the Frankfurt Declaration in repudiating any theological position that rejects the eschatological expectation of the second coming of Christ. Likewise, any ideology that loses sight of biblical historical realism and which holds naively "that all of mankind is already moving toward a position of general peace and justice and will finally—before the return of Christ—be united under him in a great world community."[83] But I must also take a stand against those who in the name of biblical realism fail to declare that history is moving toward the final consummation of God's kingdom and that the historical struggles for justice and peace are signs of this coming kingdom. These signs, of course, are not easily recognized by the world. But the church ought to discern them, under the guidance of the Spirit, and interpret them to the world. In this consists, *in part*, the church's prophetic ministry. But this is missing from the Frankfurt Declaration![84]

---

81. Italics mine.

82. *Ibid.,* p. 119.

83. *Ibid.*

84. In all fairness, it must be acknowledged that the Declaration does admit the idea of humanization as a sign of the coming messianic peace (cf. *Ibid.,* p. 120), but only as a result of conversion. And since conversion is basically a personal experience, it follows by implication that the authors consider as signs of the coming *shalom* only those humanizing deeds which result from the Christian's ethical involvement in society. They would not consider signs of the coming kingdom the historical struggles for justice and peace. Obviously, they fail to relate providence and redemption and the old idea of the Reformers of God's other hand working in accordance with his purpose in judgment and redemption through Christ Jesus in the secular structures of society. The

As a theological document aimed at standing forth for the biblical concept of mission, the Frankfurt Declaration is a great disappointment. It is too shallow, too polemic, and too negative. Surely a group of distinguished theologians could have come out with a more positive, profound, and evangelical affirmation.

It is ironic that a document aimed at helping to direct the course of the Commission on World Mission and Evan-

---

issue, then, is whether there are signs of the kingdom in the secular world (which, of course, are not understood by the world as such) and which the church is called upon to interpret to the world under the leading of the Holy Spirit, or whether the signs of the coming kingdom are to be found only in and through the church.

It is my contention that just as God is present and active in the world of nature and in the world of culture (understood in its wider sense) so he is in the struggles against the oppressive, demonic forces of this world. That these struggles are also under the judgment of God is undisputed. Nevertheless, God must be identified with the former because, in their imperfection and/or moral limitations, they represent the cause of justice and well-being, and God is the giver of all good gifts.

Further, Christ's redemptive work as a cosmic event extends even to the world of nature. Just as nature looks to the fulfillment of its redemption, so mankind groans for a new world. This which can be traced back to the events after the fall takes on a new turn after the death and resurrection of Christ. For the possibility of a new world is asserted in the work of Christ. God pronounces himself in favor of the well-being of mankind. Man's search for justice and peace not only represents a legitimate aspiration but one fed by God himself.

That man will never achieve a perfect, just, and peaceful world through himself is clearly taught in Scripture. But his search for justice and peace is, nevertheless, a sign of the coming age which the church must interpret in the light of the gospel. His struggles for a better world constitute, therefore, opportunities for the church to show forth her identity as the eschatological community of salvation and to fulfill her prophetic ministry in the world. Thus the church is faithful to her mission not only by showing forth her commitment to justice and peace but also by interpreting the meaning of the struggles of men for a better world in the light of the gospel. She thus becomes God's instrument for the final manifestation of the kingdom, which will come only through God's intervention. Participation in the coming kingdom as well as in its present communal manifestation is contingent on the acknowledgment of and commitment to Jesus Christ as Lord and Savior.

gelism should be so shallow.[85] How Peter Beyerhaus, the mastermind behind the document, thinks that such a declaration could contribute to the integration of "the ecumenical socioethical concerns and the evangelical soteriological concerns in a harmonious manner"[86] is beyond my imagination! For the fact of the matter is that rather than contribute to the continuation of the dialogue between evangelicals and the conciliar movement, which Beyerhaus himself recommends as essential for *both sides*,[87] the Frankfurt Declaration on the Fundamental Crisis in Christian Missions has intensified the polarization. Instead of engaging in a fruitful and profound dialogue, it sets out "to oppose" and denounce the conciliar movement by setting up straw men, by refusing (1) to interpret the official documents put out by the World Council of Churches and its corresponding bodies within its own particular context, and (2) to point out in a theologically responsible and profound manner the points of disagreement.

Following the adoption and publication of the Frankfurt Declaration, Donald A. McGavran introduced it in North America through an article in *Christianity Today.* Said McGavran:

> The official English translation has just reached me, and I make haste to share it with Christians in North America. Although it arose quite indepen-

---

85. In . . . *Which Way?* . . . , p. 102, 103, 104, Beyerhaus states: Our mission societies must acquire insight as to how we can concretely help direct the course of the Commission and Division for World Mission and Evangelism in a responsible theological direction . . .

A forceful attempt in this direction is the "Frankfurt Declaration on the Fundamental Crisis in Christian Missions," which was issued by a well-known group of confession-minded German theologians in March 1970. It is the German counterpart to the Wheaton Declaration. On the basis of this declaration, the Commission should be induced to listen to the objections and to answer them in a responsible way.

86. *Ibid.,* p. 93.

87. Cf. *Ibid.,* p. 92, 93.

dently, like the Wheaton Declaration . . . it speaks to a "fundamental crisis" in missions. It is a tremendous pronouncement issued to "clarify the true missionary motives and goals of the Church of Jesus Christ." It rings true to the Bible. It rings true to historic missions.[88]

He states further that since in Germany most missionary societies are related to the World Council of Churches, the Frankfurt Declaration gives the conservative elements in these churches the opportunity "to appeal to Geneva to reverse its stand that horizontal reconciliation is the only suitable mission strategy for our day. How far Geneva will yield[89] remains to be seen."[90] Referring to North American churches aligned with both the World Council and the National Council of Churches, he urges "the conservative elements in each church (the silent majority?) . . . to appoint someone to receive signatures and to flood denominational headquarters with them, demanding[91] emphasis on vertical reconciliation."[92]

THE ROLE OF
PETER BEYERHAUS

The introduction of the Frankfurt Declaration to the North American churches was followed by the publication of the English version of Peter Beyerhaus's *Humanisierung—Einzige Hoffnung Der Welt?* ("Humanization—the only hope of the world?") under the title, *Missions: Which Way? Humanization or Redemption*. The book constitutes the theological expositor of the Frankfurt Declaration for the

---

88. Quoted from *Christianity Today* in *Ibid.*, p. 110.
89. Italics mine.
90. *Ibid.*
91. Italics mine.
92. *Ibid.*

English-speaking public.[93] In it Beyerhaus expounds the crisis in the classical understanding of mission and gives the reasons behind it. He then goes on to analyze what he considers the three general answers that have been given in Protestant Christianity to this crisis, namely, that of the conservative evangelicals, that of the former International Missionary Council and that of its successor, the Commission on World Mission and Evangelism of the World Council of Churches. This leads him into an analysis of the confrontation that has been taking place ever since Uppsala between ecumenicals and evangelicals. This is followed by a chapter on the necessity of a reciprocal corrective between the socioethical emphasis on the Commission on World Mission and Evangelism and the soteriological emphasis of the evangelicals. He concludes with two chapters on the "destiny" of the ecumenical missionary movement and its implications for the German evangelical mission. In this last chapter he introduces the Frankfurt Declaration (which he includes in full in the Appendix, together with McGavran's article of introduction in *Christianity Today*) as a forceful attempt in the direction of reorienting the course of the CWME.

Beyerhaus's works, unlike the Declaration itself, are thorough and well documented.[94] The book is written in a smooth, easy-to-read form. Hardnosed words are explained in footnotes or in parentheses. In entering into the evangelical cause vis-à-vis the World Council of Churches, traditional evangelicals have found in him a sophisticated spokesman who can employ the language of contemporary theology to expound their position. His efforts, however, may not suffice for some younger evangeli-

---

93. But note: In Germany, the book preceded the Declaration. The latter was Beyerhaus, et al.'s response to the silence of the German Missionary Council vis-à-vis his *Humanisierung*.

94. Although his treatment of Cuban theologian Justo González (pp. 79, 80) and his concept of "the sacrament of social service," leaves a lot to be desired. He treats González through Peter Wagner's questionable interpretation of him in his controversial work, *Latin American Theology—Leftist or Evangelical?* (Grand Rapids: Eerdmans, 1969).

cals who insist, among other things, in keeping both word and deed intrinsically tied together and interrelated, and who are more sensitive to the concerns that have risen out of the social predicament of the "have-nots" (the poor and the exploited) of the earth and the implications of the gospel for their particular situation.

A case in point is Beyerhaus's insistence on maintaining the dichotomous language of traditional evangelicals. He insists that

> mission occurs . . . *primarily* in the proclamation of the redemptive act and of Jesus Christ's kingly lordship in all new and, as yet, untouched areas of life. It is *accompanied* by the authenticating presence of new life in the Spirit within the community of the Church, and by the transforming power of the Spirit in the believers, also in their obedient attempts to bring about better social structures.[95]

Later he goes on to state that

> the planting and growth of the Church as the body of Christ in the world remains the primary goal of mission within history. The transformation of the structures of this world is the *result*[96] of a membership which is prepared to serve.[97]

The problem with this position, as implied earlier, is that it militates against the wholeness of the gospel, which comes through in Scripture as an all-embodying message. To say that mission occurs *primarily* in proclamation and that it is *accompanied* by the church's life is to imply that mission cannot occur through the church's life; that the church's witness is bound to the primacy of *verbal* proclamation, as if *oral* communication was the only kind of com-

---

95. *Ibid.*, p. 68.
96. Italics mine.
97. *Ibid.*, p. 69.

munication available to the transmission of the gospel. Further, this position does not take into account the fact that the church herself is part of her message. By making such a cut-and-dried distinction between the gospel and the church, Beyerhaus fails to take into account the fact that the basis of the church's witness is her own life and experience with the gospel.

Alfred Krass tells how he used to think that one could separate the church, which is "the social context out of which evangelism proceeds," from her message.

> I came to see, in my experience as a pastor in this country and in Africa, that the Church is not to be separated from the gospel. The Church is part of the message. The Church which proclaims redemption is itself a redemptive community. Just as the pastor presiding over the Lord's Supper says to the people, "Ministering to you in Christ's Name, I give you the bread," so the Church says to the world, "Ministering to you in Christ's Name, we bring you the gospel." Evangelism is not just a testimony to God's acts in Christ, but participation in those acts.[98]

A second problem with Beyerhaus's position is that he writes as a North Atlantic missiologist committed to the thought categories and the continuation of the Western European and North American missionary enterprise. He does not seem to understand the dynamics of the indigenization of the church in the Third World in the last decade and a half. For him, the indigenization process among Asian and African (and although he does not mention it, among many Latin American) Christians has been "emotionally saddled with the unpleasant memory of their former second-rate status" and "mingled in the nationalistic [anti-imperialistic] reaction of their non-Christian fellow countrymen."[99] He is not sensitive to the fact that many of

---

98. Krass, Beyond . . . p. 24.
99. Beyerhaus, . . . Which Way? . . . , p. 19.

these Christians have gone through a profound stage of theological reflection which has led them to rethink the whole idea of mission in the light of biblical theology and their own particular situation. This process, which has taken a dynamic turn since the beginning of the last decade, has led Christians everywhere in the Third World in different directions. In one segment it has led to questionable theological conclusions. And with this particular segment, Beyerhaus's contention about the positive attitude of some Asians toward religious coexistence and syncretism, and about the tendency in an even wider segment of some Third World churchmen (together with other North Atlantic ecumenical theologians) to undermine certain traditional key elements of the church's mandate for mission and put them on a lower level to the church's social responsibility, is quite valid.

Yet a goodly number of Third World churchmen have remained within the framework of evangelicalism, particularly in the latter's strong orientation toward world mission, but have been increasingly criticizing the North Atlantic missionary enterprise and especially the missiology that has been linked with it. These churchmen are not alone in their criticism of the concepts of mission, the gospel, and the church which permeates the North Atlantic missionary enterprise. In the United States, an increasing minority of evangelical churchmen (such as evangelists Bill Pannell and Tom Skinner, editor John Alexander of *The Other Side,* and a group of young theology professors in respected evangelical seminaries) have been criticizing not only the missionary praxis (at home and abroad) of the North American evangelical church but its often unbiblical or theologically inconsistent theology of mission.

As has been observed, the issue of mission and the liberation of man in Protestant missiological thought since the Uppsala Assembly is not as cut-and-dried as one might think. Of course, it depends upon whom one reads. Some, like Beyerhaus, the original adopters of the Frankfurt Declaration, and the majority of British and North American evangelical churchmen who have criticized the Renewal in Mission Report, affirm that the problems are as clear as night and day. Others, among whom I include myself, do not think so, and while they may agree with many of our evangelical brethren's contentions, they see loopholes in the latter's criticism. The issue continues, especially (1) in the light of the study which the Commission on World Mission and Evangelism has sponsored in the last several years and which concluded with the World Conference on Salvation Today, held in Bangkok, Thailand, from December 29, 1972 to January 13, 1973 and (2) in view of the emergence of "the theology of liberation" which has played an important part in the idea of liberation as a dimension of the biblical doctrine of salvation and the church's mandate for mission. (In the next two chapters, we will consider the mission-liberation issue in the light of the theology of liberation and the World Conference on Salvation Today.)

ADDENDUM TO CHAPTER 9: SHAKEN FOUNDATIONS AND THE FRANKFURT DECLARATION

In his 1972 lectures at the School of World Mission and Institute of Church Growth of Fuller Theological Seminary, published recently under the title, Shaken Foundations (Grand Rapids: Zondervan, 1972), Peter Beyerhaus dedicates an entire chapter to expound "The Story of the Frankfurt Declaration." In this chapter he tells how it started, the role that Missions: Which Way? played in its formulation, the aim of the Declaration, its original signers, the tumult it produced in Germany, and its cold reaction from Geneva. He concludes this chapter by expressing the hope that the World Conference on "Salvation Today" (see the next chapters) would offer the opportunity to voice the concerns of the Declaration. He further emphasizes in the concluding pages the continuing function of the Frankfurt Declaration. He sees the latter, together with the Wheaton Declaration, as a possible rallying point for closer fellowship on the basis of a common concept of mission. He does admit, however, that the Declaration could stand a broadening and deepening in the days to come in at least two ways: (1) in the elaboration of a more popular version; (2) in the further clarification of such theological issues as the relation between verbal witness and social service as two sides of the total mission of the church, the significance of Eastern religions in the light of biblical revelation, etc. (cf. *Shaken Foundations,* p. 75).

A copy of *Shaken Foundations* did not reach me until after completion of the final draft of the manuscript of this book. For this reason I will not be able to enter into detail about the content of this chapter or the rest of the book. My remarks are therefore general and limited in scope.

Beyerhaus's suggestion of a closer world fellowship on the basis of a common concept of mission is well taken. The idea of mission as an ecumenical motif is both biblical (cf. Jn. 17:21) and historically valid. The problem, however, lies with his implication that the Frankfurt and Wheaton Declarations be taken as a basis for the definition of the common concept of mission. Both of these documents are historically conditioned to specific and concrete problems: the latter, to the problem of world mission from the particular situation of North American evangelical missionary societies; the former, to the particular and unique situation of the German missionary movement. The question is, is it valid to define mission from the perspective of such particular situations?

This leads me into a second related yet even more critical concern. As a Third World churchman and missiologist I find it hard to accept Beyerhaus's (and other North Atlantic leaders') persistent suggestion that Christians and churches in the Third World consider adopting the Frankfurt Declaration. Without wanting to be impolite, I feel that it is perhaps a bit presumptuous on their part. For it comes through as one more attempt of North Atlantic Christians to impose a theological agenda on Christians from the Third World, as if we could not think for ourselves, were not engaged in our own process of critical reflection on the crisis and challenges of world mission, and as if we did not have the theological resources to participate in defining a common concept of mission—and thus needed theological tutoring from the North Atlantic.

This may sound a bit harsh, but it seems to me something that must be said. For the situation is developing into unbearable proportions. When Beyerhaus rejoices that "largely on the basis of the Frankfurt Declaration, a world-wide brotherhood" is "emerging, of people who had found themselves to be involved in similar theological and ec-clesiastical struggles" (p. 71), he gives the impression of wanting to revive an epoch which has long passed its function, namely, the age when the North determined the theological, ecumenical, and missionary agenda of the church in the Third World. His reference to the 2,000 copies of the Frankfurt Declaration that were sent out to Indo-nesian clergymen and missionaries as evidence of the sup-port the document is receiving in the Third World does no more and no less than give evidence of the tremendous efforts that are being made to impose a theological and missiological agenda on the Third World church. A similar effort was made in December 1970 at the first meeting of the Latin American Theological Fellowship when a North American missionary brought with him 200 copies in Span-ish of the Frankfurt Declaration and proposed that the As-sembly adopt it as its own. The delegates, considering such a suggestion completely out of the question, voted to turn it down. They then went ahead to write their own declaration in the light of their own particular situation and through the use of their own theological resources.

In criticizing the continuous and persistent insistence of Beyerhaus and his friends that Christians and churches throughout the world adopt and sign the Frankfurt Declara-tion, I am not questioning at all their sincerity and com-mitment to the task of world mission. Further, I do not doubt that in spite of the serious theological questions that the latter has raised in my own mind it may be playing an important function in the missionary endeavor of the German church. What I do question is their insistence that Third World Christians and church adopt it as their own.

In this respect I see a great difference between the spirit of the Wheaton Declaration and that of the Frankfurt Declaration. The former represents a sincere attempt on the part of *a group* of church and mission leaders to express their concerns about the church's world mission. If it reached the hands of Christians around the world, it did so as a document from a gathering of Christians engaged in a process of serious reflection. It could be used as a *frame of reference,* showing how they, in a particular setting, interpreted the world situation with regard to the church's world mission. Its style is both humble and positive. While it questions and criticizes certain trends in world mission, it does so from a perspective of a positive commitment to the gospel and a spirit of confession of the past ills of their own particular involvement in world mission.

The Frankfurt Declaration, however, is dogmatic and polemic. The promotion it has received makes it come through as an attempt to recruit supporters for the theological efforts of a particular group of theologians. In so doing, it calls for a commitment to a particular style of theologizing which is in fact being questioned more and more in the Third World. (On this, see the next chapter.) Little wonder that when Peter Beyerhaus suggested in Bangkok (see chapter XI) that the conference consider the Frankfurt Declaration (as he said in his Fuller lectures that he was going to do), an African responded "that he was disgusted with such attempts to foist controversies of the West onto the Third World."[100] Although Beyerhaus argued that "consideration of a biblically based statement is not imposition of a Western controversy,"[101] most of the representatives from the Third World remained unconvinced.

If, as Beyerhaus suggests, the foundations of the missionary movements have been cracked, then it ought to be

---

100. Donald Hoke, "Salvation Isn't the Same Today," in *Christianity Today,* XVII:9 (February 2, 1973), p. 37.
101. *Ibid.,* p. 38.

a matter of concern for leaders around the world. Such an analysis and the solutions proposed must be the cooperative effort of theologians from different parts of the world. For it may be that in the process even the prominent German and North American theologians may have something to learn from the analysis and perception of their less prestigious but equally sharp and committed Asian, African, and Latin American counterparts.

10/MISSION AND THE LIBERATION OF MAN
Section 2/From Uppsala to Bangkok via Latin America— The Emergence of the Theology of Liberation

The last chapter traced the historical development in Protestant missiology of the tension between mission and the liberation of man since the Uppsala Assembly and up to the Frankfurt Declaration. This tension has intensified the polarization between evangelicals and ecumenical Christians. Nor does the situation seem to improve. Groups within both camps become more radical in their position. A good example of this is the fact that at the same time that the Frankfurt Declaration was coming out as a protest from a group of German confessional theologians, a group of young theologians was emerging with a sharp criticism of the theological undergirding of ecumenical missiology. Their writings were not only a challenge to evangelical missiology (and accordingly, a reaffirmation of the contention of the Frankfurt theologians) but also to the forth-coming World Conference on Salvation Today.

The theological endeavors of these young writers represent a critical reflection on the oppressive situation of the peoples of the Third World, particularly Latin Americans, in the light of the commitment of an increasing number of Latin American Christians to the struggle for a just society. The initial efforts of these theologians, all Latin Americans, have led to what has come to be known as "the theology of liberation."

Unlike the Frankfurt Declaration and the writings of its supporters in Europe and North America, which are a re-action against Uppsala *in preparation for* Bangkok 1973 (as I shall call, from here on, the 1973 World Conference on Salvation Today) the theology of liberation doesn't even take notice of Uppsala.[1] It does appear on the scene in connection with the Consultation on Theology and Development organized by the Society for Development and Peace (SODEPAX) in Cartigny, Switzerland, in November 1969.[2] Nevertheless, it represents an important theological trend for the debate which emerged out of Uppsala.

The importance of the theology of liberation lies in the fact that it is not simply a critical reflection on the commitment of Christians to the struggles for justice for the op-

---

1. Except as a passing reference. (This passing reference has, nevertheless, tremendous implications, as will be observed in the next chapter.) In his prologue to the publication of the documents of a consultation on the theology of liberation sponsored by Iglesia y Sociedad en América Latina (ISAL), Hugo Assmann makes the following observation:

> From the Protestant side, the initial impulses of the famous encounter in 1966 of the World Council of Churches [the World Conference on Church and Society], of the encounter at Uppsala, etc., equally drained, to a great extent, its verbal denunciation on account of the complete absence of a real tacticostrategic implementation. Hugo Assmann, "Presentación," *Pueblo oprimido, Señor de la historia* (Montevideo: Tierra Nueva, 1972).

2. For a good summary of the historical development of the theology of liberation, see Hugo Assmann, *Opresión-Liberación: Desafío a los cristianos* (Montevideo: Tierra Nueva, 1971), pp. 45-50, 79ff.

pressed. Rather, as Gustavo Gutiérrez points out, it is "a critical reflection on Christian praxis in the light of the Word."[3] As such, it interacts with the historical situation of the Third World, particularly Latin America, and the political option of the Latin American Church, but especially with the whole question of the meaning of salvation in a context of the binomial oppression-liberation and its implication for the church's mission. Accordingly, the theology of liberation posed a challenge which the worldwide studies and Conference on Salvation Today could not very likely ignore.

The purpose of this chapter is to analyze the main ingredients of this theology, particularly in relation to the mission-liberation issue. This analysis will help us to understand more clearly the dynamics and final outcome of Bangkok 1973 and its implications for the church's worldwide mission, particularly in relation to the urging demands of the oppressed masses of the world.

THE THEOLOGY OF LIBERATION AS A THEOLOGICAL REBELLION OF LATIN AMERICA

The theology of liberation is first and foremost a Latin American theology.[4] This does not mean that it is a provincial theology. Indeed, as has been shown, one of its leading characteristics is, that while all its spokesmen are

---

3. Gustavo Gutiérrez, *Theology of Liberation. History, Politics and Salvation,* translated and edited by Sister Caridad Inda and John Eagleson (Maryknoll, New York: Orbis Books, 1972), p. 13.

4. As a school of thought, the theology of liberation is not grounded on the thought of a single person. It is a movement which has achieved, nevertheless, a definite theological structure largely through the writings of Rubem Alves, Hugo Assmann, Gustavo Gutiérrez, Juan Luis Segundo, C. Alvarez Calderón, J. A. Hernández, J. Lozano, and H. Borge. Although in its earlier stages (1968) it was mainly associated with Roman Catholic reflection groups that grew out of the stimulus of the Latin America

Episcopal Congress (CELAM) in Medellín, Colombia, it has since widened its scope to include the thinking of such an avant-garde movement as Iglesia y Sociedad en América Latina (which has a Protestant origin) and such Protestant theologians as José Míguez Bonino, Luis Rivera Pagán, Julio de Santa Ana, and Emilio Castro. Some of the most unique contributions, however, have come from Rubem Alves, Hugo Assmann, and Gustavo Gutiérrez through their most important writings. Nevertheless, in reading the latter one needs to bear in mind several consultations that have been held since 1970. The fruits of these consultations appear in the following publications:

Aportes para la liberación (Bogotá: Editorial Presencia, 1970).

Liberación (Bogotá: Editorial Presencia, 1970). Volumes I and II of the first symposium of theology of liberation held in Latin America (Bogotá, 1970).

Liberación en América Latina (Bogotá: Ed. América Latina, 1971). Documents of a theological encounter of Catholic theologians and churchmen held in Bogotá, Colombia, July, 1971.

América Latina: movilización popular y fe cristiana. (Montevideo: ISAL, 1971). Papers from the 1971 General Assembly of ISAL.

Pueblo Oprimido, Señor de la historia. (Montevideo: Tierra Nueva, 1972).

There were also two important gatherings in the hemisphere (in 1970 and 1971), which deserve to be mentioned: (1) A symposium on the theology of liberation (held in Mexico), with the participation of Harvey Cox and other North Atlantic theologians, but which produced no official publication (although several of the papers have been widely circulated); (2) the Eighth Annual Conference of the Catholic Inter-American Cooperation Program (held in Reno, Nevada), which produced *Freedom and Unfreedom in the Americas,* Towards a theology of liberation, Thomas E. Quigley, ed. (New York: IDOC, 1971).

Without falling into generalizations, I shall try to characterize the particular contribution of Alves, Assmann, and Gutiérrez to the theology of liberation.

Alves, though a Protestant, can be described, nevertheless, as the *prophet* of the movement. Although he has been greatly criticized by Assmann and others for the vagueness of his language, it is acknowledged that the publication of his best-seller, *Theology of Human Hope,* marks, in the words of Assmann, the "wide globalization of the basic questions of a 'Theology of Liberation.' " (*Ibid.,* p. 80). Harvey Cox, in the Foreword, acknowledges the importance of the book for the theological world.

> With the appearance of this book, it is no longer possible for us to talk *about* the Third World theologically . . . It is now clear that first of all we must listen. After that any further discussion must be *with,* not about. In Alves's own words, the Third World is neither mute nor reflexive. It will

Latin Americans committed to and writing from the perspective of their continent's liberation, they nevertheless make a serious attempt not only to relate their critical reflection to the situation of the rest of the Third World but with the church universal. Its international and ecumenical orientation must be seen against the backdrop of the theologies of the last decades which have come out of the

---

no longer allow either its political destiny or its theological self-definition to come from somewhere else.

(Harvey Cox, "Foreword," in Rubem Alves, *A Theology of Human Hope* (Washington: Corpus Books, 1969), p. vii.)

But if Alves is the prophet of the movement, *Hugo Assmann* is the *apologist*. In his cutting and dialectical work, *Opresión-liberación: desafío a los cristianos* (Oppression-Liberation: A Challenge to Christians) he not only gives the roots of the theology of liberation, including the definition of the term liberation and the role of the theology of liberation as a political theology, and defends its theological *locus* and methodology, but launches a mounting attack on North Atlantic theologies, dismantling their vagueness and ideological presuppositions. Using an admirable guerrilla-like approach, he sets up one roadblock after another to the "ethics of order," and builds a case for the theology of liberation as an autochthonous political theology based on an "ethic of change." He then outlines the main elements which must be considered for a more precise characterization of the theology of liberation.

The latter task is undertaken by *Gustavo Gutiérrez,* the *systematic theologian* of the movement. With the appearance of his *Teología de la liberación,* the movement entered into a new stage. Gutiérrez builds a case for a theology of liberation in dialogue with nontheological disciplines, old and contemporary theologies, the history of Christian thought and biblical exegesis, in an ecumenical and international perspective. Hence, the theology of liberation becomes not a reactionary theological reflection—*i.e.,* a negation of the existing "theology of repetition" which has characterized Latin American theology for so long, or even a negation of the continued function of theology as a justification of the *status quo*—but a positive theological work wrapped up in a radically different "system." This new system encompasses the main areas of a traditional systematic theology, yet includes them in a different way and uses radically different categories. One might not always agree with him, but one cannot help but admire his sharp yet positive, synthetical yet open-ended, innovative yet historically-minded theological style. Further, the wealth of documentation and notes makes the book the most authoritative bibliographical source on the subject to date in the English language.

affluent North Atlantic World. It is in connection with them that the theology of liberation manifests its rebellious character.

A RADICAL BREAK WITH THE THEOLOGIES OF THE NORTH ATLANTIC. Just as Karl Barth's *Romerbrief* marks a break with nineteenth-century liberalism and Jürgen Moltmann's *Theology of Hope* with Barthian theology, so the theology of liberation constitutes a radical break with the theologies that have come out of Western Europe and North America in the past decades. This break has at least three leading traits.

First of all, the theology of liberation represents a radically different starting point. Unlike the majority of theologies from the North Atlantic, which start theologizing with theological categories—God, church, world—the theologians of liberation start from the poverty-stricken, oppressive, and dominated reality of Latin America. In the words of Hugo Assmann, "The greatest merit of the 'theology of liberation' probably lies in its insistence on the historical starting point of its reflection: the dominated situation of Latin America."[5]

Another starting point of the theology of liberation is the increasing consciousness of a growing number of oppressed people that their situation should not and must not remain thus. They are committing themselves to a process of negation and a struggle for liberation. In other words, they are simply becoming aware of the oppression that dominates them and are determined to struggle to liberate themselves historically.[6] This experience is having tremendous impact on the conscience of an increasing number of Christians, who now have begun to enter into the historical battleground in solidarity with the masses. It is out of this praxis that the theology of liberation arises.[7]

---

5. Assmann, *Opresión-liberación* . . . , p. 24.
6. Cf. Rubem A. Alves, *Theology of Human Hope* (Washington: Corpus Books, 1969), p. 11ff.
7. Cf. Assmann, *Opresión-liberación* . . . , p. 31ff.

In this context, theology is conceived of not simply as "spiritual" or "rational" knowledge of the faith, but as a critical reflection on the historical praxis of faith. It is out of the commitment and participation of Latin American Christians in the struggle for liberation that the theology of liberation comes into being. Thus its second characteristic, namely, that it represents a very different way of doing theology because it questions the faith on the march, in a concrete historical situation rather than abstractly. Therefore, Gutiérrez can affirm that

> the theology of liberation offers us not so much a new theme for reflection as a *new way* to do theology. Theology as critical reflection on historical praxis is a liberating theology, a theology of the liberating transformation of the history of mankind and also therefore that part of mankind—gathered into *ecclesia*—which openly confesses Christ. This is a theology which does not stop with reflecting on the world, but rather tries to be part of the process through which the world is transformed. It is a theology which is open—in the protest against trampled human dignity, in the struggle against the plunder of the vast majority of people, in liberating love, and in the building of a new, just, and fraternal society . . .[8]

Third, the theology of liberation breaks with the theologies of the North Atlantic at the level of the tools it employs. Theology as a critical reflection on the praxis of faith is preceded by previous analysis of the sociopolitical reality. This means that its primary tools are those of the social sciences, for they have the first word with respect to the concrete data of the historical praxis.[9] Hence, the

---

8. Gutiérrez, . . . *Liberation*, p. 15.

9. For those who object to this on the ground that it implies the "socialization of theology," men like Assmann reply that even if one were to start from the Bible he would have to depend on the scientific tool. He argues that

not even exegesis can do away with the resource of the hu-

social sciences are the fundamental frame of reference and the contextual starting point of the theology of liberation.[10]

This utilization of the social sciences as tools for analysis is a key idea. The social sciences are not ideologically neutral. The methodology used determines their ideological role. What determines the methodology to be used? The best possible option for the human and political dimension of the problems.[11]

For the theologians of liberation, the most viable option for the Latin American church is one that analyzes the situation from the perspective of the masses. Consequently, they reject the North American functionalistic sociological analysis since it represents a commitment to developmental theory.

According to this theory, national growth is a total process contingent upon the advantages of several interdependent factors. To the extent that all of these factors (economic, social, political, and cultural) are properly coordinated there will be a balanced growth and underdeveloped countries will be able to snap out of their limited situations. The harmonious interdependence of these factors constitutes the goal of this theory. Functionalism takes such a system at face value and seeks to discover those factors which are not *functioning* properly and are causing stagnation. Its goal is to improve the system so that it might function properly and permit growth. Its fallacy lies in the fact that it fails to challenge "the formal structure" of the system (which in this case are the existing institutions of the country). This makes it an instrument of the

---

man sciences to interrogate the biblical text. And when it does . . . not only do the true challenges contained in the Bible escape her, but, what's worse, she does not know how to make the biblical text speak to the problem-filled contemporary mind of man.
Assmann, *Ibid.,* pp. 66, 67.

10. Cf. *Ibid.,* p. 65.

11. Cf. *Ibid.,* p. 66, 67.

status quo, and hence of the establishment.[12]

Because the theology of liberation represents a critical reflection on the historical praxis of Christians out of solidarity with their oppressed neighbors, and since no scientific methodology is exempt from ideological commitment, it has no other option than that of a "structuralistic" methodology. Unlike functionalism, sociological structuralism does not accept the system at face value but questions it from the perspective of the poverty-stricken masses. It goes to the root of the problem. Accordingly, it analyzes the situation as one of economic, social, political, and cultural dependence and sets forth the necessity of deep structural changes as a condition for advance. In other words, it calls for the liberation of the masses from oppressive structures as a necessary condition for their well-being.

In taking this option, the theology of liberation commits itself to an "ideology of struggle." At the same time, it warns other theological endeavors that not to assume positively an ideology is to commit oneself to the "ideology" of the *status quo* and thus to become an alienating force vis-à-vis the struggle for the liberation of man.

A SERIOUS CRITICISM OF THE THEOLOGIES OF THE NORTH ATLANTIC. Such a radical break implies a serious criticism of the theologies of the North Atlantic. This criticism explains why the theologies of the affluent world are no longer satisfactory for Latin American theologians committed to socio-political change. Even the most progressive European and North American theologies of the last decade—those of Johannes Baptist Metz and Jürgen Moltmann—have been characterized by a Latin American theologian as "prologues in search of courage" against his characterization of the theology of liberation as "courage with primitive arms."[13]

The theology of liberation interacts critically with the

---

12. Cf. Gutiérrez, . . . *Liberation,* pp. 21ff.
13. Quoted in Assmann, *Opresión-liberación* . . . , p. 106.

respective theologies of secularization, existentialism, Barthianism, revolution, politics, and hope. Although theologians of liberation question conservative-evangelical theology throughout their writings, they do not treat specifically any one evangelical theological trend. The closest they come to this is in their treatment of the Barthian paradigm.

Briefly, how does the theology of liberation understand these theologies and why does it reject them?

While accepting the contention of the various *theologies of secularization* that the process of secularization is a legitimate fruit of biblical faith,[14] the theology of liberation rejects the latter's optimistic view of technology. Liberation theologians view this uncritical acceptance of "technologism" as an alienating ideology for the following reasons: (1) It destroys man's ability to say no to his present situation of oppression by delivering goods which commit him to that system. (2) By narrowing future hope to a matter of more production and better goods, it limits man's capacity to creatively shape his own history. (3) It reduces man to impotence through the process of automation, in which the machine takes over his duties.[15]

The theology of liberation also rejects the *existential theology* of Kierkegaard, Bultmann and his followers. While agreeing with their insistence "that man cannot remain human if he ceases to be a subject in history," it rejects their radical subjectivity as leading to the privatization of faith and the divorce of hope from politics.[16]

The theological paradigm of Karl Barth is discarded due to its otherworldly concept of God's transcendance. God's power is seen as merely touching history without actually

---

14. Cf. Arendt Th. van Leuwen, *Christianity in World History* (London: Edinburgh House Press, 1965); Harvey Cox, *The Secular City* (New York: Macmillan, 1965); Robert L. Richard, *Secularization Theology* (New York: Herder and Herder, 1967); R. Adolfs, *La tumba de Dios* (Buenos Aires: Ediciones Carlos Lohlé, 1967); L. Shier, *The Secularization of History* (Nashville: Abingdon, 1966), among others.

15. Cf. Alves, *Human Hope,* pp. 21-27.

16. Cf. *Ibid.,* pp. 34, 43.

coming to grips with and transforming it.[17]

Even the *Theology of Revolution* has come under fire by the theologians of liberation, closely linked as it may be to their own. In contrast to the generally accepted notion in the North Atlantic Community that Latin America is both the cradle and chief exporter of the theology of revolution, Hugo Assmann affirms that (1) the abundant bibliography available and (2) the intellectual-theoretical style in which the theology of revolution is dressed are "a phenomenon more characteristic of the rich world than of Latin America."[18] Latin American theologians of liberation want to disassociate themselves from the theology of revolution because of the latter's use of categories drawn from theology rather than from the social sciences to define and characterize what is and what ought to be the social revolution which must take place in situations of oppression. "Theology," insists Assmann, "does not have in itself the instruments for such a task, nor is this her function."[19]

The Political Theology of Johannes Baptist Metz,[20] and to a certain extent that of Moltmann,[21] represents one of the most influential "foreign" sources of the theology of liberation. Since the latter has characterized itself from its earliest inception as "a Latin American form of Political Theology," it welcomes the new European theology with its rejection of classical political theology (permeated with such categories as theological justification of the State and the binomial citizen-state). It further applauds (1) the fact that by underscoring the political dimensions of faith it has become a corrective to theological individualism; (2) its use of new terminology for theological reflection; (3) its concept of the church as an institution of social

---

17. Cf. *Ibid.,* pp. 44ff.

18. Assmann, *Opresión-liberación* . . . , p. 107.

19. *Ibid.,* p. 112.

20. Johannes Baptist Metz, *Zur Theologie der Welt* (München y Mainz: Mathias-Grünenwald-Verlag y Chr. Kaiser Verlag, 1968).

21. Jürgen Moltmann, *Theology of Hope* (New York: Harper & Row, 1967).

criticism; and (4) its stress on rescuing in Christian history and thought that "dangerous memory," the "subversive" content, the shouts of frustrated hopes.[22]

Nevertheless, the theology of liberation questions the vagueness of the former's socioanalytic content. "There is a sort of fear in naming directly the mechanism of domination," comments Assmann.[23] An even more serious criticism arises in relation to Metz's distinction between the task of theology (to detect the critical aspects of faith in relation to historical praxis) and ethical politics (to deal directly with the question of praxis). The theologians of liberation deem such a distinction inconceivable and unacceptable.[24]

The Theology of Hope has also had a tremendous impact on the theology of liberation, as can be observed by the treatment it has received in the major texts.[25] Nevertheless, Moltmann's emphasis on a future based on given promises has very little *concrete* influence on the present and contrasts sharply with the emphasis of liberation theology on the present condition of man and his negation of that present as the necessary starting point, the hope which arises out of his negation, and his struggle for an open future. Moltmann runs the risk of relegating man to the

---

22. Assmann, *Ibid.,* pp. 13, 14.

23. *Ibid.,* p. 116.

24. As Assmann observes:
    One cannot do real, detecting "Political Theology" of the critical aspects of the faith in so far as historical praxis is concerned without speaking an analytical language. This also means always the option for a type of analytical instrument. Such an option is an ethical step and not simply a neutral selection of an instrumentation for the analysis.
    Opresión-liberación . . . , p. 117 (cf. 116). See also Juan Luis Segundo, in "Problemática de la idea de Dios y de la liberación del hombre" (Montevideo: ISAL, n.d.), p. 5 (mimeograph), where he states that "a Political Theology exists . . . today in Latin America simply because there is a real theology and the reality is political in its decisive plane."

25. See *Ibid.,* pp. 119ff.; Gutiérrez, . . . *Liberation,* p. 217f.; Alves, . . . *Human Hope,* pp. 55ff.

role of an inactive spectator,[26] or worse yet, of replacing a "Christianity of the Beyond," with its tendency to forget the world, with a "Christianity of the Future," with its danger "of neglecting a miserable and unjust present and the struggle for liberation."[27]

This critical interaction with the contemporary theologies of the North Atlantic makes the theology of liberation the more interesting, given the fact that its spokesmen represent the largest *Christian* area of the world of poverty and that even to date this area continues to be not only socially, politically, economically, and culturally dependent on the rich countries of the world, but also theologically and missiologically. Why is it that after more than 400 years of Christianity only now an indigenous theological school begins to emerge? Why is it that the Latin American church is still *dependent* on the North Atlantic church for the supply of a heavy number of its missionary task force and its participating so little in the missionary task force of the church in other parts of the world?[28]

The theology of liberation, as stated, emerges as a critical reflection on the situation of dependence in which Latin America is living today. It sees the situation of Latin American Christianity as part of a total process of dependence-liberation. As a critical reflection on historical praxis, it is concerned with the church's life *in mission*. Accordingly, it must be seen in relation to the mission-liberation issue.

---

26. Assmann, *Ibid.,* p. 80.

27. Gutiérrez, *Ibid.,* p. 218.

28. In a recent press release, the Spanish Embassy in Costa Rica stated that at the present moment Spain has 15,000 missionaries in Latin America ("15,000 religiosos españoles trabajan en América," in *La Nación* (San José), (March 30, 1973), 64). For their part, Protestants, according to the Missionary Research Library, had 9,194 missionaries from North America. (*North American Protestant Ministries Overseas Directory,* 9th edition, compiled and written by Missions Advanced Research and Communication Center (New York: The Missionary Research Library, 1970), pp. 22-23)). Of course, the number of missionaries from the North Atlantic is much greater if one considers the rest of Western Europe.

THE THEOLOGY OF LIBERATION AND THE MISSION-LIBERATION ISSUE

The radicalism of the theology of liberation does not lie merely in the fact that it represents a theological revolution vis-à-vis the theologies of the last decade produced in the affluent world. It also constitutes a radical reflection on the mission-liberation issue. Its radical historical orientation with its situational hermeneutic leads to a redefinition of such concepts as salvation, Christology, eschatology, and the church. It is beyond the purpose of this part of the present chapter to analyze exhaustively these concepts in the theology of liberation. Limiting ourselves to the writings of the aforementioned writers, let us, therefore, consider briefly those themes which bear directly on this issue.

LIBERATION AND SALVATION. Salvation, Gutiérrez affirms, is the central theme of the Christian mystery. For this reason, the theology of liberation asks about "the relationship between salvation and the process of the liberation of man throughout history."[29] It is primarily concerned with the intrahistorical reality of salvation. Consequently, it is more preoccupied with the qualitative dimension of salvation than with the quantitative. The latter has to do with "the problem of the number of persons saved, the possibility of being saved, and the role which the Church plays in this process."[30] The former deals with "the value of human existence," or with the intensity of the presence of God's grace among men "and therefore of the religious significance of man's action in history."[31]

The substitution of the qualitative dimension for the quantitative leads Gutiérrez and his colleagues not only to a universalistic concept of salvation in the widest sense of the word but to the elimination of the other-worldly charac-

---

29. Gutiérrez, . . . *Liberation*, p. 149.
30. *Ibid.*, p. 150.
31. *Ibid.*

ter of salvation. Using the support of the "Dogmatic Constitution of the Church" and the "Pastoral Constitution on the Church in the Modern World" of Vatican II, Gutiérrez holds that man

> is saved if he opens himself to God and to others, even if he is not clearly aware that he is doing so. This is valid for Christians and non-Christians alike—for all people. To speak about the presence of grace—whether accepted or rejected—in all people implies, on the other hand, to value from a Christian standpoint the very roots of human activity.[32]

Salvation, understood as "the communion of men with God and the communion of men among themselves," is thus oriented to the transformation *in history* of human reality.[33]

The notion of a qualitative, intensive salvation is, according to Gutiérrez and others, grounded on the biblical link between creation and salvation. This link is "based on the historical and liberating experience of the Exodus."[34] Accordingly, creation is seen as the first salvific act. It marks the initiation of history and thus the opening up of "the human struggle, and the salvific adventure of Yahweh."[35] Further, creation is a salvific act because it is revealed by the redeemer himself in his redemptive action in the Exodus experience. And since the Exodus experience constitutes a political act, in which Israel is liberated from the bondage of oppression, it follows that salvation must be understood in terms of political liberation. Further, political liberation ought to be understood as the "self-creation of man."[36] "The dislocation introduced by sin is resolved"[37] by God's liberating action. Creation con-

---

32. *Ibid.*, p. 151.
33. *Ibid.*, p. 153.
34. *Ibid.*
35. *Ibid.*, p. 4.
36. Cf. *Ibid.*, p. 155f.
37. *Ibid.*, p. 157.

tinues by God's decisive action. Israel is set free not only to build a just nation but also to witness to the rest of the peoples of the earth about God's liberating concern for all humanity. The Exodus becomes, therefore, a paradigm for the political liberation of man. It witnesses to the gift of liberation: the recovery of man's God-given creative nature which, when properly exercised, makes him the subject instead of the object of his own history.

For Gutiérrez, the "work of Christ forms a part of this movement and brings it to complete fulfillment."[38] Hence the link between creation and salvation must be understood Christologically. In Christ, God sets out to recreate the world through the liberation of man from sin and all its consequences. "This liberation fulfills in an unexpected way the promise of the prophets and creates a new chosen people, which this time includes all humanity."[39] The paradigm of the liberation of man found in the Exodus experience finds its definite fulfillment in Christ. In him, God sets free all men to continue their creative vocation, to work and transform this world.

Accordingly, salvation must be understood as "the inner force and fulness of this movement of man's self-generation which was initiated by the work of creation."[40] Salvation is thus conceived of as a process "which embraces the whole of man and human history." This means that "building the temporal city is not simply a stage of 'humanization' or 'pre-evangelization,'" nor the fruit of the ethical application of Christ's saving work. Building a just, peaceful, and fraternal human society *is* what salvation is all about.[41]

CHRISTOLOGY AND HISTORY. Not only is salvation understood in intrahistorical terms, as political liberation, but Christ is understood preeminently in historical categories.

---

38. *Ibid.*, p. 158.
39. *Ibid.*, p. 158.
40. *Ibid.*, p. 159.
41. *Ibid.*, p. 160.

He is the Logos made flesh, the historization of God. The idea of the presence of God, understood in the Old Testament as being localized in the temple, is universalized and transferred to the heart of human history. In Christ, says Gutiérrez,

> the particular is transcended and the universal becomes concrete. In him, in his Incarnation, what is personal and internal becomes visible. Henceforth, this will be true, in one way or another, of everyman.[42]

The practical consequence of this last phrase is that Christ is to be found in every man. "Since God has become man, humanity, every man, history, is the living temple of God." Consequently, God is to be found among men. We meet him "in our encounter with men; we encounter him in the commitment to the historical process of mankind."[43]

Since "Christ is the Neighbor,"[44] the kingdom, understood as God's reign among men, which Jesus proclaimed as drawing near, is also historical, immanent. The experience of conversion is also materialized in the human process. "The conversion to the God of the Kingdom," says Assmann, "has to be materialized in the conversion of the historical human process."[45] Accordingly, "to be converted, to God and the perspectives of his Kingdom, it is necessary to be converted, here and now, to man and his history. It is in the struggle for the liberation of man that the love of God is materialized (cf. Mat. 25)."[46]

HISTORY AND ESCHATOLOGY. However, one must not lose sight of the biblical tension between the "now" and the "not yet" of the kingdom. On the one hand, the kingdom materializes in the concrete historical struggles of lib-

---

42. *Ibid.*, p. 193.
43. *Ibid.*, p. 194.
44. *Ibid.*
45. Assmann, *Opresión-liberación* . . . , p. 155.
46. *Ibid.*

eration. On the other, "the horizon must be kept open, toward the ultimate and definite Kingdom."[47]

What is the character of this ultimate and definite kingdom? Assmann says that it is "a horizon always open before us."[48] Gutiérrez describes it as that which is always ahead, that which keeps us from absolutizing any one historical stage, any revolution, or any human achievement. It is that which keeps the future open, full of new possibilities.[49] The permanent kingdom is thus that which keeps history open, always full of possibilities; the hope that arises out of the struggles of the present. Alves moves in this same direction in his description of Jesus' concept of the presence and futuricity of the kingdom (*i.e.,* "the now and the not yet"). According to him, the now of the kingdom in Jesus' teaching

> was not the presence of the eternal now, a present that exhausted itself. The future did not become present in an eternal now as in realized eschatology. Nor did it remain an isolated dogmatic idea, independent from and not related to the now, as a future that comes down from the heavens, as with consistent eschatology. The now was the time when a liberating activity that pushed toward the future was going on. Already and not yet were not, therefore, abstract points in the chronology of objective time. The not yet was what qualified and determined the present. It was not primarily the point of arrival but rather that which was being engendered in the future made historical through God's action . . . what God's action does is to create an explosiveness that is both present and negates the present.[50]

The theology of liberation has, therefore, an open,

---

47. Assmann, *Ibid.,* p. 154.
48. *Ibid.*
49. Gutiérrez, . . . *Liberation,* p. 233.
50. Alves, . . . *Human Hope,* pp. 95, 96.

unqualified eschatology that arises out of the present and concrete historical struggles. God's future is in the present, but only as "hope and promise," for God's kingdom is, likewise, present in the now, but not in its perfect form. But if the present cannot mediate God's kingdom in its absoluteness, neither can the future reveal its final definitive character. The future kingdom exists, in other words, to the extent that there is hope, and hope can only emerge from the now, from one's commitment to historical praxis.

CHURCH, MISSION, AND EVANGELIZATION. Salvation, it has been noted, is viewed among liberation theologians in strict historical categories, as political liberation. (It must be understood, of course, that by political they do not mean party politics, but commitment to the liberation of man from all sorts of oppression.) Further, Christ is said to be found present in all mankind. Conversion takes place only in relation to one's commitment to the transformation of human reality, while the future can only be perceived in relation to the historical now. In view of this, how do liberation theologians see the church, her missionary mandate, and the specific task of evangelization to be understood?

Consistent with their historical orientation, the theologians of liberation, particularly Gutiérrez, who is the most systematic of them, see the church as a means and not an end. Following Vatican II, Gutiérrez sees the church as a sacrament of salvation, or as a visible sign that points beyond herself to what salvation is all about. This has several implications.

For one, it means that to be consistent with her image as a sacrament/sign-bearer community, she should signify in her own internal structure the reality of salvation. And since salvation is understood as the liberation of man and history, this means that the church should witness through her life to God's presence in the struggles for liberation. In other words, the church must be a place of liberation in her concrete existence.[51]

---

51. Cf. Gutiérrez, *Ibid.,* p. 261.

Second, the fact that the church is understood as a sign-bearer community implies that she has no meaning in herself except in the measure in which she is able "to signify the reality in function for which [she] exists."[52] This means that the church has a provisional character. She is oriented toward the reality of the kingdom of God, present in history in God's liberating action among men.

Third, it follows from the latter that the church is to be understood dynamically and not spacially. The church is basically a calling, a vocation. Since basically all mankind has been saved in Christ, the idea of vocation and special service is the only way that the church can be distinguished from the world. The biblical concepts of the people of God and of salvation history are thus qualified by the notion of mission. All mankind must be understood as the people of God, and all history must be understood as a general history of salvation. Within this history, however, there is a particular history which serves a diaconate function.[53] This history is the history of Israel and the church. The latter is called to a particular task, to be a witness to the reality of God's Word as it breaks forth in history. "The Church," says Gutiérrez,

> is humanity itself attentive to the Word. It is the People of God which lives in history and is oriented toward the future promised by the Lord. It is, as Teilhard de Chardin said, the "reflective Christian portion of the world."[54]

The church is, therefore, mission, a responsive community to God's action, always *in via,* pointing through her existence to the reality of salvation in history. This action takes at least three forms, namely, celebration, denunciation, and annunciation.

The church points to the reality of salvation by cele-

---

52. *Ibid.*
53. Cf. Assmann, *Ibid.,* pp. 150, 151.
54. Gutiérrez, *Ibid.,* p. 261.

brating with joy the gift of the salvific action of God in humanity through participation in the Eucharist. This celebration becomes a vivid dramatization of what has been achieved in Christ—human liberation and brotherhood—to which the church addresses herself in the binomial denunciation-annunciation which takes place in the *historical praxis* of the Christian community.[55]

By denunciation is meant the stance the church must take against the present state of social injustice. This is the negative side of the church's missionary task. It represents the necessary confrontation that must take place wherever the gospel is proclaimed. Accordingly, the denunciation "is achieved by confronting a given situation with the reality which is *announced* . . ."[56] The reality which is proclaimed is the gospel.

What does it mean to preach the gospel? According to Gutiérrez, the gospel is the good news of the presence of God's love "in the historical becoming of mankind." He adds:

> To preach the Good News is for the Church to be a sacrament of history, to fulfill its role as community—a sign of the convocation of all men by God. It is to announce the coming of the Kingdom. The Gospel message reveals, without any evasions, what is at the root of social injustice: the rupture of the brotherhood which is based on our sonship before the Father; the Gospel reveals the fundamental alienation which lies below every other human alienation.[57]

This leads to the concept of evangelization. It has been shown how the theologians of liberation conceive of the experience of conversion (which is the product of evangelization) in political terms. Evangelization must also be seen in its political dimension, which has several aspects.

---

55. Cf. *Ibid.*, pp. 262, 263.
56. *Ibid.*, p. 268.
57. *Ibid.*, p. 269.

If to evangelize is to proclaim the good news against the reality of sin and from the perspective of God's action in Jesus Christ, then, they feel, to evangelize is to point out any situation of injustice and exploitation because it is incompatible with the gospel. This means that the proclamation of the gospel has "a politicizing function."[58] But Gutiérrez warns that such a function

> is made real and meaningful only by living and announcing the Gospel from within a commitment to liberation, only in concrete, effective solidarity with people and exploited social classes. Only by participating in their struggles can we understand the implications of the Gospel message and make it have an impact on history.[59]

These, in general terms, are the basic themes pertaining to the liberation-mission issue that run throughout the writings of the three theologians of liberation considered. Our remaining task is to evaluate them in terms of their own internal arguments, in the light of our understanding of the Scripture and the reality of the church's missionary praxis.

AN APPRAISAL OF THE THEOLOGY OF LIBERATION

A CHALLENGE. Needless to say, and apart from any criticism we may have of its theological assertions, the theology of liberation poses a tremendous challenge to contemporary missiology. For evangelicals, this challenge becomes even more serious given its biblical content. Here is a theology whose biblical integrity must be highly questioned and challenged by evangelicals and later on I will be pointing out some of its biblical deficiencies. And

---

58. *Ibid.*
59. *Ibid.*

yet, I believe, in at least two areas it proves to be closer to biblical thought than the traditional theologies of mission.[60]

A missiology which takes seriously man's concrete historical situation. The insistence on the concrete historical situation as a necessary starting point is perhaps the greatest merit of the theology of liberation—and its greatest challenge for the theology of mission. Because it challenges the naivete of so much mission thinking today, which assumes that it is possible to do theology, on the one hand, without being committed politically, and on the other, without taking seriously one's concrete historical situation. The insistence of the theology of liberation on the political dimension of faith and on theologizing out of commitment to a historical praxis dismantles *the "ideology" of the status quo* and uncovers an implied docetic worldview. For the fact of the matter is that our respective life situations have a political character. They each have a "what for?" which confronts us with ethical decisions. The notion of neutrality is an implicit commitment to the *status quo* (the existing order). To affirm our Christian faith, or missiologically, to think in terms of our missionary responsibility to the world without considering the concrete conflictive situation of the world—of which we ourselves are part—is to be ahistorical and thus docetic.

Biblical Christian faith has a historical character. Its message is firmly rooted in a concrete historical situation. Thus John's insistence on the fact of the incarnation. His is perhaps the most missionary-oriented Gospel (cf. Jn. 20:30, 31) and its one supreme truth is that in Jesus of Nazareth God became flesh! God chose to come to man in a concrete historical situation: Jesus, the incarnate Word, dwelt in a determined place, lived in a given historical

---

60. For two good examples of a traditional evangelical theological approach to mission, see Harold Lindsell, *An Evangelical Theology of Missions* (Grand Rapids: Zondervan, 1970) and George W. Peters, *A Biblical Theology of Missions* (Chicago: Moody Press, 1972). Both of these texts share the absence of a serious interaction with the concrete historical situation and the diaconate dimension of salvation and the church.

moment, and was born into a specific people and culture. And out of this profound identification with a specific historical context, Jesus wrought the redemption of mankind. In other words, he brought good news in the context of suffering humanity. Such a unique contextualization of God surely involved also the political situation of the Palestine of Jesus' day. As José María Abreü, a Venezuelan evangelical student of the New Testament, has so ably said in his study on the Gospel of John:

> . . . the Incarnation has a profound political meaning. It establishes a relation between the eternal and the temporality of each political situation. The Incarnation speaks to us about God's commitment in Jesus Christ: God commits himself to the historical realization of his plan of salvation. Such commitment is framed within a given political situation and is assumed by Jesus Christ himself: a country occupied by a foreign power in whose hands he was to suffer a violent death for the redemption of the world.[61]

To be sure, Jesus did not join one of the several political parties of his day. Neither did he start a party of his own. He never played the role of a party politician. On the contrary, he stayed away from party politics.[62]

But the fact that he was the Word of God made flesh; the fact that he was the incarnation of truth; the fact that he claimed to give meaning to history: all these made his presence in Palestine a unique political event, because it challenged the universal pretensions of the Roman Empire. Thus, while avoiding involvement in party politics, Jesus nevertheless took a political position. He relativized the

---

61. José María Abreü, "Un enfoque político al Evangelio Según San Juan," p. 36. (For the full biographical information of this work, see p. 73 of the present volume).

62. Cf. Oscar Cullman, *Jesús y los revolucionarios de su tiempo,* translated from the French by Eloy Requena (Madrid: Studium, 1971). Martin Hengel, *Was Jesus a Revolutionist?,* translated from the German by William Klassen (Philadelphia: Fortress Press, 1971).

authority of the Empire and of any earthly kingdom by underlining their temporal character and their corrupt moral nature. As Abreü points out:

> The very nature of the kingship of Jesus Christ is the light, the truth, the frank openness of love ($\alpha\gamma\acute{\alpha}\rho\eta$). The world, in turn, has to have its being in the darkness. For this reason, the kingship of Jesus cannot be of this world. Pilate cannot understand this, because he is not in the truth; he does not belong to the sphere of that which is open to God. He is rather in falsehood, in [mere] resemblance of power (19:11). Pilate represents the Empire; he is closed to the light of the Logos. Therefore, the Empire is also in falsehood, in [mere] resemblance and in darkness. And so long as it is a sphere hostile to God, it cannot belong to God's world. Under no circumstances is the Empire an absolute power. Rome must forget about the project of universal domain.[63]

Jesus not only challenged the universal claims of the Empire and underlined its corrupt moral nature. His political option involved also an identification with those who were the victims of the powerful and the mighty. He took sides with the weak and destitute. He emptied himself, Paul says, and took the form of a servant. He did not stand alongside the haughty and rich (cf. Lk. 6:24-26). Rather he stood on the side of the hungry, thirsty and naked, strangers and prisoners, harlots and publicans.[64] All these fall in the category of the "poor," for they have no one to stand on their side. They are the prototype of the heirs of the kingdom (cf. Lk. 6:20-22; Mt. 5:3). Little wonder that Jesus described his mission in terms of preaching good news to the poor, proclaiming release to the captives, and

---

63. Abreü, ". . . San Juan", pp. 71, 72.

64. Here it must be borne in mind that while the publicans were identified with the mighty, they were nevertheless exploited by the Empire. The picture the Gospels give us of them is that they were the victims of a corrupt, oppressive system (cf. Mt. 9:9-13; Lk. 18:9-14; 19:1-10).

recovering of sight to the blind, setting at liberty those who are oppressed and proclaiming the acceptable year of the Lord (Lk. 4:18, 19).

This is congruent with his own servant character and with his humiliation unto death. By humbling himself unto death, by following the course of powerlessness, by choosing the cross, Jesus identified himself vicariously with the suffering of the weak and destitute and opened the way to their exaltation, uplift, and salvation. At the cross, the triumph of the powerful became in reality their defeat, and the defeat of the oppressed became their triumph over the oppressor. Jesus stood on the side of those who suffered spiritually, socially, economically, politically, and culturally.[65]

For this reason, the way of salvation will always be the way of the cross. They who wish to enter God's kingdom must become poor in spirit, i.e., weak, destitute, humble,

---

65. Abreü, in ". . . San Juan," p. 24, 25ff., makes two important observations about the cultural dimension of the Christ event. First, the incarnation (understood in its larger context, as encompassing the life, ministry, and work of Christ), was a racial event. "Jesus was a Jew, a truly authentic Jew, and was a Jew fully identified with the culture and the time that his country had to live. This racial particularity . . . was a scandal for Greeks and Romans." Second, the incarnation was also a linguistic event and as such it carries several political implications.

   . . . The Gospels present an unquestionable fact: that the Christ event took place and was transmitted in certain determined languages. . .

   It is extremely interesting to notice that only the Gospel of John records the threefold inscription on the cross (19: 20)—as if John would want to tell us that there, on the top of Mount Calvary, God was giving himself to men in three cultures. Thus, the threefold inscription is a graphic witness of the cultural nature of the incarnation . . .

   This threefold inscription—in Hebrew (in reality it refers to Aramean (= Aramaic), Latin and Greek—join the three cultural traditions that formed the spirit of Christianity. On the one hand is the historical continuity with the people of Israel (1:17). On the other is the linguistic atmosphere in which the apostolic message was proclaimed and which results in the New Testament. And in the middle, Latin, remembering the presence of the foreign invader, the cultural imposition of the Empire, which put its seal of approval on the dead body of Jesus of Nazareth.

and open before God. And likewise, they who enter must *show forth* their commitment to Christ by being merciful and kind to those who suffer. They must stand on the side of justice (cf. Mt. 25:31ff.; Lk. 10:25ff.; Js. 1:26ff.). "Blessed are those who are persecuted for righteousness' sake, for theirs is the kingdom of heaven" (Mt. 5:10).

Therefore, when the theologians of liberation insist on the political dimensions of the gospel and on the necessity of theologizing out of commitment to the concrete historical situation of the downtrodden, they are in fact calling us, *at this one point,* back to the heart of biblical theology. They are challenging us to evaluate the political perspective of our missiology. Is it a justification for a system of domination and oppression, or is it an outgrowth of commitment to the well-being of man in obedience to the God who demands justice, who at the cross took the side of the weak and destitute and commands his people to follow his example?

In many instances the missionary enterprise has been used as a justification and a cover for the domination of people. The interrelation between mission, technology, and imperialism is well known. The expansionistic ambitions of militarily and economically powerful countries have always been accompanied by missionary interest. Thus, in ancient history the conquest of a people was followed by their religious indoctrination. This became the *modus operandi* in the West during the Constantinian age.

Kosuke Koyama describes the arrival of Christianity in Asian soil back in the 16th century with the expression "gun and ointment."[66] The same people who brought the ointment of the gospel brought the gun and vice versa. One justified and supported the other. Mission was in reality an instrument of domination. The same can be said about Africa and Latin America.

The situation continues even today between the al-

---

66. Kosuke Koyama, " 'Gun' and 'Ointment' in Asia," in *The Future of the Christian World Mission,* William J. Kanker and Wi Jo Kang, eds. (Grand Rapids: Eerdmans, 1971), pp. 43ff.

liance of a great sector of the international business community and the missionary enterprise. The gun is embedded in the economic domination of the North Atlantic while the ointment that accompanies it is a supposedly politically neutral missionary enterprise.

Not only does the theology of liberation challenge missionary theory and praxis to take seriously the political dimension of the missionary situation by evaluating its own political stance (its justification of the *status quo* through the policy of nonpolitical commitment), but also by insisting on the incarnational character of the gospel. If mission is to be faithful to the gospel it purports to communicate, it must be undergirded by a theology grounded on serious commitment to mankind in its many situations. Such a theology must have at least three characteristics: unfeigned love, faith that acts, and creative hope.

Unfeigned love is sincere and completely committed to others. It has its foundation in God's love toward man, a love that proved itself all-encompassing through the precious gift of God's only begotten Son. His was a love which did not count the cost, a love not shaken even by the reality of hell.

The missionary enterprise must be grounded on such a love. This means that it must go all-out in search for man, not *merely* to prepare him for the future, but to help him cope with his existential problems here and now. It must be a love verified by concrete acts of solidarity with all men in their historical struggles. It is one thing to theorize about one's all-out commitment to others; it is another thing to go all the way out to where they are, to live, stand, and struggle with them in their struggles for freedom and dignity. So much mission work today is done from the top balcony. Too much Christian love is wrapped up in beautiful words. Too much charity is covered up by superficial handouts. We need a theology of mission characterized by the praxis of an unconditional love toward people in their concrete historical situation.

Further, we need a theology of mission characterized by *faith that acts*. Faith is acceptance of, trust in, and committal to God. Faith that acts is unconditionally committed in praxis to everything that God is committed to. It does not rationalize Scripture; it accepts its precepts at face value. It is always willing to go the second mile on behalf of man, especially the poor and the afflicted. It is willing to denounce injustice at whatever cost. In short, it is willing to do *anything that Jesus would do for man.*

There is no doubt that in the history of the missionary movement many have lived such a faith. Many today are acting out their faith in very difficult missionary situations. Yet an objective look at the missionary praxis of the church throughout the world will reveal that in a great number of situations—more than we evangelicals would like to admit—a faith incarnated in the life struggles of people is far from a reality. It is time we evangelicals start sounding off on the imperative of *orthopraxis,* instead of spending *all* our time defending right doctrine. Orthodoxy is no guarantee of *orthopraxis,* as Jacob Spener[67] and the Pietist movement taught us. It is not even a guarantee of missionary zeal! The latter comes only from serious, loving, all-out commitment to God *and* man.

Third, we need a theology of mission grounded on dynamic, *creative hope.* Such hope would fulfill a twofold function. On the one hand, it would serve as catalyst to open up horizons filled with unlimited possibilities for the kingdom of God. On the other, it would be an incentive to action in present struggles. Such an eschatological conception of mission is possible only from the perspective of the extension of the kingdom of God among men as the goal of mission. We know that the kingdom, while it is present, is yet to come in its fullness. Accordingly, our work for the kingdom should involve at once our creative involvement in the transformation of life and society and the annunciation of a new world as evidence ("firstfruits") of the new age inaugurated by Jesus and as guarantee of the promised future.

---

67. See Phillip Jacob Spener, *Pia Desideria* (Philadelphia: Fortress Press, 1964).

Evangelicals have been surrounded by a completely other-worldly oriented eschatology. This has led to a message oriented to the "beyond" and to an escapist missionary praxis. Mission has been seen in terms of escaping the coming judgment. It has been involved in the proclamation of a hope meaningless for the here-and-now: a hope that is historically alienating and theologically distorted because it fails to take seriously the "now" and to understand the dynamics of the future kingdom. Admittedly, Scripture points toward a definitive, historical moment when God's kingdom will become a definite and final reality. This future kingdom, however, is already manifesting itself in the present. Consequently, its influence over the "now" is always dynamic and creative. It challenges and questions it. At the same time, the present reality of the kingdom is a hope-generating agent which operates in the church in a way that leads her to transcend situations of frustration and apparent defeat and to see new possibilities for the future.

This involves a present pregnant with hope and a future that activates the present. It also implies a Lord who is present in the church in mission, (1) participating in her efforts to share in word and deed the good news of the kingdom; (2) empowering her to overcome frustration and unbelief by opening her eyes so that by faith in God's promises she can see the horizon of his future drawing near; and (3) stirring up Christians to action in their concrete historical situations.

This is the kind of creative, dynamic hope that ought to undergird our theology of mission. Such undergirding would serve as a corrective for the ever-present temptation to escape to the "beyond" and to use the coming kingdom as an excuse to sit, wait, and do nothing about the "now." Such a hope reveals God as already active in the world and working toward the transformation of life. Further, it serves as a corrective for those who either become frustrated with the contradictions of life or overly enthusiastic with short-range victories—forgetting that more is to come, that history will not end with a victory of the forces of injustice, oppression, exploitation, with the frustrated efforts of those who are struggling for a better world. Such hope allows the church to renew her strength, to mount up with wings as an eagle, to run and not be weary, to continue her pilgrim march and not faint (cf. Is. 40:31).

A service-oriented salvation and a salvation-oriented church. A second challenge posed by the theology of liberation has to do with the perspective of service in which it puts both salvation and the church. Obviously, from the point of view of Scripture, there is more to salvation and the church than the idea of service. Yet this is one dimension that missionary theology and praxis have often left untouched. Salvation has often been conceived of as a personal gift and thus a *private* possession. The church, as the community of the saved ones, has been thought of as the gathering of those who have "their ticket to heaven." We tend to forget, as the theologians of liberation rightly point out, that salvation is not so much a prize won as a responsibility given. Without its "for what?" salvation is meaningless. Even the notion of holiness, which is understood in both the Old and New Testament as a definite fruit of salvation (as has been shown in a previous chapter), is conceived of in terms of a "setting apart" for service.

What makes the theology of liberation's insistence on the diaconate function of salvation challenging is the way it defines service in terms of liberation and solidarity, rather than as something which one does for someone else, as it is usually understood. In other words, to be saved is to be free to stand in solidarity with one's neighbor and to participate with him in his struggle for liberation.

Even if one's view of grace forces him to raise questions about concepts such as "self-liberation" and "self-creation," he cannot help but admire the idea of service as standing with people at the point of their inner and social conflicts and participating with them in their struggles for justice. To think of salvation in these terms is biblical: Scripture is permeated with passages that speak of expressing God's love by standing with people in need. The story of the Good Samaritan, the discourse on the judgment of the nations, John's insistence on loving one's neighbor, James's emphasis on the visitation of orphans and widows in their afflictions: these are just a few cases where the New Testament stands with the Old Testament in its insistence on doing justice as evidence of knowing the Lord.

Together with the diaconate concept of salvation is the idea of the church as a sign-bearer of salvation. The church is primarily a "showcase" of salvation. The church best demonstrates her salvation by being herself a place for liberation. What a challenge to the church's involvement in evangelism and church growth! What a difference it would make if the church, instead of transmitting a gospel of repression, subjugation, and alienation, as she has often done, would communicate a liberating gospel which restores people to their humanity, puts them on the road to creativity, and involves them in the struggle for justice and peace! What a difference it would make if national churches, local congregations, and missionary societies, instead of producing lopsided congregations subjugated to the *status quo* and engaged in the proclamation of salvation as a ticket to heaven, would plant liberated communities of believers who relate the claims and demands of the gospel to their concrete historical situation and work toward a more just and humane society! The worship of such congregations would be a celebration of the triumph of the gospel in their particular culture and historical struggles. Their evangelistic endeavors would turn out to be acts of liberation. In short, their everyday life, deeds, and verbal witness would be truly good news of salvation to a lost, oppressed, and alienated humanity. It would mean the dismantling of Marx's devastating concept of religion as an opiate of society!

A WARNING. Yet for all its challenging characteristics, the postulates of the theologians of liberation raise serious theological questions. Harvey Cox, in his Foreword to *A Theology of Human Hope,* says that for Alves "ideas are weapons whose truth is discovered only as they are used in combat." Weapons, however, are always dangerous and sometimes they explode in your own hands.[68] This I think is a good description of the theology of liberation: it is a tremendous weapon in the hands of the Third World vis-à-vis the rich affluent world of the North Atlantic. But it is an equally dangerous weapon for the Third World itself, which represents not only the lands of exploitation, oppression, and repression, but that part of the world in which millions of people have yet to be confronted with the gospel of God's kingdom. Thus, while the emergence of the theology of liberation constitutes one of the greatest contemporary challenges to the missionary enterprise, it also poses some dangers and a warning to those of us from the Third World who may be attracted by its commitment to the struggle for social justice and its sharp biblical, theological, and missiological insights.

The dangerous consequences of a situational hermeneutic. If the insistence of the theology of liberation on the necessity of taking seriously the concrete historical situation as a primary frame of reference is its greatest merit, it is also its greatest danger. For it insists on the situation as the "text" on which theology, understood as a critical reflection on the present historical praxis, is grounded. The Bible, tradition, the teaching of the church, history of doctrine, etc., are secondary frames of reference. The historical situation is, in other words, the only normative element in the hermeneutics of the theology of liberation.

However, if the biblical text has only a comparative, descriptive function, how can the theology of liberation be sure of maintaining the distinctiveness of the Christian faith? Isn't there the danger of falling into theological syncretism? This is an important question, given the insistence of Assmann on the necessary presence of the Christian faith in a critical reflection on praxis in order for the latter to be theological.

In the last chapter, the Frankfurt Declaration was criticized for refusing to consider the historical situation as a

---

68. Harvey Cox, "Foreword" in Alves, . . . *Human Hope*, p. ix.

primary frame of reference. Now the theology of liberation must be criticized for refusing to consider Scripture a primary frame of reference *together* with the situation.

Admittedly, the difference in time-space between the biblical text and our historical moment makes it necessary that it be mediated by scientific tools. The many variables that one must cope with limit his encounter with the text. This would militate against the normativeness of the text, if it weren't for the fact (of faith) that the truth of Scripture does not lie in the findings of biblical scholarship as much as in the authority of Christ and in the witnessing presence of the Holy Spirit. Since the Holy Spirit is the Spirit of the risen Lord and since Christ is not only the central theme to Scripture but the ground of its authority and the key to its understanding, it follows that he is the one who mediates the truth of the Word in history.

Only a hermeneutic that takes seriously the authority of the Word of Christ mediated through the witnessing presence of the Holy Spirit can assume the preservation of the distinctiveness of the Christian faith. Without the norm of Scripture (the canon), the Christian faith runs the risk of losing itself in the concrete situation or emerging out of it amalgamated with other non-Christian ideas.

In the case of the theology of liberation, the danger of syncretism lies in the ideological postulates of the scientific methodology used to analyze the situation. While it cannot be denied that any methodology is committed to an ideology, and that therefore the best methodology is one with an ideology that favors the oppressed in their struggle for liberation, it is possible, nevertheless, that the primacy which is given to the analysis of the situation may result in the infiltration of foreign ideas into the *Christian faith*. This danger arises because the so-called Christian presence in the process of critical reflection does not have anything to test itself by to make sure it is maintaining this identity and not confusing itself with the ideological postulates of the methodology used (which may be totally foreign to the faith).

The issue becomes even more alarming when we realize that the theology of liberation rejects from the start the possibility of going directly to the heart of Christianity,[69] *i.e.,* to its original sources. This would seem to imply that Christianity has been influenced by so many ideas that about all we can have is a very limited perception of what it is all about. Hence it is quite possible that from the beginning of the critical reflective process the Christian perspective is so intoxicated that syncretism may not be a "dangerous consequence" but a fact. Thus, the failure to take seriously the biblical text puts the content of the presence of the Christian faith in the critical reflection about praxis on very shaky ground.

The fallacy of a Spirit-emptied Christology. A second problem with the theology of liberation has to do with the absence of a doctrine of the Holy Spirit. Just as the action of the Spirit is not taken into consideration in the treatment and interpretation of Scripture, so its Christology is virtually empty of any reference to the Holy Spirit. This leads to the contention that

> any Christ *a priori,* before the salvific act lived in history, can very easily result in a pre-fabricated Christ, possessed beforehand, therefore, previous

---

69. In a very important passage, Assmann (*Opresión-liberación . . .*, pp. 62, 63) says quite frankly:
   If it is impossible to go directly to the "heart of Christianity," because the latter only exists in mediating concretizations; if the Bible itself is not a text of direct criteria, but rather the history of successive configurations of these criteria always partial and dialectically conflictive in themselves; if the conjunction of act and word is essential to the conception of Revelation; more, if all of it reached us formed, deformed, reformed and deformed again by the concrete history of Christianity, and if within these circumstantial contextures of history and dogmas, ecclesiastical law and pastoral [theology] are verbalized, how is it possible to speak with such simplicity about a criterion "in the light of faith"? How can [one] speak so candidly of the Gospel, when there is so much truth in what a Christian committed in the struggle was saying to me on one occasion: The Bible? It doesn't exist. The only thing that exists is the sociological Bible of what appears all around us as Christian!

and sometimes placed before and opposed to the facts, which means, purely and simply: not real.[70]

In other words, any reference to the biblical Christ (the man Christ Jesus) can only be made after one's encounter with him in the neighbor. To speak of Christ before that moment is to run the risk of referring to a prefabricated Christ who may be an unreal Christ.

Such a contention faces us with a similar problem to the one previously discussed. If the man Christ Jesus is not a norm, how can I really determine the validity of the "Christ" I discover in the neighbor? After all, I can have encounters with my neighbor in which the "anti-Christ" rather than Christ is present (e.g., the neighbor as an oppressor, who is also oppressed, but who refuses to acknowledge this fact, and thus rejects the moment of salvation). Further, the New Testament explicitly claims a link between Jesus of Nazareth and the Christ of faith, and this link is attributed both to valid and convincing testimonies of eyewitnesses (cf. Acts 1:11) and the witnessing action of the Holy Spirit. In fact, it is impossible to know Christ, even in the neighbor, except through the witness of the Holy Spirit (e.g., cf. Mt. 16:17; 1 Cor. 12:3 and other passages). Accordingly, if it is true that Christ is often present in the neighbor, it is also true that his presence, at least from the perspective of Scripture, is attributed to the witness of the Spirit. Thus Christ is mediated through the Spirit and not through the neighbor. Admittedly, at times *the witness of the Spirit is* mediated through the neighbor, *i.e.,* the Spirit makes Christ present through the neighbor, but he also uses the mediation of the word, the sacraments, providence, etc.

To say, then, that Christ is mediated through man alone is, from the point of view of the New Testament, a fallacy. Consequently, if it is true that an *a priori* Christ can be a fabricated Christ, it must also be asserted that an *a posteriori* Christ can be a distortion beyond recognition of the

---

70. *Ibid.,* p. 157.

biblical Christ. For what makes the biblical Christ real is not an *a priori* or an *a posteriori* reference but the man Christ Jesus, risen and crowned Lord over all things and made present through the Holy Spirit acting sovereignly *in* the world. A Spirit-emptied Christology is like a Christ-emptied Bible: neither can be understood.

The result of an anthropocentric theology. A third problem lies in the anthropological orientation of the theology of liberation. Man in his historical praxis is the *locus* of theology. Christ is defined in terms of man, as he who is present in the neighbor. The church is viewed as part of the world of man. Above all, salvation is seen in terms of man's liberation from anything that keeps him from creating a new world. In short, theology itself is defined, in the words of Gustavo Gutiérrez, as "man's critical reflection on himself, on his own basic principles."[71] Such an orientation would seem to have a definite negative effect on the Christian doctrine of grace.

Alves, however, appears to take a positive view of grace. For him, the difference between humanistic messianism (*e.g.,* Marxism) and messianic humanism (*e.g.,* biblical faith) is the fact that for the former the task of humanization is the result of man's sole effort while for the latter it is conceived of as a gift. He builds on the Protestant doctrine of grace in its critique of all movements that are dominated by the messianic obsession about what man can do through his activity and on the affirmation of God's grace as liberating us from anxiety and fear for the future.[72] He criticizes classical Protestantism for being inconsistent with this affirmation, because "it concluded that there was no room for human creativity in history. Grace, instead of making man free for creativity, makes creativity superfluous or impossible. Work is therefore not a tool to be used in creating the new, but rather an expression of obedience to the command of the One who was the only creator."[73]

---

71. Gutiérrez, . . . *Liberation,* p. 11.
72. Alves, . . . *Human Hope,* p. 142.
73. *Ibid.*

Without entering into the validity of Alves's interpretation of Protestantism, let us see where this takes him. He says that it is necessary to preserve both grace and creativity. Hence he concludes that "salvation is achieved through a politics in which God makes man free to create."[74] Elsewhere he states:

> God's grace, instead of making human creativity superfluous or impossible, is therefore the politics that makes it possible and necessary. This is so because in the context of the politics of human liberation man encounters a God who remains open, who has not yet arrived, who is determined and helped by human activity. God needs man for the creation of his future.[75]

Note that while salvation is conceived of in terms of an act of grace, God is seen as needing man to help him create the future. We have here a sophisticated new form of Pelagianism. In Pelagianism, grace is what makes possible the forgiveness of sin to those who believe. But after this, grace has no meaning, because man can do everything himself.[76] In Alves, however, grace is what makes possible man's freedom to create. It liberates him from the anxiety of the past and the fear of the future. Man thus is set free to *help God* build the future.

The problem with this view is that it makes God dependent on man. God is so historicized that he loses his otherness. Salvation is a process which is only partially dependent on God's grace.[77] Man thus "earns" his future in part through his work.

For Alves, the latter is the only alternative between the two extremes: humanistic messianism, which has no no-

74. *Ibid.,* p. 144.

75. *Ibid.,* p. 136.

76. Cf. Paul Tillich, *A Complete History of Christian Thought,* edited by Carl E. Braaten (New York: Harper and Row, 1968), p. 125.

77. See Gutiérrez, . . . *Liberation,* pp. 159, 160.

tion of the gift of grace, and classical Protestantism, which does have a clear notion of the gift of grace but reduces work to a mere preparation for death (Luther), an act of "obedience" (Calvin), a "valuable safety valve" (Harnack), or an "extracurricular activity" (Barth).[78] Alves's alternative, however, ends up reducing grace to an initial act and God to a mere participation in a partnership. The new creation, which in the New Testament is a salvific concept, is seen by Alves as a cooperative enterprise in which God reduces himself to being man's co-worker.

It seems to me, however, that in Scripture God doesn't appear as needing man, but as one who in love gives himself to man. In his grace, he has willed that man work the earth. Work is, then, a gift of creation. In the exercise of this gift man becomes a co-worker with God. This is both a privilege and an opportunity that God offers man to find fulfillment *as man*. It is a new opportunity for man to be man, that is, God's viceroy, and to respond to his love. When properly put into practice and understood, work becomes an act of worship and a ministry. God, however, remains God and man remains man. Further, man continues to depend on God for strength and wisdom, and ultimately it is God himself who is responsible for the completion of creation. Thus man is a co-worker but God still remains *the Worker*. Without his sustaining grace man cannot function.

Rather than reducing work to a mere preparation for death, an act of "obedience," a "valuable safety valve," or an "extracurricular activity," Scripture sees it as an opportunity for man to participate with God in the building of the new creation, and thus to fulfill his vocation as God's viceroy. It maintains man's ever-dependence on God's grace and God's sovereign rule over creation. While Scripture does not stop man's creativity, neither does it put it on an equal footing with God.

The danger of a qualitatively defined salvation. The theology of liberation lights a fourth warning light. This has

---

78. Cf. Alves, . . . *Human Hope,* pp. 142, 143.

to do with its preoccupation with the qualitative dimension of salvation. As has been observed, this leads the theologians of liberation to an absolute universalistic salvation, an all-inclusive salvation. All men are saved, whether they know it or not. The question now is whether they are going to take advantage of this salvation wrought by Christ for their "self-creation" or not.

This is where the theology of liberation reveals its *partial* support from Scripture. For while it acknowledges the fact that the New Testament teaches the "for allness" of salvation, *i.e.,* salvation as an offer to all men, it fails to take into account the equally valid teaching that salvation is not appropriated automatically but through an act of faith, and that those who do not respond in faith to the good news of salvation remain in their trespasses and sins. To put it in the words of the Gospel of John: "He who believes in the Son has eternal life; he who does not obey the Son shall not see life, but the wrath of God rests upon him" (Jn. 3:36).

The problem of absolute universalism has been with the church ever since the days of Origen. Many arguments have been offered pro and con.[79] It is not my intention to enter into the controversy except to point out that ultimately the issue hinges on the reality of the gospel, the seriousness with which the New Testament treats the communication of the gospel, and especially the inescapable fact, as noted above, that the New Testament teaches both a salvation made available to all and a judgment which continues upon all who reject this offer.

As to this last item we need not enter into detail. A multitude of passages teach directly and indirectly, explicitly or implicitly the universality of salvation *and* the certainty of coming judgment. The "narrow gate" saying of Jesus (Lk. 13:23f.), the Johannine passages that deal with the universality of both God's love and his wrath (Jn. 3:16, 36, etc.), the universal reconciliation and judg-

---

79. For a good summary of the problem, see G. C. Berkouwer, *The Return of Christ* (Grand Rapids: Eerdmans, 1972), pp. 387ff.

ment passages in Paul (cf. 1 Tim. 4:10; 2 Thess. 1:9), the warnings of the epistle to the Hebrews (Heb. 2:2f.; 4:1ff., etc.), and the story of the judgment day in Rev. 19:11ff.[80] suffice as examples.

In addition to this evidence, the gospel itself points to the possibility of judgment. Earlier in this volume it was said that the content of the gospel stems from the postponement of God's wrath for a time (known only to him) and the revelation in Christ of God's gift of grace. This implies both a positive and a negative side to the gospel. The positive side is the declaration of God's gift of grace and the postponement of the coming judgment. The negative side has to do with the fact that God's final wrath has been *postponed, not revoked.* Thus the gospel *always* leads to a call to repentance. If all are saved, if there is no judgment, why call people to turn from their wickedness? Why does the element of judgment appear in almost all the sermons recorded in the Book of Acts? Why does John emphasize the terrible peril of unbelief? Why does Paul equate not knowing God with failure to obey the gospel and state bluntly that those who disobey the gospel will suffer the wrath of God (cf. 2 Thess. 1:8)?

This leads to a brief consideration of the seriousness of the communication of the gospel to those who have not responded in faith to its announcement. On the one hand, mission results from the moral and existential failure of the human race and, on the other, from the abounding love of a creator who is also judge of the world. This God who is all-compassionate does not wish that any should perish. He is willing to postpone his final judgment and provide the way so that man can be forgiven of his moral and existential failure, have abundant life, and thus triumph over the power of sin and death. Mission represents the urgency of this tension: a lost race and a searching God. This is why the Gospels describe the task of mission as an im-

---

80. For a fair treatment of many of these salvation-judgment passages in the findings and arguments of many outstanding contemporary exegetes and theologians, see *Ibid.,* pp. 403-413.

perative. No option is here available to the church; to be the church signifies commitment to this enterprise. This is also the reason why the communication of the gospel is not simply an informative task but a passionate plea, like that of Paul (cf. 2 Cor. 5:20), for men to respond in faith to this unique opportunity which God is offering them to be liberated from their moral and existential failure and experience a creative, victorious, and fulfilled life.

But if all men are saved, why this missionary urgency? Why all this talk about the church's missionary responsibility to the world? In the New Testament, the experience of salvation is linked to the witness of the Spirit (cf. Rom. 8:12ff.). The same Spirit who operates in redeemed man operates in redeemed inanimate nature. If all men are already reconciled to God, wouldn't it be logical to think that Paul's statement about the Spirit witnessing to the redeemed man's spirit would be applicable to *all* men? In which case there would not be any need for the church as a sign-bearer of salvation, for all men would be made aware of their salvation by the Spirit.

The absolute universalism of the theology of liberation constitutes a serious warning for those who would be tempted to emphasize the qualitative dimension of salvation at the expense of the quantitative. Such an emphasis only distorts the seriousness with which the New Testament treats the problem of the lostness of *all* men, the possibility of their salvation, and God's passionate concern for their salvation as expressed in the cross of Christ and in the church's mandate for mission. It also pays no attention to the New Testament's stern warning about the perilous consequences of unbelief and the certainty of God's coming judgment.

The vagueness of an unqualified open future. As has been observed, the theology of liberation is grounded on an open eschatology. It holds to the tension between the now and the "not yet." The coming kingdom is that horizon always before us. In fact, the theologians of liberation are so committed to an absolutely open future that they wind up in vagueness and generalities. The weapon they use against Moltmann's treatment of the present, namely, a lack of preciseness about the present, explodes in their own hands. For they too are vague about the so-called "definitiveness" of the coming kingdom.

This vagueness about the future stems, I think, from the fact that in the theology of liberation hope emerges only out of the present. It is not grounded also on a God who is ahead, coming to us, and pulling us toward him, but on a God who has come along with us and is leading us to the future which is in the making. In other words, it is based on the incarnation and not on the resurrection. It is a prophetic future (because it projects itself from the present to what is yet to come) and not an apocalyptic future (which irrupts from the future to the present). In the theology of hope, however, hope is basically apocalyptic. It irrupts into the present from a God who is always ahead. The consequences of both approaches is vagueness about either the present or the future.

Both the prophetic and the apocalyptic vision seem to be supported in the New Testament. In the incarnation, God becomes man. This *kénosis* has its greatest expression in the struggle of the cross. Out of the feeling of forsakenness, however, emerges hope for the future ("Father, into your hands I commend my spirit"). Thus, the present is negated in the liberating action of the cross and pushed unto the certainty of God's future.

The resurrection, however, deals with the category of the future. It represents the future invading the present. Hence Christ is seen as the "firstfruits" of them that sleep.

These two eschatological visions are integrated in the ministry of the Spirit. On the one hand, he is the continuation of the incarnation, the one who makes Christ present in the concrete historical situations of life. On the other, he is the Spirit of promise.

Both paradigms may be also observed in the Revelation of John. There he was in Patmos, suffering on account of the Word of God and the testimony of Jesus with *patient endurance,* when he was caught up in the Spirit. The future invaded his present endurance (in hope) and he was invited to see what must still come to pass. Out of the vision of the future, John gained better perspective of his present situation. But likewise, his commitment to Jesus permitted him to endure patiently and thus to overcome the temptation to despair. He endured patiently because he refused to accept his present as determinative for his future. He was encouraged and was better prepared to go on saying "no" to the present and working toward the coming future because he was able to see what was coming to pass.

The Book of Revelation is not a blueprint for the future. It is, nevertheless, an interpretation of history from the perspective of a present which is negated and a future which is promised. It sets forth a kingdom already present,[81] but not in its fullness. It also describes in concrete terms the definite character of the coming kingdom, namely, God's *shalom,* a state of well-being in which the world of man and the world of nature will be at last reconciled by him who made them in the first place. Liberated from the sting of death, man will be able to live up to the fullest of his creative capacity. What we now have in part will become reality in its fullness.

For John of Patmos the final revelation of the future kingdom will come from outside of history. The revelation itself will take place *in* history. Nowhere does the apocalyptic vision of Patmos anticipate an end to history. Rather it implies the renewal and transformation of history. Hence the final reference to the new heavens and a new earth. Little wonder that John's response to Jesus' promise, "Surely I am coming soon," is a marveling, "Amen. Come, Lord Jesus!" No escapism here! It is rather a cry of hope uttered by faith. Such a cry must be translated in terms of commitment and action. For this reason the book ends with a benediction: "The grace of the Lord *be* with all the saints." Where? In their life struggles as witnesses to

---

81. See for example the reference to the kingdom in 1:9, the description of Jesus in 1:13ff., the reference to the seven churches in 2:1—3:22, and the struggle of the church in the tribulation in 4:1ff.

him who died and is alive for evermore and has the keys of death and hades, even Jesus the Christ.

Thus while the New Testament maintains the openness of the future (no one knows the hour nor the day, is a repeated warning), it qualifies it by a precise characterization of what is to be expected to come to pass. When the future is absolutely open, eschatology becomes nothing more than an "ideal" and thus falls into the category of vagueness and generalities.

These are some warning lights that I see in the theology of liberation. While it constitutes one of the most challenging contemporary theological reflections, especially for those of us who are part of the struggle of the Third World, it poses a serious warning to the church as she seeks to fulfill God's mission in the world. Its sharp insights on the mission-liberation issue make it very enticing. However, the price that a mission-minded and biblically oriented Christian must pay is too high.

We must not, however, throw aside its challenging insights simply because there is in it too much we simply cannot buy. We must have the courage to stand with the theologians of liberation in those things which are faithful to biblical revelation and which are congruent with the latter's vision of a just and humane society. Anything short of this is neither wise nor Christian. After all, we *are* commanded to be "wise as serpents", to "test everything" and "hold fast that which is good" (Mt. 10:16; 1 Thess. 5:21).

In conclusion, from the perspective of the mission-liberation issue, the theology of liberation represents a radicalization of the humanization imbedded in the Renewal in Mission report of Uppsala. Thus, without consciously planning it, the theology of liberation turned out to be a radical challenge to the missiology of Uppsala and a strong contender, in the measure that it became influential in the thinking of theologians and churchmen concerned about the meaning of salvation for the world and for the church's world-mission, to clash with the supporters of the line taken by the Frankfurt group at the 1973 World Conference on Salvation Today. In the following chapter, the documents of Bangkok 1973 are analyzed to see whether these two forces clashed and further polarized the contemporary Ecumenical Movement, as expected, or whether the Conference was able to transcend their radical differences and open the way for an understanding of mission in the context of the struggles for man's liberation which would not jeopardize the basic concerns of either of these positions. Above all, we attempt to evaluate the missiology of Bangkok 1973 in the light of the impending challenge of world mission.

11/MISSION AND THE LIBERATION OF MAN
Section 3/ Bangkok 1973 and Beyond

The World Conference on Salvation Today held in Bangkok, Thailand, from December 29, 1972, to January 9, 1973, marked the conclusion of a four-year worldwide Study coordinated by the Commission on Mission and Evangelism of the World Council of Churches. Study groups and discussions were held on all six continents, many of which produced written reports. Two consultations were held, one on the biblical concept of salvation and the other on the orthodox understanding of salvation. In addition, there was "a collection of texts illustrating the search for salvation which is going on today."[1] Individual papers were also

---

1. Jean Fraser, Steven Mackie, and Thomas Wiser, "Editorial," *The International Review of Mission*: Vol. LXI, No. 241 (January, 1972), p. 5.

written, many of which were published in the *International Review of Mission.*

The Study stimulated the publication of several books[2] as well as articles in such conservative-evangelical periodicals as *Christianity Today, Church Growth Bulletin* and *World Vision Magazine.* Such statements as the Frankfurt Declaration and the promotion given it around the world were meant to stir up sufficient pressure on the Conference so that either of two things would happen: (1) the Conference would shift radically toward a more conservative evangelical position (perhaps adopt the Frankfurt Declaration?), or (2) continue on the logical course of Uppsala and therefore leave conservative evangelicals with no other choice than once and for all to pull out of the organized ecumenical movement and create a new organism that would pick up the "lost pieces" of the old International Missionary Council.[3]

As we come into this last section of the mission-liberation issue we are interested in determining whether Bangkok further radicalized the theology of "humanization" imbedded in the Renewal in Mission Report of Uppsala (following more or less the line of the new theology of liberation). Likewise we are interested in determining whether Bangkok sought to present a balanced perspective on salvation, and consequently on the mission-liberation issue.

Such an undertaking requires interpretative analysis

2. In addition to those already referred to in previous chapters, see, for example, Donald McGavran, *Crucial Issues in Missions Tomorrow* (Chicago: Moody Press, 1972) and Peter Beyerhaus, *Shaken Foundations: Theological Foundations for Mission* (Grand Rapids: Zondervan, 1972).

3. This affirmation is based primarily on a between-the-lines interpretation of the latest writings of men like Beyerhaus and the dialectics that have characterized the relationship of anti-conciliar and pro-conciliar evangelicals in the past decades. With regard to this last point, see Arthur Glasser's interesting interpretation (referred to in chapter IX), in the *Evangelical Missions Quarterly,* of the stance of evangelicals in Great Britain and North America in relation to the ecumenical movement: "What Has Been the Evangelical Stance, New Delhi to Uppsala?" pp. 129ff.

of the testimonies of those who were present and have since given their own particular perspective on what took place there. Yet since everyone sees reality through his own "grid," it is imperative that the Conference first be allowed to speak for itself through its official documents.

THE THEME AND OBJECTIVES OF BANGKOK 1973

"Salvation Today" is perhaps one of the most important themes in contemporary world Christianity. In spite of the fact that the choice of the theme provoked some concern (especially on the part of those who, following the general line of the theologies of secularization so prevalent in the North Atlantic during the 60s, considered it a stumbling block to secular man), it nevertheless became apparent as the Study advanced that the theme was both timely and relevant. As stated in the January 1972 issue of the *International Review of Mission*: ". . . in the last two to three years not only the notion but the very word salvation has come to be used again more and more, not only in church circles but also in such secular contexts as newscasts and Broadway plays."[4] Thus at Bangkok, Thomas Wiser, director of the Study, could report:

> The choice of the theme was welcomed as a return to the essentials of the Christian faith and of mission, or it was understood as the challenge to make explicit, in the midst of missionary involvement in the world, the basis of the faith. It was furthermore found that in the dialogue with people of different religious faiths the notion of salvation, far from being a stumbling block, came into the center of the conversation as one of the points around which the dialogue could be clarified.[5]

---

4. Fraser, *et al.*, IRM, p. 5.
5. Thomas Wiser, "Report on the Study" (Bangkok: World Con-

To concentrate on the notion of salvation was a wise decision. First, because the big controversy at Uppsala had to do precisely with the meaning of salvation. Second, because in the last several years, the myth of secularization has been demythologized by several trends in Western religiosity: the revival of the occult, the fascination with eastern religions and cults, the Jesus Movement, and the resurgent interest in evangelism in mainline denominations. Third, because the church has to examine periodically the biblical understanding of salvation in order to fulfill faithfully her missionary mandate. And fourth, because the many situations in which contemporary man finds himself challenge Christians all over the world to reflect critically both on the ways by which people can experience salvation today and the specific ways by which the church should respond in her life and missionary action to these experiences.

In short, the theme of Bangkok was important not only because it dealt with one of the most crucial issues in the missionary mandate (what is the meaning of the salvation the church is sent to proclaim?), but also because it sought to explore the meaning of salvation *today,* in the light of the concrete historical situations of contemporary mankind.

This is further corroborated by the objectives of the Conference, which had a threefold aim:

    (1)   to celebrate and proclaim the richness of salvation as a gift of God through the Holy Spirit, as witnessed to by the Scriptures, and as experienced by men and women today, in their struggle for meaning and fullness of life and for social justice;

    (2)   to consider the implications of Salvation Today

---

ference on Salvation Today, December 29, 1972—January 8, 1973), (mimeograph), p. 2. For a published edition of the major documents, see *International Review of Mission,* Vol. LXII, No. 246 (April 1973).

for the churches and the ecumenical movement;
(3) to help participants and their sponsoring bodies to act on these implications.[6]

Note the liturgical, kerygmatic, missiological, scriptural, ecclesiastical, and praxeological character of these objectives.

The Conference was structured to be both a liturgical and kerygmatic event. It was meant to be a great celebration through which God's gift of salvation through the Holy Spirit would be proclaimed to the world. This was to be accomplished through worship services, Bible study groups, which would permit serious confrontation with the witness of Scripture, and discussion groups, which would engage in the analysis of the varied ways by which men and women are experiencing salvation in their life struggles.

Further, the Conference was to be a symposium on the implications of Salvation Today for the life and mission of the church, both in her local and worldwide manifestations. In other words, it was structured to create a critical reflective experience on the meaning of the missionary mandate today and its implications for the life and mission of individual Christians, local congregations, denominations, missionary and service agencies, and ecumenical bodies. This was to be accomplished through three general work sections which would encompass the following areas: I. *Culture and Identity* (with sub-sections on Dialogue with People of Living Faiths; Christian Identity and Racial Identity; and Cultural Change and Conversion); II. *Salvation and Justice* (with sub-sections on Violent Revolutionary Change; Economic Exploitation and National Planning; and Local Struggles); and III. *Churches Renewed in Mission* (with

---

6. Leon Howell, "Summary-Part I" (Bangkok: World Conference on Salvation Today, December 29, 1972—January 8, 1973), (mimeograph), p. 1. Henceforth, all references to the official summary statements will be identified by the following code: Bangkok I or II. Reference to the Sections' reports will be identified: Bangkok, Doc. 39, 40, or 41.

sub-sections on the Local Mission of Each Church; Growing Churches and Renewal; and Churches in Relationship).

Third, the Conference was designed with a praxeological orientation. That is, it was hoped that the activities planned would focus on the praxis of salvation and that the Conference would produce specific suggestions to implement the findings of the Study and the resolutions made at the Plenary Sessions at the level of each local situation.

Hence from the perspective of the theme and the established objectives, Bangkok had every reason to be looked upon with expectancy. Looking back to Bangkok we must now ask whether these objectives were met and whether the Conference lived up to its expectations.

THE STRUCTURE AND DYNAMICS OF BANGKOK 1973

Bangkok was so organized as to allow for maximum participation. For the first time in an ecumenical missionary conference the Third World had an equal representation, although many Latin Americans felt they were not adequately represented.[7] Formal speeches were reduced to a minimum—three. The major portion of time was dedicated to small study groups and work sessions where individuals had a chance to share their views, hear others, challenge and be challenged in a way not possible in meetings dominated by speeches. At the same time, there were sufficient plenary sessions to allow for maximum interchange of ideas.

Three days were dedicated to small study groups, of which the majority were engaged in Bible study. So many participants wanted these (from a total of seven options: Bible Study, Meditation, Music and Arts, Health and Heal-

---

7. According to the official Report, only 16 Latin Americans were present (although this was disputed by a member of the Latin American delegation who said only 13 came) as against 30 from North America, 22 from Africa, and 56 from Asia.

ing, Suffering, Ill-Health and Death) that three additional groups were required.

The rest of the Conference was spent in sections considering the three areas mentioned: Culture and Identity, Salvation and Justice, Churches Renewed in Mission. These were said to be key areas "where the attitudes and decisions of Christians" are believed to "affect the way in which the message of salvation is presented and understood."[8]

The choice of these areas as well as the particular methodology used in the Conference was based on the three worldwide studies conducted in the last twelve years by the Commission and Division of World Mission and Evangelism: (1) the World Studies on Churches in Mission (which helped shape the course of Section I: Culture and Identity); (2) the recent study program on the Role of Christians within Changing Institutions (which affected Section II: Salvation and Social Justice); and (3) the study which preceded the latter on the Missionary Structure of the Congregation (which gave form to Section III: Churches Renewed in Mission).

Each of these studies was action oriented. A significant portion of the work sections was devoted to listening to "action reports." The three sections were divided into sub-sections which dealt with specific issues related to each main area. The function of each sub-section was to enter into the situations described by the action-reports. They had to seek out the practical problems the action-reports raised and draw up an agenda for future discussion. Together with other sub-sections they were expected to raise the theological principles underlining their area of concern. They then worked on their own agenda to develop practical recommendations.[9]

On the basis of the work of each sub-section, each

---

8. Steven Mackie, "For the Sake of Action: Notes on Conference Methodology," in *International Review of Mission*, LXI: 243 (July, 1972), 288.

9. Cf. *Ibid.*, p. 294.

section prepared a report and submitted it on the last day of the Plenary Session. Each report was introduced by a brief statement outlining the basic objectives of that particular section. It included a summary of the major issues outlined by each sub-section together with their specific recommendations. The Plenary Session, in turn, discussed each report, modified and/or approved it, and referred each resolution and recommendation to the General Assembly of the Commission on World Mission and Evangelism who met immediately after the Conference.

The internal dynamics of the meeting reflected the tremendous variety to be expected in an international ecumenical gathering. It also reflected some of the expected tensions. One Summary Document stated that while there is great value in working through small groups, it involves also a lot of risk.

> . . . the dynamics can appear confusing, if not messy, and anxiety usually arises when no one seems to know how things are going overall . . . If the groups feed dynamically into a creative process at the end, participants are gratified; if the meeting bogs down, the whole may seem a waste of valuable time. Further, conferences seem to draw forth set speeches from people with strongly held views they wish all participants to hear. *Bangkok seemed overburdened.*[10] Even on the seventh day some were still giving their own speeches rather than interacting creatively with others.[11]

On the one hand, there were those who had gone to Bangkok hoping to influence the Conference toward a conservative evangelical stance on mission. Beyerhaus, for example, had challenged the conveners at Geneva, several years before, "to integrate the ecumenical socio-ethical concerns in a harmonious manner."[12] C. Peter

---

10. Italics mine.
11. Bangkok, I, p. 3.
12. Beyerhaus, . . . *Which Way?* . . . , p. 93.

Wagner, commenting on the outcome of the Conference, said shortly after:

> Evangelicals had hoped that the Bangkok meeting would be a watershed in missions focusing the thrust of the conciliar movement once again on biblical evangelism and Great Commission missions. It could have sounded a clarion call to churches all over the world to rise to the challenge of the two billion-plus people on this planet who have not yet committed themselves to Jesus Christ. It could have become a launching pad from which a renewed missionary force would move out to proclaim the gospel of salvation to all nations.[13]

It was no surprise, therefore, to see Peter Beyerhaus and other participants who followed more or less his line of thinking press "for a new dialogue about what mission really is."[14] Beyerhaus's insistence, both during the discussion on Section III and in the Plenary Session, that "the assembly come to grips with the theological issues raised in the Frankfurt Declaration"[15] was challenged each time by participants with opposing views. For Beyerhaus, however, the issues at stake were crucial. Thus, in a statement he submitted to Section III as a whole, he stated:

> I think this conference should not be concluded without unequivocally reaffirming what Uppsala Section II only stated by way of admission: that it is definitely our aim in Christian mission to work towards the growth of the church and thereby secure the salvation of man today.[16]

---

13. C. Peter Wagner, "Two Evangelicals Look at the Bangkok Consultation—More Horizontal than Vertical," *World Vision Magazine* (March, 1973), 16.

14. Bangkok, I, p. 5.

15. Wagner, ". . . More Horizontal . . . ," p. 16.

16. Peter Beyerhaus, "Growing Churches and Renewal" (Appendix II of the Report of Section III), Bangkok, Doc. 41, p. 14.

In other words, what Bangkok needed to produce was an *unequivocal statement* defining church growth and the reconciliation of man with God as the chief and irreplaceable task of Christian mission.[17]

At the same time, others were not so interested in the production of statements. They were ready to move beyond the verbal denunciation of Uppsala to specific and concrete action. They would agree with Mackie "that the framing of resolutions by ecumenical bodies is not necessarily a form of action, but all too often is a substitute for it."[18] Not only were they in theological disagreement with many conservative evangelicals (*e.g.,* they would not consider "church growth" the chief and irreplaceable task of Christian mission; rather they would emphasize the liberation of man as the main thrust of the Christian message); they were also in disagreement about the main contribution of a conference such as Bangkok 1973. If Hugo Assmann had been present, he would have warned the participants not to repeat the experience of Vatican II, Medellín, Geneva, and Uppsala: a lot of words but no strategic implementation.

Assmann was not at Bangkok, but some of his Latin American colleagues were, namely, Gustavo Gutiérrez, Rubem Alves, Emilio Castro, and Ana Cecilia Jimenez (a Catholic social worker from Costa Rica who has been very active as a laywoman in the theology of liberation movement). Especially Gutiérrez and Jimenez, together with other militant colleagues from Europe, Asia, and Africa, working out of Section II (the sub-section on Violent Revolutionary Change), tried to press for strategic implementations.[19]

In spite of all their efforts, neither conservative evangelicals of the persuasion of the Frankfurt Declaration nor

---

17. Cf. *Ibid.,* p. 7.

18. Mackie, "For the Sake of Action . . . ," p. 295.

19. This statement is based on an interview I had with Miss Ana Cecilia Jimenez in San José, Costa Rica on April 3, 1973.

those who followed more or less the thinking of the theology of liberation came out of Bangkok satisfied. For Bangkok produced neither an "unequivocal statement" on the purpose of mission nor the type of strategic action that the latter would have liked to see. In a sense, the outcome of the Conference was imbedded in Mackie's article:

> If there is not to be confusion and frustration throughout the conference there must be explicit agreement regarding the type of action that is possible and appropriate. It must be made clear that the framing of resolutions by ecumenical bodies is not necessarily a form of action, but all too often is a substitute for it. This does not mean that the only kinds of action possible are what delegates can do when gathered together by using their hands or feet. Marches and protests can also be a substitute for action. Indeed the only form of action which a conference can take is a joint decision. That decision must be expressed in *words* which will *lead*[20] to action. Such decisions may be those which an ecumenical body can and must take regarding the use of its own resources of money and staff-time. Since the CWME, and indeed the WCC as a whole, has strictly limited the resources in both kinds, it is important to realize that such action may be of greater symbolic than actual value.[21]

For the two opposing forces in development since Uppsala, Bangkok turned out to be no more than a mental exercise, full of possibilities but frustrating. We shall return to this point further on. For the moment, the words of a Latin American delegate will suffice to describe the internal dynamics of the Conference: ". . . conferences," he said,

---

20. Italics mine.
21. Mackie, *Ibid.*

are "for mental exercise." But "in the Assembly [of the CWME, which met immediately after the Conference] and the real centers of power what was proposed" at Bangkok "would not really be dealt with . . ."[22]

THE THEOLOGY
OF BANGKOK 1973

What were the main theological concerns expressed at Bangkok? Did the Conference as a whole take a theological stance? If so, how was it expressed?

Perhaps the place to begin to answer these questions is with the last one. As indicated, Bangkok did not produce any specific theological statement. The theological perspectives must be found in the different activities, statements, and reports produced *throughout* the Conference: addresses, worship experiences, conversations, drama and art, reports of the sections and sub-sections, as well as individual statements.

For this reason, one must be careful in referring to the theology of Bangkok. As an ecumenical gathering, sponsored by a Commission of a conglomerate (the World Council of Churches), it could not produce a carefully defined theology. The different traditions represented, the plurality of mental structures and categories, and the varied Christian experiences of the participants make difficult the selection of a theological language satisfactory to the great majority. Perhaps this is why neither the organizers nor the participants as a whole bothered to consider the possibility of formulating a definite theological statement. Rather the Conference sought to let the participants speak for themselves about *their* understanding of salvation. In this respect, the theological perspectives of Bangkok are descriptive rather than prescriptive. This means that in order for one to appreciate these insights he

---

22. Bangkok, II, p. 2.

had to be there. Only from within, as an observer-participant, could one really interpret the theology expressed at Bangkok.

It is possible to get a glimpse of what went on there through the limited written materials that came out and from the testimony of those who were there and had the benefit of noting from within all the different theological perspectives expressed in the eight days of activities.

Given the fact that Bangkok was an ecumenical *missionary* conference, it is obvious that its theological perspectives had to do preeminently with the theology of mission. It must therefore be asked, what were the principal missiological insights expressed?

ON SALVATION, CONVERSION, AND EVANGELISM. The Conference, of course, was primarily concerned with the meaning of *salvation* in today's world. It asked about the form and content of the salvation that Christ offers men and women *today*. Perhaps the most succinct and clearest answer to this question came from the statement prepared by Jürgen Moltmann and adopted by Section II ("Salvation and Social Justice in a Divided Humanity"). In it, salvation is described in four dimensions.

> Within the comprehensive notion of salvation, we see the saving work in four social dimensions:
>
> 1. Salvation works in the struggle for economic justice against the exploitation of people by people.
>
> 2. Salvation works in the struggle for human dignity against political oppression by their fellow men.
>
> 3. Salvation works in the struggle for solidarity against the alienation of person from persons.
>
> 4. Salvation works in the struggle of hope against despair in personal life.[23]

---

23. "Report of Section II: Salvation and Social Justice"—2.

Such a description of the work of salvation puts the latter in a holistic perspective. It is based upon a comprehensive notion of salvation that takes seriously the New Testament concept of "newness of life." Such a salvation involves the

> soul and the body . . . the individual and society, mankind and the "groaning creation" (Rom. 8:19). As evil works both in personal life and in exploitative social structures which humiliate humankind, so God's justice manifests itself both in the justification of the sinner and in social and political justice. As guilt is both individual and corporate, so God's liberating power changes both persons and structures. We have to overcome the dichotomies in our thinking between soul and body, person and society, human kind and creation. Therefore we see the struggles for economic justice, political freedom and cultural renewal as elements in the total liberation of the world through the mission of God. This liberation is finally fulfilled when "death is swallowed up in victory" (1 Cor. 15:55). This comprehensive notion of salvation demands of the whole of the people of God a matching comprehensive approach to their participation in salvation.[24]

This holistic emphasis is echoed in other documents. Take, for example, the following testimonies and statements recorded in the Section I Report:

> In my country I am a second-class citizen, a leper. When I met the man Christ who is God, I became a different person. I had no walls and became a full man. I can give of my culture to others and receive from them. If I was not a Christian I would not be so

---

"Salvation and Social Justice in a Divided Humanity," Bangkok, Doc. 40, pp. 2, 3.

24. *Ibid.*, p. 2.

sensitive to my wholeness as a person. Christianity has opened my eyes to the evil of being made less than a person.

. . . . . .

To speak of SALVATION IN JESUS CHRIST pre-supposes the existence of at least two persons who meet:
—Christ bringing salvation
—the person who receives salvation.

. . . . . .

The Christian conversion relates to God and especially to his Son Jesus Christ. It introduces people into the Christian community, the structure of which may differ greatly from one culture to another, and which may include different persons. Christian conversion gathers people into the worshiping community, the teaching community and the community of service to all men. Even if people are not called out of their culture and separated from the society in which they were born, they still will form cells of worship, or reflection and of service within their original cultures.[25]

Note the emphasis on the personal experience of *conversion*, its contingency on a faith-response ("called-out") to Jesus Christ, its orientation toward the church, worship, spiritual growth, and service. In other words, conversion is at once personal and social. It results from an evangelistic action and leads into the formation of churches. It brings about a transformation in one's lifestyle without alienating him from his culture.

This integral theological orientation is seen further with regard to *evangelism*. In the Report of Section III, evangelism is seen in the perspective of church growth. At the same time, growth is defined in terms of "the numerical growth of the church and the development of a new man in every person, the rooting of Christians' faith in local realities and their commitment to society."[26]

---

25. "On Racial Identity," Bangkok, Doc. 39, pp. 1, 3, 5, 6.
26. "Growing Churches and Renewal," Bangkok, Doc. 41, p. 7.

Farther on, the Report defines salvation as "Christ's liberation of individuals from sin and all its consequences" and "a task which Jesus Christ accomplishes through His church to free the world from all forms of oppression."[27] One can ask whether this task is performed by Jesus Christ *only* through the church, given the intrinsic relation referred to in chapter IX between God's providence and Christ's redemption; bearing in mind Paul's reference in Rom. 8 to the groaning of creation which is related to the work of the Holy Spirit; and taking into account the "spiritual" character of the battle with the demonic forces, of which Paul speaks in Ephesians 6. In spite of the slight touch of "ecclesiastical triumphalism" evident in the Report's definition of salvation, the fact remains that the view of church growth and salvation reflected therein is congruent with the previous statements. In other words, Section III comes forth for a *pro-church concept of evangelism and salvation together with a pro-world concept of the church.*

ON THE INDIGENIZATION AND INTERNATIONALIZATION OF MISSION. The same Report comes forth also for a pro-indigenization and a pro-internationalization of the task of mission. Recognizing that "a church which is the bearer of a gospel of liberation to others must first be liberated from all that hinders its true self-expression or robs it of a true sense of its own responsibility," the report states that

> the single transfer of power from one church to another is not the answer. What we must seek is rather a mature relationship between churches. Basic to such a relationship is mutual commitment to participate in Christ's mission in the world.[28]

27. *Ibid.*
28. "Churches in Relationship," *Ibid.*, p. 10.

The Report of Section III thus reasserts the concept of "partnership in mission" of previous world and regional meetings, but by pointing to concrete steps and by calling attention to a specific model. Accordingly, it urges mission agencies to make

> provisions for representation on their governing bodies from the churches to which they relate. The representation should be more than token if it is to be really meaningful. There should be full participation even in the setting of the agenda for mission. And if genuine reciprocity is to be realized, the representation should be extended to those bodies which govern the life and work of the church to which the mission agency itself belongs.[29]

As an example of what can be done, the Report points to the Evangelical Community for Apostolic Action. The latter, very much like the Latin American Community of Evangelical Ministries considered in chapter VIII, is the by-product of a missionary society (The Paris Evangelical Missionary Society) which was dissolved and replaced by a consortium of churches in Africa, the Pacific, France, Italy, and Switzerland. The purpose of the Community

> is to carry forward and transform the former missionary work of the Paris Society and to undertake new enterprises together, e.g., in Dahomey and France. The Council [sic] formed by the presidents of the participating churches [sic] decides on the action to be undertaken and the use and deployment of funds and personnel placed at the disposal of the Community by the various members. The Council also engages in theological reflection, which, for example, has resulted in directing questions to the churches of Europe regarding their own work and priorities.[30]

---

29. *Ibid.*, p. 11.
30. *Ibid.*

ON DIALOGUE WITH PEOPLE OF LIVING FAITHS. Finally, one can observe in the same Report a very wise, balanced position, undergirded by an evangelistic motif, on "dialogue" with people of non-Christian religions. For example, it was affirmed that

> the call to dialogue arises out of our faith: the affirmation of Salvation in Jesus Christ in all its aspects of forgiveness, liberation from injustice and oppression, fulfillment in personal and community life and the development of an inner spiritual life, is our starting point.[31]

At the same time, "The need to listen in order to understand *and communicate*[32] was acknowledged."[33] No tendency toward syncretism nor any surrender of the biblical imperative of evangelism is here noted. On the contrary, such a dangerous possibility is totally discarded.

> Is there an inescapable tension between [dialogue and evangelism] as some fear? This is not necessarily so. We will be faithful to our Lord's command to mission and witness, which is part of our title deed and which people of other faiths know as a duty for Christians as their own faith-relationship with the Ultimate gives them a sense of universal significance. A desire to share and a readiness to let others share with us should inspire our witness to Christ rather than a desire to win a theological argument. We were glad to note that increasingly mission is being carried on in this spirit of dialogue *without the subsequent decrease* in the sense of urgency in evangelism.[34]

---

31. Bangkok, Doc. 39, p. 8.
32. Italics mine.
33. *Ibid.*
34. *Ibid.*

BANGKOK 1973 AND THE
MISSIONARY ENTERPRISE

Bangkok 1973 was the ninth ecumenical missionary conference held in the 20th century.[35] As such, what did it have to say to the world missionary enterprise? Or to put it in other terms, how did it evaluate the missionary enterprise?

In a sense, it can be said that Bangkok stood on the shoulders of Mexico 1963, which dealt with mission in six continents. It reaffirmed, but in concrete action, the reality of the (relative) missionary presence of the church in all six continents. As has been observed, for the first time there was equal representation between the old "mission" fields and the old "Christian" world. There were also representatives from large nonmissionary churches in Africa, Asia, and Latin America.

Yet is was obvious that serious problems were still to be overcome, particularly at the point of church-mission relationships, the harsh reality of a divided world *and* a divided church, the still impending challenge of millions who have yet to be confronted with the gospel, and the emptiness and meaningless of life in the Western world and the apparent powerlessness of the church.

Moreover, there was a considerable absence of pastors, evangelists, and missionaries. Fifty percent of the delegates were church officials, 20 percent belonged to the staff of the Commission on World Mission and Evangelism, 15 percent were theologians, 7 percent Roman Catholics and 8 percent mission-related personnel. Granted that the latter do not necessarily represent people "at the cutting-edge" of mission—but neither do church officials!

To a certain extent, Bangkok had an ironic stance before the missionary enterprise. On the one hand, it recognized the need for renewal at the level of church-mission

---

35. The other eight were: Edinburgh (1910), Jerusalem (1928), Madras (1938), Whitby (1947), Willingen (1952), Ghana (1958), and Mexico (1963).

relationships; on the other, it provided very little participation from "decision-makers" in the missionary enterprise.[36] It reaffirmed the reality of mission in the six continents; and yet it was reminded (by the witness of many of the participants from all points of the globe) about the millions who have yet to hear the gospel message, the new frontiers for mission in the Western world, and the receptiveness in many segments of human society toward Jesus Christ.

This stance was also manifested when in his official introduction as new director of the Commission on World Mission and Evangelism, Emilio Castro stated: "We are at the end of a missionary era; we are the very beginning of world mission. . . ."[37] When I first read these words I interpreted them rather darkly. I discovered later that other evangelicals had been tempted along the same line.[38] Castro himself clarified what he meant, first in a personal conversation, and later, in an article in the *International Review of Mission.*

In this article, Castro reformulates his original statement: "We have seen the end of one missionary era; we are beginning a new one in which the idea of world mission will be fundamental."[39] He then goes on to underline several implications that further clarify the meaning of his original statement.

> 1. It is no longer possible to make a clear-cut distinction between the foreign missionary enterprise and home missionary activities. In the interrelated world of today we all belong together. The mission of the churches in the United States of America has more importance for the situation of the church in many

---

36. Cf. Mackie, "For the Sake of Action . . . ," p. 295.

37. Bangkok, II, p. 2.

38. Cf. Arthur Glasser, "Bangkok: An Evangelical Evaluation," a paper read at the annual meeting of the American Society of Missiology, held at Concordia Seminary, St. Louis, Missouri (June 9, 1973), p. 8.

39. Emilio Castro, "Bangkok, The New Opportunity," in *International Review of Mission,* LXII:246 (April, 1973), p. 140.

countries of the world than the act of sending of missionaries from these particular churches. In fact, what will help to make credible the testimony of the missionary is the attitude of the sending churches in relation to their own national problems. . . .

2. It does not mean that mission across national borders is ended. On the contrary, new possibilities of international cooperation open up once we realize the importance of seeing the whole world as mission territory. In Mexico City the phrase was coined: Mission in six continents. Now we realize that the missionary situation in Sweden is also the responsibility of the Christian Church in Africa, Asia or Latin America, and that when we come to reflect on the possibilities open to us in the local situation we must remember that we have at our disposal the resources of the world church. . . .

3. The Western countries need the aid of the formerly so-called "mission lands" to help them in the fulfillment of their missionary duty in the midst of secularized societies. This was a new factor in Bangkok: the joy of discovering the Church universal in this dimension and the honesty of asking for reciprocal help in our missionary situation. Nobody is so sure of himself that he does not need the help of brothers and sisters from other countries. No church should so concentrate on its own affairs that it forgets that it bears a missionary responsibility for the rest of the world. . . .

4. In the light of our awareness of the dramatic reality of the Church planted all over the world and rooted in different national cultures, values that have been taken for granted in recent missionary history were not only questioned but bluntly rejected. We are at the end of the westernization of the Church and are going through a process in which in a multiplicity of different identities the Church universal will appear. This process will breed tension but it is also

full of promise. "The universality of the faith does not contradict its particularity." Christians discovering their roots in particular races, nations, cultures accept this as their contribution to the ecumenical dialogue and to the world missionary enterprise.[40]

I agree wholeheartedly with such a statement. That mission must be conceived in terms of the whole world as a mission territory; that once such a vision is caught, new possibilities of international cooperation open up; that churches from the North Atlantic world need the help of their sister churches in the Third World in the fulfillment of their respective witnessing responsibilities at home; and that the rediscovery of lost cultural values and the emergence of indigenous lifestyles on the part of Third World churches constitute a tremendous enriching experience for the world missionary enterprise: all are a necessary corrective to the often parochial, triumphalistic, culturally bound, and theologically distorted missionary perspective of many churches and missionary societies in the North Atlantic.

Yet one cannot help but wonder why the emphasis on the comprehensiveness and factuality of mission in the six continents was not matched by equal emphasis on the impending challenge of the millions of people around the globe who are still beyond the frontiers of Christianity. One wonders why Bangkok did not take notice of one of the greatest missionary facts of our era: the tremendous missionary movement from all over the Third World, including the great ethnic "forgotten" minorities of the North, particularly in the USA.[41]

---

40. *Ibid.,* pp. 140-142.

41. See Edward C. Pentecost, "Third World Missionary Societies," in *Church Growth Bulletin*, Vol. IX, No. 2 (November, 1972), pp. 275ff. The author reports on the research carried out in the Spring of 1972 by three research associates of the School of World Mission at Fuller Theological Seminary on the outreach of the gospel being carried on today by missionaries from the Third World. Although only "forty percent of the addresses in Africa and only thirty-seven percent in Asia responded," nevertheless,

It is interesting to note that while Bangkok called for "a moratorium on sending funds and personnel while receiving churches sought their own identity and worked out their own understanding of mission,"[42] it failed to call the churches to an all-out effort to evangelize those outside the frontiers of the gospel. In fact, Phillip Potter's contention, early in his report, to the effect that any debate over "proclaiming the Gospel to the two billion or more who have never heard it . . . is totally futile" seems to have set the pace for the conference's overall attitude toward the urgency of the evangelistic mandate. Accordingly, James Sherer could state several months later in his evaluation of the conference: "No call to evangelism was issued at Bangkok, and the priority of making the Gospel known to all men was not sufficiently emphasized, even if it was not specifically repudiated."[43] Castro's contention that the Bangkok proposal for a moratorium on funds and personnel "is justified only when we come to the conclusion that in this particular place and moment it is the way best to fulfill our Christian mission" and should not be construed as an "abandonment of our missionary mandate" is well taken.[44] But the fact that such a proposal was not

---

the researchers were able to identify a total of 2,533 missionaries from 34 different countries representing a total of 179 missionary agencies from the Third World (p. 276).

In the USA, black churches and denominations have been engaged in the sending of missionaries to Africa and the Caribbean ever since the 19th century. In the East coast, the Asambleas de Iglesias Cristianas, the Iglesia "La Sinagoga," and other Puerto Rican Pentecostal groups have missionaries all over Latin America and in Spain. In the Midwest, the Asociación de Iglesias Bautistas de la Región Lagunera have a missionary in Yucatán, México, and have participated in missionary projects in El Salvador, Nicaragua, Costa Rica, and Puerto Rico. On the West Coast, there are several *chicano* missionary agencies with work in Mexico.

42. Bangkok, I, p. 5.

43. James Sherer, "Bangkok: a Lutheran Appraisal," a paper prepared for the annual meeting of the American Society of Missiology, held at Concordia Seminary, St. Louis, Missouri (June 8-9, 1973), p. 6.

44. Castro, "Bangkok . . . ," in IRM, pp. 142, 143.

matched by an equally strong proposal calling the church to make the gospel of salvation known among the millions of unreached people around the world makes Bangkok's stance on the missionary enterprise ironic and bordering on contradiction.

AN APPRAISAL OF
BANGKOK 1973

How should Bangkok be evaluated? With such categories as good, bad, or mediocre? In the light of the agreement or disagreement of the participants in their deliberation? From the perspective of the theological insights imbedded in the documents produced? On the basis of its final outcome—in relation to world evangelism, the missionary enterprise, and the church?

All these criteria are valid. Yet none of them suffices in itself. First, it is much too soon to determine the effect of such a Conference on the church as a whole, world evangelism, the missionary enterprise, the ecumenical movement, the Commission on World Mission and Evangelism, and the spheres of influence of the participants. Second, it is almost impossible to make an objective evaluation of an event such as this because of the tremendous interaction of the many variables that enter into a world ecumenical meeting. About all that can be said, is that the value of Bangkok varies according to everyone's "grid." Let us, therefore, analyze some of the reactions that have been voiced.

AN AMBIVALENT REACTION. Some have had ambivalent reactions. Arthur Glasser, for example, has written about his "deep feelings of ambivalence." He rejoiced, on the one hand, at the direct, explicit commitment to biblical evangelism expressed in several documents. On the other, he wondered whether the delegates really agreed on what "salvation today" is all about. He admired the courage of the conveners on their determination not to manipulate the delegates "with a heavy succession of canned speeches" and on the involvement of so many representatives from the Third World, many of whom "were evangelical in faith and obedience." Nevertheless, he questioned many of Bangkok's emphases, especially its lack of missionary personnel and its seeming indifference to the fact that two billion-plus are still without the gospel of Christ.[45]

An equally ambivalent reaction was expressed by some of the Latin American participants very much committed to the theology of liberation. For them, Bangkok remained in the sphere of the theoretical and conceptual; it never landed on the concrete sphere of strategic action. Thus while they rejoiced in the stance of Section II, they were disappointed with the vague, imprecise language in which the latter's position was expressed. They came out with the feeling that Bangkok had been another "good" ecumenical conference, full of frustrated possibilities because the so-called "action" of which Mackie had written about months before was reduced to words which most likely would not lead to concrete action.[46] As stated above, had Assmann been at Bangkok, he would probably have said that it was no more and no less than Geneva 1966 (Church and Society), Medellín 1968 (Latin American Episcopal Council) or Uppsala 1968 (World Council of Churches).

NEGATIVE REACTIONS. Some have reacted rather negatively. Chandu Ray, for example, in the "Newsletter" of the Coordinating Office for Asian Evangelism, expressed the view that Bangkok appeared as a confusing situation "be-

---

45. Arthur Glasser, "Two Evangelicals Look at the Bangkok Consultation: Deep Feelings of Ambivalence," in *World Vision Magazine* (March, 1973), 17. For a further elaboration of Glasser's views on Bangkok, see his "Bangkok: An Evangelical Evaluation," p. 5. In this article, Glasser shows forth his positive, albeit critical attitude toward those at Bangkok who had a different view from his on mission and salvation. "At Bangkok I felt that I had to come to terms, not with heretical universalism or a secularized, humanistic Gospel, but with the Christians whose priorities were different from my own."
46. Cf. Interview with Ana Cecilia Jimenez.

cause men were speaking from their own backgrounds rather than a world view." He felt that "the overall result of the Conference was not the liberation of the Gospel for the hundreds of millions who are perishing." "Salvation Today," said Ray,

> was more addressed to political and economic issues rather than man who is imprisoned by his own pride and prejudices. And because conditions vary in different parts of the world, there appeared to be no affirmation of a universal Gospel for salvation today.[47]

This same line was followed by C. Peter Wagner in his *World Vision Magazine* report. His fundamental reaction was that "delegates appeared more inclined to promote social justice than to avoid the final judgment." The horizontal dimension of salvation was emphasized at the expense of the vertical dimension. While evangelicals "were willing to concede that the Bible contains a cultural mandate," they insisted, to little avail, "that the evangelistic mandate be given at least equal time." Wagner felt that

> . . . for every word that stressed the urgency of men and women being reconciled to God, 100 seemed directed to the horizontal dimensions of the gospel . . .
> Evangelicals left Bangkok unconvinced that salvation is more horizontal than vertical and that the missionary task of the church is obsolete.[48]

For Donald Hoke, Bangkok marked a situation of "theological confusion" particularly with regard to the theme itself. According to him, there was no clear or definitive statement given on "salvation today, yesterday, or tomorrow." Moreover, the reaction of most delegates to the challenge of Beyerhaus that the Conference consider the

---

47. Chandu Ray "Newsletter" (Singapore: Coordinating Office for Asian Evangelism, January, 1973), p. 1.
48. Wagner, "More Horizontal than Vertical," p. 16.

Declaration (in an attempt to stop the "infection of faith" that was spreading throughout the world) was negative. He further complained:

> What was left unsaid was perhaps more significant than what was said. There was no call for justice and liberation of the subjugated people in Iron Curtain countries, no adequate recognition of the evangelical revolution (the international spread of the Jesus movement, revival in many lands, Key '73, Explo '72, the congresses on evangelism, the surging Pentecostal phenomenon), and no emphasis on reaching the world's two billion people without Christ.[49]

The most negative reaction I have come across thus far—matched only by that of Harold Lindsell[50]—is that of Peter Beyerhaus. Basically, Beyerhaus's evaluation falls into three general categories. The first is theological.

The fundamental problem with Bangkok, according to Beyerhaus, was the fact that "Scripture . . . was not allowed to play its majestic role in Bangkok. It was . . . substituted . . . by a situationalist approach . . . called 'contextuality'."[51]

---

49. Donald Hoke, "Bangkok Consultation—Salvation Isn't the Same Today," *Christianity Today*, Vol. XVII, No. 9 (February 2, 1973), 37, 38.

50. For Lindsell's view see his article, "Dateline Bangkok," in Ralph Winter, *The Evangelical Response to Bangkok* (South Pasadena: William Carey Library, 1973), pp. 121ff. This book contains all the major evangelical reactions on Bangkok to date (July 1973) that I have come across. I do not interact with Lindsell because much of what he says overlaps with the other reactions considered.

51. Peter Beyerhaus, "The Theology of Salvation at Bangkok," in *Ibid.*, p. 111. Compare, however, Beyerhaus's evaluation about the role which Scripture played at Bangkok with the evaluations of such rank-and-file evangelicals as Arthur Glasser and Paul Rees. According to Glasser, in "Bangkok . . . ," p. 5,

> . . . not a little time at Bangkok was spent in Bible study. So many delegates wanted to participate in these studies that

Such a weak view of Scripture would lead, naturally, to a weak theological workout. Accordingly, Beyerhaus complains that

> . . . from the theological point of view, Bangkok was a frustrating experience. . . . Although it was convened under a highly theological heading, serious theology was to be excluded from this conference from the very beginning.[52]

No serious theological statements were produced either before or as a result of the conference. As a result, says Beyerhaus, the theology of Bangkok was reduced to a collection of experiences. Salvation was so broadly defined and "deprived of its Christian distinctiveness, that any liberating experience at all can be called 'salvation.' Accordingly, any participation at all in liberating efforts would be called 'mission.' "[53]

Second, Beyerhaus criticizes Bangkok not only for its weak theological basis but also for its methodology. According to him, one of the pities of the program was that it

---

> the program had to be rearranged at the last minute to accommodate them. For three successive days we spent the mornings in small groups examining primarily a number of Old Testament passages. This was a very exhilarating experience. No holds were barred; differences were real, passions were aroused and on occasion arguments were bluntly presented. But we listened to the Bible. And I believe God spoke to us.

For his part, Rees states that

> Bangkok appears to have been marked by a more serious grappling with what the Bible has to say to us on the theme of salvation than perhaps any previous meeting of the CWME, perhaps indeed than most comparable conferences held by non-Council Christians.

Paul Rees, "Thinking Aloud about Bangkok," in Winter, . . . *Evangelicals* . . . , p. 139.

52. Beyerhaus, "The Theology . . . ," in *Ibid.*, p. 113.

53. *Ibid.*, p. 120.

"provided very few public lectures and still less opportunity to discuss the advertized theme."[54] He characterized the group approach as "brain washing" and condemned the fact that "it was done in the name of the working of God's Spirit" as bordering on blasphemy.[55]

Third, Beyerhaus's criticism was political in nature. For him, Bangkok was an ecumenical plot against those who defend a biblical view of salvation and mission.

> To arrive at a proper theological evaluation of the Bangkok conference it would be necessary to discern between two different conferences, which partly overlapped in Bangkok. The first and decisive conference had started long before the opening of the Bangkok meeting. It was the continuous consultation of the Geneva staff members and their accredited ecumenical fellow-workers in other parts of the world. This conference elaborated both the theology for "Salvation Today" and the strategy for Bangkok. The second, more representative, conference was the one in which the official delegates found themselves, carefully guided and guarded at every step by highly disciplined people who served as chairmen, secretaries, reflectors, consultants, artists, musicians, newspaper editors or rather anonymous sensitizers in the group meetings. The purpose of this official meeting, I'm afraid, was to arrive as nearly as possible at the predetermined results without giving the impression that they had worked them out by themselves.
>
> This master plan succeeded, but partly got stuck due to the still intact biblical convictions of a great number of the delegates from many different countries and ecclesiastical traditions.[56]

---

54. *Ibid.,* p. 114.
55. *Ibid.,* p. 113.
56. *Ibid.,* pp. 117, 118. Cf., however, Beyerhaus's attitude with that of Glasser:

Of course, what really disturbed Beyerhaus was the fact that the conference not only questioned the validity of a debate around the Frankfurt Declaration but bluntly rejected it. Interestingly enough, those who criticized the document the hardest were delegates from the Third World. He deplored (together with Glasser) the fact that Potter had not even mentioned in his report the ecumenical-conservative controversy on the theology of mission as pinpointed by the Frankfurt Declaration. He further deplored the fact that his suggestion to the Conference to call an international theological consultation between ecumenical and non-conciliar evangelical theologians in order to resolve the "fundamental crisis in Christian missions"[57] was met by such bitter and blunt rejection by Third World leaders.

Consequently, he questions whether the "loudest Afro-Asian speakers at the Bangkok meeting were really representing the faith of the masses of Afro-Asian church members." He adds:

> They have so often enjoyed the privileges of VIP's at ecumenical meetings around the world that they have lost the vital contact with their fellow Christians at the grass root level of the congregations. The influence of ecumenical sensitivity training with all its humanistic and syncretistic vocabulary has become tighter and tighter within their minds. Thus mentally and ideologically they have become even more depen-

---

I feel that as an Evangelical I should not speak darkly of ecumenical plots, of conspiracies to sow seeds of doubt, stab at true faith, and sabotage all those who accept the Bible as the Word of God. I should be willing to initiate efforts to bridge those gulfs that separate Evangelicals from the conciliar movement. I should seek to listen and learn as well as bear witness and serve. For, in many ways, what I do with my brethren in the CWME is not unrelated to making my contribution to the task of reaching the two billion that have yet to hear of Jesus Christ.

Glasser, "Bangkok . . . ," p. 8.
57. Beyerhaus, "The Theology . . . ," in Winter, ". . . *Evangelicals'* . . . ," p. 115.

dent on the West than they were under the influence of so-called Western scholastic theology, which in most cases simply was plain biblical theology.[58]

Whether Beyerhaus's perception of these leaders from the Third World is just and valid is open to question. Even so, it suffices to point out the politico-cultural character of his criticism.

SOME DOWN-TO-EARTH REACTIONS. Not all reactions were so cautious or negative. One of the most practical and down-to-earth reactions came from those who served as reflectors.

> They decided that the result of this meeting [was] not embodied in neat messages as in other conferences but "firstly, in the lives of those that have participated and, secondly, in the concrete actions of churches, missions, and ecumenical agencies which will follow from it."[59]

This was substantiated by Alfred Krass who, although not present at Bangkok, participated in the Salvation Today Study as an evangelical reactor and followed through all the events leading to Bangkok. Krass was able to receive a firsthand report from colleagues who were present and has since worked his way through the major documents. For him, Bangkok was not meant to be a Conference where a clear, succinct definition of salvation would be produced. Its chief value lies in the measure that it will be able to stimulate further discussion and action through the lives and influence of those who were there and shared in the experience. Bangkok, nevertheless, proved to be a step forward—in contrast to Geneva and Uppsala—toward a more balanced view of the church's role in God's mission. In this respect, Bangkok did not turn

---

58. *Ibid.,* p. 117.
59. Bangkok, II, p. 2.

out to be what many conservative evangelicals had predicted. It did not further secularize the theology of salvation. On the contrary, it served as a forum for both the horizontal and the vertical dimensions. And in so doing, Krass said, it opened the way for wholeness in mission and for more balance and greater sharing of both perspectives.[60]

A REACTION TO THE REACTIONS. To understand and appreciate what took place at Bangkok, one must not lose sight of what was discussed in the previous two chapters. Only against the backdrop of Uppsala and its subsequent developments can Bangkok be truly appraised.

As has been observed, Bangkok did not satisfy those who followed the general orientation of the Frankfurt Declaration nor those who were more inclined toward the theology of liberation in its missiological thrust. It came forward for a personal salvation without reducing it to a "private one-way ticket to heaven." It affirmed the interrelatedness between God's salvation and social justice; between salvation of the soul and of the body, of the individual and society, of mankind and the groaning cosmos.

If this is the case, how can Wagner assert that Bangkok was more concerned with the horizontal aspects of salvation than with the vertical? How can Hoke say that no clear statement on the meaning of salvation came out of Bangkok? How can Chandu Ray say that "Salvation Today" was "more addressed to political and economic issues rather than man who is imprisoned by his own pride and prejudices"? How can Peter Beyerhaus affirm that salvation was deprived of its "Christian distinctiveness"?

Perhaps one of the greatest tragedies reflected at Bangkok is the incapacity of some evangelicals to participate wisely and positively, not polemically, in pluralistic ecclesiastical meetings. At the bottom, the reaction of so many evangelicals to the main thrust of Bangkok shows a

---

60. Cf. Interview with Alfred Krass in San José, Costa Rica, April 4, 1973.

hermeneutical crisis, *i.e.,* a refusal to interpret people in the light of their own terms, experiences, and categories.

To be sure, a lot of absurd things were said at Bangkok. As Paul Rees reminds us: this "is almost inevitable, given the fantastic doctrinal pluralism that has overtaken the [member] denominations in recent years."[61] But to take these various and dispersed statements and make them the yardstick for the theology of the entire Conference is tragic, unfair, and even absurd.

As stated, one of the strongest feelings of Beyerhaus, Hoke, and others was that Bangkok should have produced an unequivocal statement on salvation today. The main purpose of the Conference, however, was not to define salvation. Even so, strong evangelical statements were produced in each of the Sections. These statements, of course, were not always expressed in the *exact* language that evangelicals use. Nevertheless, they were *theologically* sound.

Take, for instance, the "Salvation and Social Justice in a Divided Humanity" statement of Section II. It describes salvation as operative in four contemporary struggles of life. It provides hardly any proof texts, nor does it reveal any detailed exegetical effort, nor is it expressed in traditional evangelical terms. Yet its context is sufficiently clear to avoid any theological misunderstanding or to dispel any suspicion of a secular theology.

Yet Beyerhaus has challenged Jürgen Moltmann (author of the statement) on three points. His argument reflects his dichotomous theological eyeglasses (discussed in chapter IX) and is a good example of reading into a statement things which it *does not* say.

> First, [Moltmann] . . . failed to acknowledge the basic distinction between the primary restoration of fallen man to the love of God with social reconciliation as its consequence. Second, his concept of anticipated

---

61. Rees, "Thinking . . . ," in Winter, ". . . *Evangelicals'* . . . ," p. 139.

eschatology makes man here and now the acting participant of that final salvation of the "groaning creation" (Rom. 8:19) which God has reserved for his own final redemptive act in the return of Jesus Christ. Third, Moltmann's yielding to the ecumenical idea of "contextuality" dissolves the concept of salvation into a number of widely disparate experiences.[62]

As has been indicated, the either/or theology of Beyerhaus is very questionable from the perspective of biblical theology. We need not argue the case that salvation is as operative in man's reconciliation with God as in man's reconciliation with his neighbor, since this has been dealt with at great length in previous chapters. Neither do we need to respond to Beyerhaus's second point, given the fact that it has been clearly shown (at least so it seems to me!) that the eschatological salvation is already manifesting its "firstfruits" in the life and mission of the church and in the signs of the kingdom (which take place in history) but which the church is called upon to interpret to the world. The issue is not whether man is here-and-now the acting participant of that final salvation of the "groaning creation," but rather whether God's coming salvation is already manifesting itself in the world, both through the church's seasoning, enlightening, and restraining function as well as through God's action in secular history. It is in this context that Moltmann's phrase, "It is a salvation of the soul and the body, of the individual and society, mankind and the groaning creation," should be understood.

As to Beyerhaus's affirmation that contextuality "dissolves the concept of salvation into a number of widely disparate experiences," this must be questioned in the light of Moltmann's statement. For he makes quite clear that he is not equating salvation with any "disparate experience." Rather his comprehensive concept of salvation encompasses all the four dimensions *together.* Beyerhaus would do well to take note of Moltmann's cautious words.

---

62. Beyerhaus, "The Theology . . . ," in *Ibid.,* p. 120.

In the process of salvation, we must relate these four dimensions to each other. There is no economic justice without political freedom, no political freedom without economic justice. There is no social justice without solidarity, no solidarity without social justice. There is no justice, no human dignity, no solidarity without hope, no hope without justice, dignity and solidarity. But there are historical priorities according to which salvation is anticipated in one dimension first, be it the personal, the political or the economic dimension. These points of entry differ from situation to situation in which we work and suffer. We should know that such anticipations are not the whole of salvation, and must keep in mind the other dimensions while we work. Forgetting this denies the wholeness of salvation.[63]

Of course, as evangelicals we feel we ought to emphasize the personal dimension as a number-one priority. But should this mean that we ought to consider the others expendable? Does the fact that Moltmann discusses salvation in these dimensions warrant Beyerhaus's contention that the former is reducing salvation into "a number of widely disparate experiences"? It certainly does not! In fact, what it does is show once again the loose tendency of some evangelicals to react negatively to anybody who theologizes in terms different from his own.

Conservative evangelicals obsessed with the need to produce "unequivocal statements" would do well to remember that for all the value of the Wheaton Declaration, the declaration of all the congresses on evangelism, and even the Frankfurt Declaration, their *praxeological value* remains yet to be proven. In other words, for all the talk about these declarations the latter have not sparked any significant, concrete, and effective worldwide evangelization movement. With the possible exception of the Asian Congress on Evangelism (out of which emerged the Coor-

---

63. Bangkok, Doc. 40, p. 3.

dinating Office for Asian Evangelism) and the US Congress on Evangelism (which played a decisive role in the launching of Key '73), the significance of the evangelism and missionary congresses of the past seven years has lain at the level of the inspiration it has produced on those who participated in the experience.

BEYOND BANGKOK

If it is true that "Popes and bishops rarely launch evangelistic or missionary movements,"[64] as Glasser has said, it is no less true that conferences and "unequivocal" missionary statements hardly spark evangelistic movements either! They may be temporary catalysts for renewal and mission, but they do not have in themselves the power to be launching pads for renewal and mission. Only the Spirit of God can do this, at the time and place he chooses.

As a conference, Bangkok was of relative value to world mission. No doubt it played a significant role in the life of many of its members. It certainly marked a step toward wholeness in mission. It focused on a gospel that proclaims an all-comprehensive salvation, which liberates man not only from his inner struggles but from his outward collective struggles as well. It called attention to the indispensable need of renewal in the church for effective mission. It pointed to the responsibility of each generation to evangelize its own generation. Above all, it affirmed:

> With gratitude and joy we affirm again our confidence in the sufficiency of our crucified and risen Lord. We know Him as the one who is, and who was, and who is to come, the sovereign Lord of all. To the individual He comes with power to liberate him from every evil and sin, from every power in heaven and earth, and from every threat of life or death.
>
> To the world He comes as the Lord of the uni-

---

64. Glasser, "Deep Feelings of Ambivalence," p. 17.

verse, with deep compassion for the poor and the hungry, to liberate the powerless and the oppressed and to liberate the powerful and oppressors in judgement and mercy.

He calls his church to be part of his saving activity both in calling men to decisive personal response to his Lordship, and in unequivocal commitment to movements and works by which all men may know justice and have opportunity to be fully human.[65]

But the ultimate effect, if any, of Bangkok remains to be seen.

One thing remains clear. It takes more than the deliberation of conferences, congresses, councils, and commissions, more than the refined language of theological statements, for the gospel to penetrate the many life situations of man and liberate him from the power of sin and death, from the state of oppression and repression, from poverty, hunger, starvation, and despair. It takes the outpouring of the Spirit of God upon all flesh. It takes the absolute commitment of the church to the gospel, expressed in her obedient response to the Spirit's call. It takes the humiliation of the church: her voluntary impoverishment for the sake of Christ and the world for whom he died. For only thus can the church be used as an effective instrument of God's liberating mission to the world.

---

65. "Affirmation of Salvation Today" (adopted by the voting delegates of the Conference), quoted in Glasser, *Ibid.*

CONCLUSION

12/THE IMPENDING CHALLENGE OF WORLD MISSION

THE MISSIONARY MANDATE AND THE NEEDS OF MAN

This book was begun with a reference to the world of man as the object of God's redemptive mission. Mission, it was said, is interested in man's many life situations. To this changing, heterogeneous, yet homogeneous world of man God sent his only Son to give his life a ransom for many (Mk. 10:45). This was followed by the sending of the Spirit to make the risen, living Lord redemptively present in all of life's situations. The Spirit was thus defined as the dynamic movement from the one to the many. Out of this dynamic movement, the church is born. She too is caught up in the manifold action of God and is used as an instrument of the Spirit to bring God's word of salvation to the world.

As God's instrument, the church has been entrusted

with an all-comprehensive mandate. She has been sent to witness to her miraculous origin, to disciple the nations of the earth by teaching them to observe whatsoever Christ has commanded, and by making known in season and out of season the good news about God's kingdom.

Imbedded in her mandate is the promise of Christ's presence and power. An atmosphere of joyous expectation surrounds the command to go to the uttermost parts of the earth. Throughout the Book of Acts one can find evidences of the power of God in drawing men and women to Christ through the witness of the church.

Yet the basis for the Spirit's persuasive action through the witness of the church is grounded on the relevance of the church's message to man's varied situations. The church can expect people to respond to her missionary endeavor because men and women need what she has to offer.

The problem lies, on the one hand, with the church's limited perception of the needs of men and women today, and on the other, with her limited, sometimes distorted vision of her role as God's missionary agent to the world.

THE CHURCH'S PERCEPTION OF THE NEEDS OF MAN. There are those in the church who see the world through the eyes of the so-called "individual." For them the needs of the world are basically those of individuals. If the world is sick, it is because those who dwell in it are sick. The needs of individuals determine the needs of the world.

The issue for these Christians is, therefore, what are the most pressing needs of individual human beings throughout the world? While they would not deny the fact that the world is infested with poverty, starvation, injustice, and exploitation, they insist that the cause of such a situation is man's spiritual depravity. Accordingly, in order to attack these problems, one must first deal with the problem of sin. And since sin is basically an individual reality, although it may have its social, collective, or structural implications, it follows that our number-one priority ought to be man's spiritual need.

Others, however, argue that man is not an island to himself: that he lives and moves in a world of structured interrelationships. These interrelationships shape his life. They either work for or against him, they can be instruments of human fulfillment or of oppression and alienation. It is in the midst of these structures where sin is most real. Sin, they affirm, is always social, collective, structural. Accordingly, God's salvation is first and foremost social.

That those who champion the cause of the individual have not understood the social reality of sin, they say, may be evidenced by the fact that individual conversion does not always lead to a more humane and just society. Too many people, in spite of their conversion, continue to engage in acts of exploitation and oppression against their neighbor, refuse to stand against injustice, and reflect little or no change in their lifestyle in society.

Both views shape the on-going lifestyle in mission of its adherents. Each view becomes the "optic" through which each one sees the church's missionary role. It constitutes the measuring stick for defining missionary priorities.

In the third part of this volume, the tension between both of these views was seen, first, in relation to the problem of church-mission relationships, and second, with regard to the liberating objective of God's mission.

To be sure, the issue of church-mission relationships involves more than this tension. As was pointed out in chapter VIII, it is an issue as old as the church. Moreover, it focuses on a complex problem which ranges from the ambiguous origin of the modern missionary movement to the problem of determining the particular form which the church must take in order to be God's missionary agent in the world.

Yet, complex as the problem may be, one cannot help but notice the tension between the individual and the collective across the different alternatives proposed. Those who see God's mission from the first perspective see church-mission relationships in terms of the advance of the gospel among those who have yet to hear it. Those who lean toward the second view see the problem in terms of the people themselves and their right under God to be themselves, an indigenous community through which God's love becomes incarnated in a concrete culture and historical setting.

The tension increases when it moves into the sphere of the soteriological. As indicated in chapter IX, ever since Uppsala 1968 the issue of whether the primary objective of mission ought to be the redemption of individuals or the transformation of society has become the number-one concern in missionary circles. Both perspectives have been getting more and more radical. Some felt that the final clash would come at Bangkok 1973, but as was underlined in the last chapter, Bangkok turned out to be a step in advance of Uppsala. Even so, there are those who have continued a mounting attack on the other side, charging the latter of diluting the biblical concept of salvation.

One of the theses of this book has been that both views have positive and negative qualities in their respective emphases. Their rightness and wrongness lies in the fact that, at least from the perspective of biblical theology, God's mission is oriented toward the world of man, which is both a personal and a structural reality. Sin has affected both man and his structured interrelationships. The aim of the gospel is to liberate man from his total situation. Accordingly, God's mission must be conceived in holistic terms. Scripture knows no other priority than that of man's entire life situation. Even such passages as "Seek ye first the *kingdom* of God and his *righteousness*" (Mt. 6:33) emphasize the comprehensiveness of God's call in Christ to all men and women. For the kingdom is not a "welfare agency," but a community of right-doing (that is, of justice, peace, and love). It is a new order of life which becomes at once the model of what the new society must look like and a measuring stick to judge the present order, without being at the same time a "governmental program." It proposes values to undergird society in order that it might be truly just and humane. When the values of the kingdom become operative in the personal and structural life of people, "all the other things" become a viable possibility.

THE COMPREHENSIVENESS OF THE MISSIONARY MANDATE. We are called in Christ to share with men and women, personally and collectively, the good news of God's kingdom. We are sent to call them to enter into this new order of life through faith in Christ and his gospel. *At the same time,* we are sent to proclaim, in word and deed, the good news of this new order of life *in* the multitudinous structures of society—family and government, business and neighborhood, religion and education, etc. In doing so, we must stand as Christ did, in solidarity with the poor and the oppressed. Further, we must engage actively in their struggle for life and fulfillment. No dichotomies here: not a vertical vs. a horizontal emphasis of mission; not redemption vs. humanization—but a holistic vision of God's mission to the world and the church's role in it.

THE INTRINSIC RELATIONSHIP BETWEEN THE CHURCH'S NATURE AND MISSIONARY RESPONSIBILITY. In the first part of our study, the church's role in God's mission was analyzed in the light of her fundamental character, her calling, and the message with which she has been entrusted. The one fundamental truth which appeared over and over again was the intrinsic, inseparable unity between the church's nature and missionary responsibility. As was pointed out, there is no other church than a missionary church. Accordingly, the church's on-going life must be understood missiologically. No aspect of the church's life can be viewed apart from her missionary responsibility. This means that *all* of the church's functions must have top priority and must be so coordinated that they are complementary to each other. The church, in accordance with her character as the people of God, the body of Christ, and the temple of the Spirit, manifesting herself in concrete human situations, must be a prophetic, priestly, and royal community in the world. Her message must be proclaimed, taught, and witnessed to all mankind. Her involvement in God's mission must be understood in terms of worship and service, presence and proclamation, Christian nurture and fellowship. It must aim at personal conversion and social transformation, standing in solidarity with the poor and the oppressed in their struggle for liberation, and calling men and women to repentance and faith in Christ Jesus—*i.e.,* building up the body of Christ and mobilizing it for witness in the world.

THE HOLISTIC IMPERATIVE OF CHURCH GROWTH. Only from this perspective can we think of the church's growth as a necessary result of mission. Not that the growth of the church is to be the absolute goal of mission. Rather it must be understood as a *temporary* end and a *sign* of a missionary enterprise that is oriented to the *world.* Church growth must be a criterion for testing the effectiveness of the church's missionary action. But likewise, the needs of the world and the biblical model of the church must serve as criteria for testing the validity of the kind of church growth that is a legitimate expression of *God's* mission.

This means that not all church growth is good. There is good and bad, positive and negative, healthy and unwholesome, Christian and demonic church growth. Only to the extent that the growth of the church takes place in a liberating context; only when it affects *in depth* both the personal life of men and women and their structured life situations can the growth of the church be understood as a legitimate expression of God's mission.

This is the reason why in the fourth chapter, church growth was defined holistically, as encompassing four major areas: the numerical, organic, conceptual, and incarnational. Each of these areas deals with variables that involve a holistic missionary interaction with the world. The numerical deals with the personal life and struggles of the people of the world, their coming into repentance and faith in Christ, and their incorporation into the community of faith. The organic deals with indigeneity and culture, *i.e.,* God's mission manifesting itself at the level of community life in terms of cultural and structural development. In other words, the community of faith takes form in culturally relevant terms, not as a foreign entity but as an indigenous organism. The conceptual penetrates both the psychological as well as the logical spheres of the life of the community in the light of her own identity, her image, and understanding of her faith and of the world. The incarnational affects the church sociologically, for it deals with her involvement in the collective and structural problems and struggles of society.

This is the only type of church growth that can legitimately be said to reflect God's missionary action to the world. Such growth is a missionary imperative. It is the type of growth that God wants and that the world needs. For it makes the church what it should be—the community for others; and the gospel what it was meant to be—the joyous, glad tidings of a new order of life. Such a church is a servant of the world for God's sake. Her growth is therefore neither imperialistic nor alienating. It is an expansion in service, in liberating action, that *generates hope and announces the advent of a new world.*

THE RIPENED CONDITION OF THE WORLD

RESPONSES OF LARGE SEGMENTS OF PEOPLE TO THE CHRISTIAN FAITH. We are standing at the threshold of a new era in God's mission to the world, an era of unprecedented opportunities and challenges for the outreach of the gospel. All over the world large segments of people are responding to the Christian faith, from the rebellious youth of the counter culture in North America, to thousands of Moslems in Indonesia, to large segments of the working masses in Latin America, to thousands of animists in Africa, Asia, and Oceania. These responses point to the ripened condition of our world for the gospel.

RENEWED INTEREST IN WORLD EVANGELIZATION. Such openness on the part of the world has been met by the church with renewed interest in evangelism. To put it in the words of Emilio Castro:

> The Church is alive today . . . with a renewal of interest in evangelism. Jesus conferences in Sweden, a world conference on evangelism called for July, 1974 in Lausanne, the ever-present band of Jesus People engaging others in conversation about their faith in the streets of the world's cities, the recent Bangkok conference on salvation, the interdenominational Key '73 evangelism campaign in the United States—all bear witness to present-day Christians' concern for their central vocation: bearing witness to the faith.[1]

This renewed interest in world evangelism raises several important questions. Is this witness to Christ of Christians all over the world as comprehensive as the gospel itself? Is it an international, united witness that aims at leaving no geographical corner of the world, no strata and structure of society, nor any individual person outside the frontier of Christianity—or is it a parochial, docetic or ebionistic,[2] individualistic, either/or witness? What role ought North Atlantic Christians to play in this new era of world evangelism? Ought they simply to concentrate on the situation at home, given the fact that for the last several centuries they have borne the burden of world evangelization, or ought they to venture out in partnership with their brethren in the heretofore "mission lands" so that the missionary enterprise can become once again the business of the whole church and not simply of one segment of the church, so that the missionary situation can be defined in terms of wherever people stand, personally and collectively, spiritually and socially, in need of the gospel of Jesus Christ?

---

1. Emilio Castro, Letter to Orlando Costas (June 25, 1973).

2. If the "docetic" are those who emphasize the "spiritual" at the expense of the material, the "ebionists" are those who emphasize the material, social, and horizontal at the expense of the transcendent, personal, and vertical encounter with God.

THE CHALLENGE BEFORE THE CHURCH. These questions summarize the basic concern of this book. The challenges and opportunities throughout the world for the outreach of the gospel involve not merely a quantitative mobilization of all the resources of the Christian church around the world, but an all-out concern for the many situations in which people find themselves and to which the gospel must be addressed. The ripened condition of our world must be understood in the light of the comprehensiveness of the Christian missionary message. The world needs a holistic, not a compartmentalized, distorted-beyond-recognition, docetic, or ebionistic gospel. The world needs to hear and see a united church witnessing and preaching, in word and deed, the liberating message of Jesus Christ, worshiping and serving him and discipling its peoples on all six continents.

Let us, therefore, mobilize all our resources—manpower, finances, talents, imagination, contacts, and opportunities—to meet this open door which the Lord lays open before his church in this hour of history. Let us give ourselves to be a prophetic, priestly, and royal community, in season and out of season. Let us proclaim, teach, and witness to, without reduction or apologies, the whole gospel of the kingdom to the whole man in the whole world. Let us strive for the integral growth of the church to the end that all the peoples of the earth might experience God's salvation in Jesus Christ in their struggles for hope and life everlasting, reconciliation and forgiveness, inner brokenness and guilt, solidarity, justice and dignity. *Amen!*